**NO RICH AND NO POOR:
The Populist Goal We CAN and Must Win**

By John Spritzler

Copyright © 2017 John Spritzler

ISBN 9781521326299

Imprint: Independently published

Dedicated to the memory of Dave Stratman, who made it possible for me to write this book

INTRODUCTION

The children of a janitor and the children of a physician or of anybody else should enjoy the same standards of education, healthy food, quality health care, comfortable living space, quality clothing, leisure time, fun vacations, and healthy and attractive environment.[1]

Practically everybody in the United States[2] knows that we live in a fake democracy.[3] They know that the important economic and government decisions that affect us are made by the very rich, not by ordinary people. They know these decisions reflect the values and aims of the very rich—inequality, domination of the many have-nots by the few haves so the haves can enjoy enormous wealth and privilege and power at the expense of the have-nots, and pitting ordinary people against each other in dog-eat-dog competition so as to more easily control us.

Most people, in sharp contrast with the very rich, want society

---

[1] These words were contributed by Dave Stratman to the online pamphlet "Thinking about Revolution," co-authored by him and myself in 2011, at http://newdemocracyworld.org/revolution/Thinking.pdf .

[2] I believe that the general statements in this book about what most people want and know apply to virtually all the people of the world, but I focus on the United States because that is where I've lived and gained the personal experiences on which this book is based. I hope, and expect, that people outside the United States will find this book useful for building a movement to win No Rich and No Poor in their part of the world. To succeed anywhere, we need these movements to be strong globally, not just in the United States.

[3] Most adults in the United States don't vote, as shown at http://newdemocracyworld.org/revolution/most.html . About one in five who are eligible don't register to vote, and only about 60% or less of registered voters actually vote. But even those who do vote do so with little expectation that the government will use its power to shape society by the values of ordinary people such as themselves; people vote hoping to elect a "lesser evil" or just because they yield to the intense propaganda that tells them it is their civic duty to vote.

shaped by what I call egalitarian values: equality in the sense of no rich and no poor, and mutual aid—people helping each other.

If the above assertions, about what most people know and want, were false then I would not have written this book. Why not? Because this book is about not only why we must, but also how we can (see Chapter Eighteen) make what I call an egalitarian revolution to actually remove the rich from power to have real—not fake—democracy with no rich and no poor. This would be impossible if most people thought we were living in a genuine democracy and thought there should be some rich and some poor. The standard wisdom holds this wrong view of people. If it were true then this book would be just a lot of nonsense based on a false premise—not worth writing.

This book is entirely based on the fact that most people know we live in a dictatorship of the rich and would LOVE to replace that with a genuine democracy with no rich and no poor where people helped each other and were not pitted against each other to be made controllable by the rich. This book is about: 1) How, because it's what most people want, we can actually make the world be the way most people want it to be despite the obvious financial, governmental, police and military power of the very rich who disagree, and 2) Why the way most people want the world to be is a) very different from Communism (which people rightly don't like because it is so anti-democratic), b) extremely democratic, c) economically very practical, productive and desirable, and d) far more desirable in all other ways than our present society for almost everybody. This book, in other words, is about the need for, desirability of, and possibility of egalitarian revolution, and none of the arguments made in this book would make any sense if most people did not already know and want what I claim they do. I provide evidence for these claims in Chapter One and in Chapter Sixteen I discuss how you, dear reader, can verify for yourself—easily and without interrupting your daily life routine at all—that these claims about people are true.

The assertions I make about what most people know and want fly in the face of standard wisdom. One never hears these assertions about people made anywhere in the mass media or the "alternative" media, whether these media cater to a conservative or liberal audience or anything in between. These media, because they are controlled by the very rich, also censor any expression by anybody of egalitarian aspirations. Why? To make it seem to those (the vast majority) who have such aspirations that they are all alone and should not waste their time (or risk ridicule or ostracism) by even talking about wanting to remove the rich from power and creating an egalitarian society.

So what's my evidence for the assertions I make about what most people actually know and want? How can I be so sure the standard wisdom is wrong?

My first piece of evidence is this. Others and I have asked thousands of random people if they think the message on the button shown below ("Let's remove the rich from power, have real, not fake, democracy with no rich and no poor") is a good idea or a bad idea.

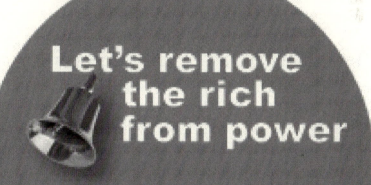

No matter where we have gone—be it five different neighborhoods of Boston, or a rally of Trump supporters (all white, mostly from western/rural Massachusetts, many wearing Trump "Make America Great" caps and NRA apparel and holding American flags), or a Bernie Sanders rally or a rural New Hampshire town where the people listen to Rush Limbaugh and not NPR—the response is consistently that at least 80% and often 90% of the people (86% at the Trump rally) say the message on the button is a good (or a great!) idea. The button's message, "Let's remove the rich from power to have real—not fake—democracy with no rich and no poor," is the heart of what egalitarian revolution—the subject of this book—is all about.

Although one would never know it from the mass or alternative media, egalitarian revolution is what most people want, regardless of whether they consider themselves to be on the Left or the Right of the so-called "political spectrum." Chapter One is about our[4] experiences asking other people—often strangers on a sidewalk or encountered while shopping, *etc.*— what they think about the message on the button.

My second piece of evidence about what people value comes from realizing what the significance is, in this regard, of how people live their everyday lives. I learned about this from reading Dave Stratman's book, *"We CAN Change the World: The Real Meaning of Everyday Life."*[5] As Stratman points out, the capitalist class is clearly in power and its values of greed and self-interest and domination of others control all the major institutions of society. Everyday we're told how important it is to make the world a "level playing field," which means a place where people (individually or as parts of businesses, nations, races, genders, ethnicities, *etc.*) compete against each other

---

[4] By "our" I am referring to those who have worn the button shown above and asked other people if they thought its message was a good idea or a bad idea.

[5] Online at http://www.newdemocracyworld.org/old/Revolution/We Can Change the World book.pdf .

(like opposing teams on a soccer field) instead of helping each other (with mutual aid, a.k.a solidarity). The message is that of course you're in competition with others; the only thing you have a right to ask for is that the playing field be fair, *i.e.,* "level."

If everybody shared these capitalist values and were thus always knifing each other in the back in ruthless competition to make a buck and trying to dominate and cheat others to profit at their expense and never acting out of concern for others, not to mention love for some, we would be living in a veritable nightmarish hell. But we're clearly not living in that kind of hell. Why not? This is the extremely insightful question Stratman asks, and answers in his book.

We're not living in a nightmarish hell because most people reject capitalist values and try in their everyday lives in the small corner of the world over which they have any real control to act on the opposite values of mutual aid (a.k.a. solidarity and concern for others) and equality. Without consciously thinking of it in these terms, people's everyday lives are implicitly a resistance to capitalism. The evidence that people have these values is that nothing else can explain why our society ruled by capitalism is not a nightmarish hell. Most people know that if they challenge capitalist values too overtly or on too large a scale—if they get too visibly "uppity"—they will be attacked by capitalist corporate and government power. So people mostly act on a small scale, in their personal sphere, in ways that only implicitly challenge capitalist values; but it is enough to make our world far better under capitalist rule than it would otherwise be.

Examples of this behavior are so common and ubiquitous they are like the proverbial water that the fish never notices. Examples are ridiculously easy to find if only one decides to look for them. Here's one example I saw just an hour before writing these words. I was carrying bags of groceries from my parked car to my condominium across the residential street, in heavy rain. I saw that I was going to have to wait in the rain to cross the street for an approaching car to pass. Despite the fact that the car was traveling pretty fast, and luckily for me, the driver of the car saw my situation and stopped to let me cross in front of it. Why did the driver do that? There's only one explanation—the driver valued concern for other people (mutual aid), even for a total stranger who would likely never have a chance to return the favor. One might say, "Sure, that driver was nice, but many others aren't." True. But the point is, why are <u>any</u> drivers nice like this one? If everybody truly shared capitalist values then that nice driver could not have existed. That driver's kindness (and the existence of the countless similar acts of kindness) shows that there is an essentially invisible but large anti-capitalist force in our society.

Acts such as that of the nice driver happen all the time (especially among family members and co-workers and neighbors but also, as this example illustrates, among total strangers) and, although they are virtually never noted nor their significance discussed, these acts are the reason we are not living in the hell it would be if most people had capitalist me-first-and-screw-you values. Did the driver of the car think he or she was resisting capitalism? Almost certainly not. But the fact is that the driver was, implicitly, resisting capitalism. Hundreds of millions of Americans, likewise, implicitly resist capitalism in their everyday lives without realizing it. When this implicitly revolutionary force gains self-awareness of its profound significance and makes explicit its aim to shape all of society, not just the personal sphere, by its values, that's when revolution becomes very possible.

My third piece of evidence concerns specifically the fact that most people know we do not live in a genuine democracy (not even a genuine representative democracy or "republic"). During the election campaign season when Al Gore was running against G.W. Bush for president, I decided to do a little experiment. I printed a leaflet with just thirteen words in very large font; it said, "America is not a democracy. What are we going to do about it?" I went to a busy corner[6] near where I lived, in the early evening as people were getting off the subway there, and held up my sign in order to converse with people about it. I wanted to see if, even in the midst of a presidential election campaign when our fake democracy was doing its utmost to appear like a real democracy, anybody disagreed with the first sentence saying, "America is not a democracy." Of the fifty people who stopped to talk, not a single one disagreed with the assertion that America was not a democracy. Not one! All but one person took my sign, and my subsequent words in conversation, to mean something that they agreed with—that ordinary people, in contrast to the very rich, have no real say in what our government does, in contrast to how it would be in a real democracy. One single person out of the fifty I spoke with interpreted my sign to mean that America was a "republic" and thus not a "democracy"; he argued that this was a good thing because democracy is "mob rule" and as little real say as ordinary people have in our "representative" government it is the most that they should have. As for "What are we going to do about it?" people's responses were all over the map.

Perhaps the strongest evidence for all of my assertions about what people know and want is that I and others discovered that when we asked people in public places such as the entrance to a supermarket, in liberal Boston and also conservative rural Unity, N.H., to sign a statement of belief titled "This I Believe" (see Chapter One for the full text), at least 80% of those who stopped to read it signed it. The statement reads in part: "In the United States we have a fake democracy. Big Money owns the media and political parties, controls the electoral process and politicians, and determines government policies, which have nothing to do with campaign promises or what most people want. This is not right! ... We should all equally own and enjoy the benefits of the earth's resources and the wealth that we produce by working

---

[6] Coolidge Corner, in Brookline, MA, a comfortable middle-class town inside of Boston.

together, with nobody being rich or poor. The principle of our economy should be, 'From each according to ability, to each according to need,' a Golden Rule idea as old as the Bible (Acts, 4:34-35). Work should be for shared goals, to produce things that people need and want, to share freely, not buy and sell. A greedy, rich and powerful minority, who were never elected and therefore cannot be unelected, prevents Americans from making ours a more equal and democratic society, which is why we need a revolution to remove them from power."

To see if perhaps the people who stopped to read "This I Believe" (we displayed the text on a large poster) were an unrepresentative self-selected group, we went door-to-door to hundreds of residences in the neighborhood of one supermarket where we collected a lot of signatures. Again, among those who came to the door when we rang the bell or knocked, more than 80% signed the statement. It would be hard to argue that people who agree with the statement would be more likely to come to the door than those who disagree with it. Since the people who came to the door probably included people who didn't stop to read "This I Believe" at the supermarket, it follows that those who did not stop to read the document at the supermarket are as likely as those who did stop to read it to agree with it.

The rich control the media and they use it to make us believe that if we think we live in a fake democracy and if we want an egalitarian revolution then we are essentially all alone, and should therefore give up any hope of building an egalitarian revolutionary movement, because if we tried nobody would join it. The very rich don't care if we love them or hate them, as long as we are paralyzed by hopelessness from doing the only thing that threatens the very rich, which is to reach out to our fellow Americans to build an egalitarian revolutionary movement that could gain the support of a large majority of Americans.

There are five key obstacles to the growth of an egalitarian revolutionary movement.

The first obstacle is that, as discussed above, people don't know that it is the vast majority—not a hopelessly small and hence impotent minority—that would love to live in an egalitarian society. People who think they are too few numerically to matter remain too paralyzed by lack of confidence to even think about building an egalitarian revolutionary movement to remove the rich from power—a goal that seems ludicrously impossible and hence not worth taking seriously. The flip side of this obstacle is that people do not know how truly possible it is to remove the rich from power, despite the existence of the highly armed police and military forces, when an egalitarian revolutionary movement of a large majority of Americans exists. This is what Chapter Eighteen is about.

The second obstacle is that many people think that an egalitarian society sounds wonderful but unfortunately it cannot really exist for one reason or another. Some think it is incompatible with human nature, or that it would result in an economy that was too unproductive, or that a new upper class would inevitably emerge and make things unequal again, or that equality requires Communist-style dictatorship that is worse than what we have currently. This book (especially Chapters Nine through Thirteen) is largely devoted to overcoming this second obstacle by addressing these understandable concerns people have about whether egalitarianism is a realistic and desirable alternative to what we have today.

The third obstacle is that many people think that even if egalitarianism is much better than what we have today, it's so hard to achieve it that it makes more sense to work only for modest, but easier-to-win, reforms of our present capitalist society and give up on trying to win egalitarianism. This book addresses this "reform or revolution?" issue by showing that a) even reform struggles are motivated by egalitarian revolutionary aspirations and b) reforms that fail to remove the rich from power to have real—not fake—democracy with no rich and no poor result in the rich remaining in power and treating ordinary people like dirt; such reforms don't solve the problem at its root and keep us on the treadmill of defeat. Chapter Fourteen discusses this.

The fourth obstacle is the ruling class's success up till now in pitting people who want egalitarian revolution against each other with "social issues" so that instead of acting in solidarity with each other for egalitarian revolution we are divided into hostile camps, each viewing the other with contempt and even fear. How the ruling class does this, and how we can break free from this divide-and-rule strategy is discussed in Chapter Fifteen.

The fifth obstacle is fear. Many people are understandably afraid that if they do anything to help build an egalitarian revolutionary movement or even express support for such a thing, that something bad will happen to them. Maybe they will end up on a "list of troublemakers," *etc*. Some people also fear that revolution will just mean more violence, either repression by the rulers, or wrongful violence by the revolutionaries themselves. This concern is discussed in Chapter Seventeen.

Chapter Eighteen is about how we can make an egalitarian revolution, despite the fact that the very rich control the government and the government has well-armed police and military forces that are more powerful than any popular revolutionary militia is able to become. The related issue of violence versus nonviolence is discussed in Appendix VI.

References

Many of the footnoted references in this book are web addresses (URLs) that, in the Kindle version, are also live links to the respective online article; in some cases these are articles I wrote that this book asks you to read. This book was written as an e-book, intended to be read with a device (such as a smart phone or tablet or computer) that has a web browser so that you can read the linked online articles. These devices, with the Kindle app, can read this book and also read the online articles that it links to.

As of May 10, 2017 the links in this book were live. But over time some may be broken. If you encounter a broken link there are two ways you may be able to nonetheless access the article. One way is to use a search engine (*e.g.,* Google, *etc.*) and search for either a text fragment (if you have one) from the article, or for the author's name. Often articles are moved from one URL to another but are still online. If the article is no longer online, however, you may still access it by going to https://archive.org/web/ (the Wayback Machine) and entering the broken URL, which may provide you with the article from a date before it was removed.

An Apology

Because some readers read just selected chapters instead of reading a book from cover to cover, I have erred on the side of redundancy and repeated things such as definitions of key words in some chapters to make them more "stand-alone" in nature. I apologize to those who do read this book cover to cover for this possibly annoying redundancy. Please consider it a kind of mutual aid to the other readers.

Table of Contents

INTRODUCTION 4

CHAPTER ONE: EVIDENCE THAT MOST PEOPLE WANT TO REMOVE THE RICH FROM POWER TO HAVE REAL—NOT FAKE—DEMOCRACY WITH NO RICH AND NO POOR 19

CHAPTER TWO: WHY HAVE NO RICH AND NO POOR? (WHY WE NEED TO ABOLISH CLASS INEQUALITY) 39

CHAPTER THREE: WHAT EQUALITY DOES NOT MEAN 78

CHAPTER FOUR: WHAT IS AN EGALITARIAN SOCIETY? 82

CHAPTER FIVE: INDIVIDUAL FREEDOM AND AN EGALITARIAN BILL OF RIGHTS 98

CHAPTER SIX: WHY ABOLISH THE USE OF MONEY? 123

CHAPTER SEVEN: WHY SHOULD ONLY EGALITARIANS MAKE THE LAWS? 130

CHAPTER EIGHT: WHY SHOULD LAWS ONLY BE MADE BY LOCAL ASSEMBLIES? 135

CHAPTER NINE: IS EGALITARIANISM'S SHARING ECONOMY PRACTICAL ON A LARGE SCALE? 142

CHAPTER TEN: IS EGALITARIANISM'S VOLUNTARY FEDERATION PRACTICAL FOR A LARGE COUNTRY-SIZED REGION? 162

CHAPTER ELEVEN: IS EGALITARIANISM COMPATIBLE WITH HUMAN NATURE? 169

CHAPTER TWELVE: EGALITARIANISM IS <u>FUNDAMENTALLY</u> DIFFERENT FROM COMMUNISM 185

CHAPTER THIRTEEN: HOW DOES EGALITARIANISM PREVENT THE ABUSE OF POWER? 210

CHAPTER FOURTEEN: REFORM OR REVOLUTION? 225

CHAPTER FIFTEEN: HOW THE RULING CLASS DIVIDES-AND-RULES US WITH "SOCIAL ISSUES" AND HOW TO OVERCOME THIS 231

CHAPTER SIXTEEN: WHAT CAN INDIVIDUALS REALISTICALLY DO TODAY TO START BUILDING AN EGALITARIAN REVOLUTIONARY MOVEMENT? 243

CHAPTER SEVENTEEN: WHAT ABOUT FEAR AND REPRESSION? 252

CHAPTER EIGHTEEN: HOW WE <u>CAN</u> REMOVE THE RICH FROM POWER 262

APPENDIX I: EXAMPLES OF POSSIBLE EGALITARIAN LAWS 271

APPENDIX II: EYEWITNESS REPORT OF A LOCAL ASSEMBLY OF EGALITARIANS IN REVOLUTIONARY SPAIN, AROUND 1937 297

APPENDIX III: EGALITARIANISM VERSUS THE OTHER "ISMS": SOCIALISM, COMMUNISM, ANARCHISM, LIBERTARIANISM, CAPITALISM 299
    SOCIALISM 299
    COMMUNISM 307
    ANARCHISM 312
    LIBERTARIANISM 318
    CAPITALISM 319

APPENDIX IV: THE FLYER WE GIVE TO PEOPLE WHO SAY THE PDR BUTTON'S MESSAGE IS A GOOD IDEA 325

APPENDIX V: WHY WE CANNOT VOTE THE RICH OUT OF POWER 327

APPENDIX VI: NONVIOLENCE OR NON-CRUELTY? 335

APPENDIX VII: A BORING TECHNICAL DETAIL REGARDING THE SHARING ECONOMY 341

APPENDIX VIII: WHO IS IN THE RULING CLASS? WHO RULES AMERICA? 346

APPENDIX IX: GLOBAL WEALTH EQUALITY: WHAT WOULD IT MEAN? 351

APPENDIX X: RACE, CRIME AND EGALITARIANISM 357

APPENDIX XI: EGALITARIAN MILITIAS 378

APPENDIX XII: TRADE BETWEEN DISTINCT SHARING ECONOMIES 379

APPENDIX XIII: WHY DOES THE ROCKEFELLER FAMILY FUND WANT YOU TO REDUCE YOUR CARBON FOOTPRINT? 381

APPENDIX XIV: HOW THE AUTHOR LEARNED WHAT CAUSES A POLITICAL SEA CHANGE 412

APPENDIX XV: WHY SOLDIERS WILL JOIN US 417

APPENDIX XVI: AN EGALITARIAN FOREIGN POLICY 421

BIBLIOGRAPHY 422

ABOUT THE AUTHOR 423

CHAPTER ONE: EVIDENCE THAT MOST PEOPLE WANT TO REMOVE THE RICH FROM POWER TO HAVE REAL—NOT FAKE—DEMOCRACY WITH NO RICH AND NO POOR

The title of this chapter contains the message on the PDR (short for PDRBoston.org[7]) button shown below:

---

[7] https://www.pdrboston.org/

To see if people think the message on the button ("Let's remove the rich from power, have real, not fake, democracy with no rich and no poor") is a good idea or a bad idea, others and I asked them, by doing something we call "buttoning." "Buttoning" means going to a public place and asking passers-by, while handing them the PDR button, "Do you think the message on this button is a good idea or a bad idea?" and, when they say it's a good idea (as most do), giving them the button and a flyer (Appendix IV) that explains why we "button." "Buttoning" also means doing the same thing, but with individuals one may know personally or individuals one encounters during the normal routine course of one's day at work or school or while doing errands.

Buttoning Trump Supporters

On July 23, 2016 I went buttoning at the Gun Owners Action League (GOAL, at goal.org, a chapter of the NRA) rally at the (Massachusetts) State House in Boston. The rally was focused on opposing the Massachusetts Attorney General's decision to eliminate a loophole that allowed people to purchase certain kinds of so-called "assault" weapons, and defending the 2nd Amendment more generally.

I arrived at 10 am when the rally was already well underway, with about three hundred or so people listening intently to the speeches. Everybody was crowded tightly together facing the speakers, so when I arrived I could only see people's backs, and had to somehow get their attention so they would turn around and look at the PDR button and answer my "Good idea or bad idea?" question. It wasn't too hard though.

The rally only lasted 45 minutes after my arrival and then dispersed. During that time I "buttoned" people, many of whom were holding American flags or flags supporting the right to bear arms, or NRA caps or shirts. A fair number of people wore Trump "Make America Great Again" hats. This crowd was all white and mostly from out of town—Western (and rural) Massachusetts mainly I believe.

Buttoning Results

When I asked people if the message on the button (or my PDR T-shirt with the button image on its front) was a good idea or a bad idea here's what happened.

Four people said it was a bad idea. Their remarks included, "The rich have a right to be rich—we're a capitalist nation," and "I like some rich people," and "Now we've got a billionaire on our side" (referring apparently to Trump's support of the 2nd Amendment) and "I want to be rich one day."

Three people said they didn't know what they thought about the button's message.

Forty-three people agreed with the button and took one and also took the flyer, many very enthusiastically, and at least three that I recall pinned the button on themselves immediately, one of whom offered me a cold bottle of water (it was a very hot day) from the three that she had with her. I told these forty-three people that they would enjoy the article on the PDR website titled "Guns and the Working Class" near the top.

Some Thoughts about the Significance of This

Be honest! When you were reading this report, before you got to the part about 43 people agreeing with the button, what were you guessing that number was going to be?

The numbers above mean that 86% of these people at the GOAL rally—essentially a pro-Trump rally—agreed with the PDR button—with the goal of egalitarian revolution—some very enthusiastically so. Only 8% of these people said the PDR button was a bad idea, which means that 92% of them did NOT think it was a bad idea.

Clearly GOAL's focus, very narrowly defending the right to bear arms, attracts both people who agree with and people who disagree with egalitarianism, and this extremely narrow focus obscures the fact that within the GOAL membership there is a FUNDAMENTAL conflict of values: pro- versus anti-egalitarian, with the pro-egalitarian side vastly outnumbering the anti-egalitarian side.

GOAL is typical of organizations in the United States. Virtually all of them avoid any explicit advocacy of egalitarianism and instead focus narrowly on some issue that obscures the fact that most people want an egalitarian revolution.

Buttoning in Boston Neighborhoods

In 2015 I buttoned in five different neighborhoods of Boston: Brighton, West Roxbury, Hyde Park, Jamaica Plain and Roslindale, some more low-income working class and others more higher-income "middle class." I stood on the sidewalk in the busy commercial center of each neighborhood and asked whoever walked by if they thought the message on the PDR button was a good idea or a bad idea. There is a YouTube video I made of me doing this[8]. It shows sixty-eight individual people (or in some cases a group of two or three friends) responding to the button, and it also shows a sample of people who said they didn't want to stop to talk. I included the people who didn't stop to talk to illustrate that these people gave reasons that had nothing to do with what they thought of the button (if they even read it), such as "I'm late and don't have time to stop." Everybody who agreed to be videotaped is included in the video: there is no "cherry picking." Of the sixty-eight people (or groups of friends) who agreed to be interviewed, 62 (91%) said the message on the button was a good (or great!) idea. Five (7%) people said the message was a bad idea (or at least would not say it was a good idea) and one person agreed with the button in part but not totally.

In 2016 and 2017 several of us buttoned again a half dozen times in Brighton and once in the relatively wealthy town of

---

[8] https://www.youtube.com/watch?v=95b3SmBYwfU

Brookline (which is surrounded by Boston) and twice at Northeastern University (in Boston.) On every occasion, of the thirty or forty people who stopped to give their opinion, substantially more than 80% (often more than 90%) of them said the button's message was a good (or great!) idea and eagerly accepted a button (in some cases pinning it on immediately) and the flyer.

Buttoning Bernie Sanders Supporters (one person's report)

Pennsylvania, April 4, 2016
On Friday, I was roped into canvassing with my son in a poor neighborhood of Pittsburgh for Bernie Sanders. It proved to be an exercise in futility and most people did not answer the door or were out. I only distributed one of the fifty buttons I had on me. On top of this, I was worn out from all of the walking and climbing steps. But I did not let this discourage me. The next morning my son, my daughter in law and I went to a pro-Sanders rally and I was not sure how things would turn out. I had 49 buttons and I was determined to distribute them.

There were a couple of hundred people at this rally, many young, Black and white and some older folks like me. I began by approaching one fellow supervising the door and asked him if he would be interested in taking a button. He wanted to know what it was about and I let him read it. His response was positive and he took one. Then he asked me what the PDR stood for and I explained this to him. He said that this sounded great. I was also enthused and began approaching all sorts of people in the hall where the rally was taking place. I did not have one negative response to the button and everyone actually seemed grateful for receiving one. There was not a lot of time for any discussions, as things were busy with the speakers and a folk singer. But they all seemed to like the message of the button and some of them actually seemed quite happy to get the button. I distributed 48 buttons at this rally and I also put some stickers up at various locations throughout that area.

Needless to say, I was more than pleased with the buttoning and felt like people really were for an egalitarian revolution. When I left the rally, I had only one button left. We went to a Thai restaurant to celebrate and when I was leaving the restaurant, I noticed a restaurant worker sitting out back having a smoke. I figured what the hell and showed him the button. He stated that he liked it and immediately put it on his shirt. It turns out that he was a cook at this restaurant. I can only hope that this might encourage others to attempt buttoning. People really do respond in a positive fashion to the message of the button. Actually, I could have easily used fifty more buttons and would have had no trouble distributing them on Sunday when I went to a union meeting with my son, who is a union organizer and I could have also distributed some to striking Verizon workers. [Nick B.]

Reports from People Who "Buttoned" People They Met Here or There

We have had countless experiences asking people we meet while doing errands what they think of the button. Here is a sample of reports of such experiences:

Cambridge, MA
I had to have a routine blood test today. After she drew my blood (it was red, phew!) I asked the phlebotomist if she thought the message on my PDR button was a good idea or a bad idea. She said, "Of course, it is a good idea" and she gladly took a button and pinned it on her. Then I was in an elevator and a woman was inside it cleaning it: same question and same response. [John S.]

Boston, MA:
I stopped into a Walgreens Drug and showed my button to the manager and cashier. The cashier liked it but seemed unsure if he could wear it at work. When the manager saw the button and chatted with me about it she put it on right away and told the cashier he could wear it. She asked for another one for her 9 year old son's backpack. The other thing about the Walgreens experience is that the Mgr wanted a button for her

son's backpack! 10 years old. She was planning to explain it to him.

Then I went to a huge supermarket where I passed out about 10 to 15 more buttons to great enthusiasm.

I ran out of buttons at that point.

Yesterday I stopped by another store and the guy behind me in line asked if he could read my button. He said it would be a much better world, so I gave him my button and he put it on then and there. [Kathy F.]

Enthusiastic response to button in rural New Hampshire:
Hello folks,
   As I went through the check-out line at my supermarket here in Claremont NH the cashier said she really liked my button and agreed with it 100%. I gave her a button along with one of the "Thank-You" sheets that I keep folded in my pocket -- and told her to please wear it with pride and spread the word, because it's important that people know that they're not alone in wanting an egalitarian revolution. I had to keep moving along and so wasn't able to talk more with her. I hadn't even asked her what she thought of the button; I suspect that another cashier, to whom I'd given a button a week or so ago, had shown it to her. [Jim R.]

Rural Pennsylvania:
Today was my day for the food bank and I do not like to go there. However, we have no choice, if we want to eat. The line was quite long and I figured that I should attempt to button. I had five with me, including the one that I wear near my anti-Sexism button. I went up to people, handed them a button and asked them what they thought of it. I was able to distribute all four of the buttons, two men and two women took them. I have had a lot of luck at the food bank distributing the button, due to the fact that the people there are suffering economic hardships. [Nick B.]

Boston, MA
Today I was in an independent bookstore, shopping for a couple of birthday gifts. The proprietor himself (whose "day job" is with Google) helped me, quickly, efficiently and pleasantly. I was wearing my coat with button on the lapel. Because this small business entrepreneur had been so nice, I asked him to read the button; although, because he was so successful, I thought that many people would consider him to be "rich." He obligingly read the button, first saying that "I don't wear buttons"; and then he said he liked it, and he took one.

So it goes.   Let's get the word out! [Bob C.]

People READILY Sign the Egalitarian Revolutionary Declaration, "This I Believe"

One of the first things we did to find out if people supported the idea of egalitarian revolution was to write a one-page statement of belief, titled "This I Believe," and see if anybody would sign it. "This I Believe," as you can see below when you read it, is not the typical kind of statement that people write when they want to get a lot of signatures. Instead of being a watered-down "lowest common denominator" statement that avoids saying anything too "controversial," "This I Believe" is, at least according to the standard wisdom about what people believe, extremely controversial.

The statement is explicitly against capitalism. It says we have a fake democracy. It says "Laws should only be made by meetings at the local level open to all who support equality and democracy. Social order on a larger scale—such as complex economic coordination—should be achieved by voluntary federation of local communities and workplaces, not by laws written by so-called "representatives" in distant capital cities or by commands from CEOs imposed from above."

It not only calls for no rich and no poor; it goes further with these words: "We should all equally own and enjoy the benefits of the earth's resources and the wealth that we produce by working together, with nobody being rich or poor. The principle of our economy should be, "From each according to ability, to each according to need," a Golden Rule idea as old as the Bible (Acts, 4:34-35). Work should be for shared goals, to produce things that people need and want, to share freely, not buy and sell."

It concludes by calling for a revolution, declaring: "A greedy, rich and powerful minority, who were never elected and therefore cannot be unelected, prevents Americans from making ours a more equal and democratic society, which is why we need a revolution to remove them from power."

Immediately after composing "This I Believe" I printed a copy with lines at the bottom for signatures and stepped outside my condominium building and asked the very first person I saw walking down the sidewalk if he would read it and sign if he agreed. Somewhat to my surprise (I'll admit!), he signed it. The next three pedestrians on the sidewalk did too. Then I walked to the local reservoir that people jogged aground and asked them, and of a dozen people I asked, ten signed it. I realized that the standard wisdom about what people thought was wrong.

To my neighbors near and far:

This I Believe

Something is very wrong about our society today. It should be based on the Golden Rule: "Do unto others as you would have others do unto you." But instead it is based on the opposite: "He who has the gold makes the rules." The ones with the gold celebrate greed and looking out for #1, destroy the environment for personal gain (like BP did to the Gulf), and pit people against each other to control them.

In the United States we have a fake democracy. Big Money owns the media and political parties, controls the electoral process and politicians, and determines government policies, which have nothing to do with campaign promises or what most people want. This is not right!

Our capitalist economy is based on, and perpetuates, enormous economic inequality. Most people are merely "hired hands" working for, and required to obey, employers who claim, illegitimately, to personally own the earth's land and minerals as well as the material and intellectual wealth produced by millions of working people. The poorest people do the hardest work and enjoy the benefits of socially produced wealth the least; the richest do the easiest work in great luxury or do no work at all, and enjoy the lion's share of these benefits. This is wrong!

We the undersigned want real democracy and an economy based on equality and concern for one another and generations yet unborn.

Laws should only be made by meetings at the local level open to all who support equality and democracy. Social order on a larger scale—such as complex economic coordination—should be achieved by voluntary federation of local communities and workplaces, not by laws written by so-called "representatives" in distant capital cities or by commands from CEOs imposed from above.

We should all equally own and enjoy the benefits of the earth's resources and the wealth that we produce by working together, with nobody being rich or poor. The principle of our economy should be, "From each according to ability, to each according to need," a Golden Rule idea as old as the Bible (Acts, 4:34-35). Work should be for shared goals, to produce things that people need and want, to share freely, not buy and sell.

A greedy, rich and powerful minority, who were never elected and therefore cannot be unelected, prevents Americans from making ours a more equal and democratic society, which is why we need a revolution to remove them from power.

We then went to public places to collect signatures for "This I Believe" (this was before we came up with the idea of making the PDR button.) We discovered that almost everybody who agreed to stop and read the statement readily signed it. "Where do I sign?" was the common reaction to reading it. Every time we "set up shop" (displayed a large poster with the text of the statement and had a clipboard handy for people to sign it) in front of supermarkets or bus stations in liberal urban Boston or at a town fair (called Unity Old Home Day) in rural conservative Unity, New Hampshire (where people listen to Rush Limbaugh, not NPR) and nearby rural Lempster, N.H., more than 80% of those who read it signed it, often more than 90%. In Unity, N.H. the co-chair of the town fair and one of the trustees of the town library were included among the twenty-four people who signed in one afternoon. Photos of people collecting signatures for, and people signing "This I Believe" are online.[9]

While rural conservatives and urban liberals were both eager to sign "This I Believe," it was interesting to hear how their questions about it tended to differ. The urban liberals wanted to know if the "laws only made by meetings at the local level" idea meant that bad people, such as racists, could make racist Jim Crow-type laws. (The answer is "no" and is discussed in Chapter Four and Chapter Eight.) The rural conservatives wanted to know if they would be less free personally. (The answer is "no" and is discussed in Chapter Five.)

We collected 1,855 signatures, 1740 of which are (at the time of writing anyway) clearly visible online[10] if one uses one's browser to zoom in. As mentioned in the Introduction, we determined that the people who did not stop to read "This I Believe" in front of a supermarket were just as willing to sign it as those who did stop when it was presented to them at their

---

[9] https://www.pdrboston.org/photos

[10] http://newdemocracyworld.org/banner-1.pdf

home's front porch when we went door-to-door in the neighborhood of the supermarket.

What Did We Learn From Buttoning and Collecting Signatures for "This I Believe"?

From both buttoning and collecting signatures for "This I Believe" we learned that ordinary people overwhelmingly agree with the idea of egalitarian revolution, not only the short version in the button but also the more detailed version in "This I Believe." The standard wisdom that says the ideas in this statement are "too radical" and will "scare people away" is just false.

From buttoning we learned that lots of people will wear an explicitly egalitarian revolutionary button when offered one.

We learned that the barber one of us goes to wanted to collect signatures, and did indeed collect thirty-three from his customers in one week. We learned that a woman we met wanted to collect signatures from members of her church, and that she collected twelve right away.

While we did encounter people who wanted to join our effort, we also learned that very few people, despite loving the button or "This I Believe," want to "button" or stand in a public place to collect signatures for "This I Believe." It is important to understand why this is. One reason no doubt is that people think the standard wisdom about people is true; they think that they would encounter mainly negative reactions if they "buttoned" or tried to collect signatures in a public place or by going door-to-door. Why, most people likely ask themselves, subject oneself to a negative experience? Those few who have agreed to "button" have been surprised at seeing the positive reactions totally exceeding the negative ones. This is the value of buttoning—it is a way for a person to discover the truth about what most ordinary people think no matter if they are conservative or liberal. But most people are reluctant to give it a try.

Another reason people shy away from getting involved in actively building an egalitarian revolutionary movement is that they think that even if most people want it, an egalitarian revolution is still impossible because the ruling class is too powerful. Some may even doubt that an egalitarian revolution, nice as it seems on paper, could remain good, or even be good to begin with, or be practical. All of these concerns are addressed in subsequent chapters.

You Can Find Out For Yourself What People Think about Egalitarian Revolution

Don't take my word for it. Find out for yourself what most people think about egalitarian revolution. Here's how. Either get some PDR buttons by going online[11] or use any online button-making company to order some made with the same words on it, and start "buttoning." See for yourself what happens. You may also make copies of "This I Believe"[12] and ask people to sign it and see what happens.

The Gallup Polling Company Won't Ask People What they Think about Egalitarian Revolution

I contacted the Gallup Poll company division of Gallup, Inc. in October of 2016 to pay for a national poll of all United States residents (not just registered voters) asking just two yes-or-no questions. (I didn't tell them what the questions were at first; the questions asked if the message on the PDR button was a good idea or a bad idea.) I spoke to Gallup representatives on two occasions by telephone. They were very friendly, said they could do what I wanted, and seemed pleased to take my money. But as soon as they heard what the exact questions were that I wanted in the poll, they said they would not do it. Here are the exact questions I put in my last email to the Gallup representative:

---

[11] https://www.pdrboston.org/why-wear-a-pdr-button

[12] http://newdemocracyworld.org/this.pdf

> *Some people say, "Let's remove the rich from power, have real--not fake--democracy, with no rich and no poor."*
>
> *Q #1. If this were really possible, would you like it to happen?*
>
> *Yes or No (or not sure)*
>
> *Q #2. If you knew that an organization sincerely wanted this to happen, would that make you think better or worse of the organization?*
>
> *Better or Worse (or not sure)*

Here's the reply I received after I sent the exact questions I wanted:

> **From:** "Joe Daly" <Joe_Daly@gallup.com>
> **To:** "John Spritzler" <spritzler@comcast.net>
> **Sent:** Friday, October 14, 2016 1:17:26 PM
> **Subject:** RE: Draft of two questions for national public release poll (all adult Americans)
>
> Hi John,
>
> Thanks for providing this information. Upon review this is not a project we can move forward with. For the reasons we discussed yesterday – scope or work and length of engagement. Additionally, the questions and subsequent data would not be the right fit for Gallup.
>
> Thanks again for your interest in our organization.
>
> All the best,
> Joe

There were no "reasons we discussed yesterday—scope or work and length of engagement"; that was just a dodge.

Clearly however, as Joe Daly said, *"the questions and subsequent data would not be the right fit for Gallup."* Gallup is not in the business of undermining the power of the ruling class by informing the public that the vast majority wants to remove the rich from power to have real—not fake—democracy with no rich and no poor.[13]

Dave Stratman's Insight About the Revolutionary Significance of Everyday Life

Most people, of course, do not wear an egalitarian revolutionary button or even know about the existence of, never mind signed, "This I Believe." Nonetheless, there is immense evidence, based on how most ordinary people behave in their everyday lives, that they want the world to be shaped by the egalitarian values of equality (no rich and no poor) and mutual aid (people helping each other, not pitted against each other in ruthless competition.) This is what the late Dave Stratman wrote about in his book, *We CAN Change the World: The Real Meaning of Everyday Life* (online[14]).

I summarized Stratman's insight in the Introduction. Dave and his wife had children in the Boston schools during the famous Boston school busing conflict. Dave got involved with black and white parents at this time who were trying to make the schools both integrated and better. Dave was initially a Leftist who, typical of the Left, believed that the white working class parents were racists with values the opposite of those of the black parents. He discovered that this was just factually wrong. With the help of the parents he met at this time, Dave

---

[13] Other polling companies informed me they could only poll registered voters or people online, which is not suitable in this context.

[14] http://www.newdemocracyworld.org/old/Revolution/We%20Can%20Change%20the%20World%20book.pdf

gained the insight that became the basis of his book: most people want to shape the world by equality and solidarity and resist as best they can the contrary capitalist values that control our society in every major institution.

Class conflict, Stratman came to see, is not what he had been taught as a Marxist. Class conflict is primarily over what values will shape society, not (as Marxists believe) a contest between classes that are each motivated by the same value of self-interest but happen to have conflicting interests. Ordinary people, because of their efforts that are usually on a small, personal, scale but occasionally break out into large scale efforts such as a strike, are the force that prevents the capitalist class from shaping society thoroughly by its values of greed and self-interest and oppression of the many by and for the benefit of the few. Because the capitalist class is so strong and ruthless, and yet has clearly failed to make our society the veritable hell it would be if it were entirely shaped by capitalist values, the conclusion is that there must be some very powerful anti-capitalist force at play. This force, though not even aware of itself subjectively, and not generally even noticed or remarked upon, is ordinary people with their positive values.

Stratman uses this insight to gain an understanding of all sorts of things, from the meaning of teenagers spending so much time on the phone with each other (it's about solidarity) to the major events in the world when he wrote in 1990. One such event was the large U.S. strike by Hormel meatpackers. Stratman writes of this strike:

> *"The strikers fought for more than a year, through tremendous hardships. Over 200 were arrested, and hundreds more were tear-gassed or otherwise attacked by police. Many lost their homes and cars. Others lost their health and life insurance and had their utilities cut off. All lost their jobs…The striking meatpackers understood that far more was at stake than their specific demands. In a speech to supporters in Boston in February, 1986, Pete Winkels, business agent of [the*

meatpackers' union] Local P-9, made this clear:

> *"Our people are never going to get back what we've already lost financially. We know that. But we're fighting for our families and for the next generation. And we're not going to give up."*

Stratman reports similarly on his meetings with people involved with the huge coal strike in England and the uprisings against the Soviet Union in Eastern Europe.

Stratman's book, in other words, is about why egalitarian revolution is possible because it is what most people actually want. It is about why the main task of a revolutionary is first, to know that revolution means shaping society by the values most people already have; and second, to help the vast majority of people gain the confidence in themselves--from knowing they are not alone and that their values are the ones that ought to shape society—that will enable them to make a revolution.

The Chief Obstacle To Building An Egalitarian Revolutionary Movement Is That People Think Hardly Anybody Else Wants It

By censoring any expressions of egalitarian revolutionary aspirations in the media and in other ways making them invisible (such as Gallup refusing to even ask people about it) the ruling class makes us doubt that many people even have such aspirations. But the ruling class also works hard to make people doubt that, even if it happened, an egalitarian revolution would improve things. This doubt is also an obstacle to building an egalitarian revolutionary movement.

One of the main tasks of an egalitarian revolutionary movement, in addition to helping people see they are not alone in having egalitarian revolutionary aspirations, is to make the egalitarian vision so clear and widely known that people will be confident it is indeed a goal worth fighting for.

For example, American school children are assigned George Orwell's book, *Animal Farm*, to read; they are told (incorrectly, by the way) that the story is a parable about what happens whenever people try to make society based on equality. If students as adults remember nothing else from that book they remember the famous line: "All animals are equal, but some animals are more equal than others." Moral: You can try to make it so that people are equal, but a new ruling elite will always emerge, so don't even try.

What students are not told, and what an egalitarian revolutionary movement would tell them, is that Orwell wrote his book as a sharp attack not on the idea of equality but on the hypocrisy and anti-egalitarianism, specifically, of the Bolshevik rulers of the Soviet Union. This movement would also inform them that Orwell wrote another nonfiction book, *Homage to Catalonia*, about his personal experience with egalitarians (who called themselves anarchists) in Spain in 1936 fighting for a society based on equality, how inspiring he found it in the areas where the egalitarians were in power, and how the Soviet rulers intervened in Spain to attack the egalitarians who were truly making a large part of Spain egalitarian.

Because of centuries of pro-capitalist propaganda, from the 17th century Thomas Hobbes and the 18th century Adam Smith to the present pundits filling our newspapers and airwaves, many people are not sure that the values of equality (no rich and no poor) and mutual aid (a.k.a. solidarity) could, or even should, shape all of society? What exactly, we wonder, would that mean? Is it even possible? Would it turn out to be better or worse than what we have? The next chapters shed light on all of these questions.

As I discuss in these next chapters, however, all of the lies that the ruling class spreads about the impossibility of making a much better, genuinely equal and democratic society, derive their credibility from a false premise. The false premise is the negative, standard view, of people. An egalitarian revolutionary movement can defeat these lies. The question is, Will there be such a movement large enough to matter? Who will build such a movement? The answer is, only people who, themselves, have (by "buttoning" or something equivalent) gained total confidence that they are not alone but rather part of the vast majority in having egalitarian revolutionary aspirations; only people who are mentally prepared to start acting like the majority they really are, instead of being so paralyzed by hopelessness that they see no point in even trying to build an egalitarian revolutionary movement.

CHAPTER TWO: WHY HAVE NO RICH AND NO POOR? (WHY WE NEED TO ABOLISH CLASS INEQUALITY)

First, to avoid misunderstanding, "No rich and no poor" here means that society is such that the economy is based on "From each according to reasonable ability, to each according to need or reasonable desire, with scarce things equitably rationed according to need." "Some rich and some poor" here means that, instead, it is a society in which some people, with no obligation to contribute reasonably according to ability, nonetheless are able to take far more than what is according to need or reasonable desire while others who do contribute reasonably according to ability are not able to take according to need or reasonable desire or have equitable access to scarce things rationed according to need.

A society with some rich and some poor is a class society, one based on class inequality. It is a society with an upper class and a lower class.

The very worst thing about a class society is that the upper class has to treat the lower class like dirt.

The upper class must do this in order to make lower class people "know their place," to make lower class people internalize the notion that they are an inferior lot that does not deserve to enjoy life the way upper class people do, and to accept their position at the bottom of an unequal society where they must unquestioningly do what they are told to do by their "betters"--the upper class folks.

If lower class people were treated with the full dignity and respect that upper class people take for granted as their due, then before long the upper class would be in serious trouble. Lower class people would begin to question--even more than they do already, which is a lot!--why society is so unequal with a privileged few lording it over everybody else.

The upper class knows very well that most working class people value equality and think the inequality of our society is morally wrong. The upper class knows that working class people, if left to themselves, would make a far more equal society. This is why the upper class dares not leave working class people to themselves. The upper class is forced to control the working class intensely. Treating the working class, especially the poorest working class people, like dirt is a strategy of social control that the upper class must use or risk revolution.

Almost all of the problems that the upper class creates for working class people are ways that the wealthy ruling upper class treats working class people like dirt. The upper class motive for this is not simply to maximize profits; it is to assert social domination over the working class.

When our rulers treat us like dirt, it is for the same reason that slave owners in previous centuries treated their slaves like dirt--to make them know their place. It is the same reason that the royalty and aristocracy treated peasants like dirt. The way that we're treated like dirt has changed over the years, but it's still a fact that we're treated like dirt, especially the poorest of us.

Treating working class people like dirt is what all of the following things, to select just some of many, have in common:

1. Paying low wages with minimal, if any, benefits and threatening to move jobs overseas if workers don't agree to even lower wages and reduced benefits.

2. Subjecting retail workers to "on call shifts" [15]--"periods for which an employee must keep an open schedule but might not end up working. Instead of simply reporting for work, the employee has to check in with a supervisor a few hours in advance. If she gets called in, she may have to scramble for a babysitter. If she doesn't get called in, she doesn't get paid, and it's too late to get a shift on a second job. 'People will be scheduled for eight on-call shifts in a pay period and only get called in for one shift,' says attorney Rachel Deutsch of the Center for Popular Democracy, a labor advocacy group." [*Boston Globe*, April 19, 2015]

3. Making people pay through the nose for health insurance, which may not even cover crucial health care needs when they are very sick or very old.

4. Telling our children in public schools that unless they score high on some absurd "high stakes" standardized test (that is designed so that children from poorer[16] families get lower scores[17]) they don't deserve to have a decent-paying job or perhaps any job at all.

---

[15] http://www.bostonglobe.com/opinion/editorials/2015/04/18/dante-ramos-call-shifts-string-workers-along/admOznKJNCM4YFuUced1QI/story.html

[16] https://www.theatlantic.com/education/archive/2014/07/why-poor-schools-cant-win-at-standardized-testing/374287/

[17] https://www.tucsonweekly.com/TheRange/archives/2015/05/15/standardized-test-scores-and-family-income

5. Having the police treat the poorest people like dirt, as discussed in numerous online articles, especially about police brutality[18].

6. Incarcerating people for things like smoking marijuana. More than two million people are behind bars in the U.S., and about half[19] of federal prisoners were convicted of drug related (marijuana more than any other drug) but not violent crimes, and are subjected in many cases to utter brutality such as long solitary confinement.

7. Making decent paying jobs, or any jobs at all, artificially scarce so people who are more than willing to work cannot find work that enables them to support themselves and a family, thus forcing them to rely on welfare or unemployment compensation and suffer being looked down upon and accused of being a free-loader or worse.

8. Using a combination of lies (like "Saddam Hussein's Weapons of Mass Destruction" and "Saddam was behind 9-11") and the poverty draft ("If you want a job your only hope is to enlist") and the offer of citizenship to non-citizens if they first serve in the military, thereby manipulating young men and women to join the military where they are ordered to kill innocent people abroad and risk being killed themselves, resulting for many in post traumatic stress disorder, deep remorse and suicide.

9. Telling people who smoke (who are disproportionately working class) who live in publicly subsidized housing that they cannot smoke in their own home, and (in some towns) having the government give a grant (a bribe, really) to landlords who order their tenants to quit smoking in their home or be evicted. Working class smokers are being increasingly

---

[18] https://www.pdrboston.org/police-brutality-and-oppression and http://www.huffingtonpost.com/2014/11/25/ray-lewis-ferguson-protests_n_6223102.html just for starters.

[19] https://www.bop.gov/about/statistics/statistics_inmate_offenses.jsp

treated like dirt[20]. Whatever the health argument[21] is for banning smoking in some places (and by the way, there is no persuasive evidence[22] that exposure[23] to second hand smoke increases the risk of lung cancer, despite the fact that many people just assume it does), the fact is that wealthy people can stay in expensive hotels[24] that have rooms where smoking is permitted, and they can smoke in their own expensive houses, but working class people are increasingly being denied the option of smoking at home and in this way they are being treated like dirt. The Affordable Care Act (Obamacare) treats smokers like dirt by allowing insurance plans to levy a surcharge of up to 50%[25] on tobacco users' premiums, while not allowing such a surcharge on other "high risk" behaviors or conditions. (The Cambridge Citizens for Smokers' Rights organization alerted me to these facts.[26])

10. Having hospitals treat working class people with far less respect and dignity than upper class people, as described in this *Boston Globe* article[27]. The article begins:

> *"He wanted the best medical care and came to the posh Pavilion at Brigham and Women's Hospital to get it, taking over two penthouse rooms with sweeping*

---

[20] http://thebaffler.com/salvos/off-our-butts-thunderstorm

[21] https://cfrankdavis.wordpress.com/2014/11/08/anti-smoking-experts-paid-by-big-pharma/

[22] http://www.acsh.org/news/2013/12/11/two-stories-one-link-found-secondhand-smoke-lung-cancer-one-seems-care

[23] http://www.nycclash.com/CaseAgainstBans/OSHA.html

[24] http://www.smokers-united.com/smoker-friendly/hotels/index.php?ln=en&coco=us&city=27

[25] https://www.sciencedaily.com/releases/2016/07/160706172008.htm

[26] https://www.facebook.com/ccsr.org/

[27] https://www.bostonglobe.com/lifestyle/health-wellness/2016/04/02/hospital-loses-its-way-care-for-vip-patient/YNCtmYKxtHQid17M58a9hN/story.html

views for a seven-month stay. The new patient had apparent ties to Middle Eastern royalty, and brought along a personal chef and an entourage of seven attendants. This, by itself, is not unheard of in the cost-is-no-object world of VIP medicine, in which elite hospitals in Boston and other cities accommodate wealthy patients, some from distant lands, who can afford the full tab for care — and for premium amenities like deluxe rooms that cost up to $800 a day more than regular ones."

11. Treating people who deliver the *Boston Globe* newspaper like dirt, both physically and mentally. The *Boston Globe* newspaper in 2016 switched to a new company to deliver its papers and the result was a catastrophe of Biblical proportions, forcing the owner of the *Globe* to publish an abject apology[28] from_that paper's owner *("First, I want to personally apologize to every Boston Globe subscriber who has been inconvenienced. We recognize that you depend on us, and that we've let you down")*, requiring the paper to hire 100 people just to handle (barely) all of the phone calls of outraged subscribers who were not getting their paper delivered at all, never mind on time, and forcing the owner to ask *Globe* reporters and columnists to help deliver the paper (*i.e.*, using their car to drive to unfamiliar neighborhoods throughout Massachusetts with stacks of papers to throw out the window.) It was a continuing weeks long disaster. Thousands of subscribers were cancelling every day. What is the significance of this?

First, if you read this article[29] **(headlined** "Long hours, little pay, no vacation for delivery drivers"**)** you will see how the

---

[28] http://www.bostonglobe.com/opinion/2016/01/05/apologize-our-loyal-readers/S0uNqQOjkx3UD7jD3WbbgL/story.html?p1=Article_Related_Box_Article_More

[29] http://www.bostonglobe.com/metro/2016/01/09/delivering-paper-long-hours-low-pay-vacation/QrlavPpVa8Qli3B2lz7B4N/story.html

people who deliver the *Globe* are treated like dirt. It is really disgusting. The article includes this description of one delivery worker:

> *"Juliani, who is 75 and has been delivering papers since 1984, is the picture of the perfect delivery man, the stalwart that thousands of subscribers were suddenly crying out for when their Globes stopped arriving last week. He knows the routes, he knows the streets, and he puts the paper right where it should be, with an efficiency that seems downright mechanical.*
>
> *"But Juliani is not a machine. And his life evokes how hard it is to make a living as the perfect delivery man. The job, once the bastion of neighborhood kids looking to make a few extra bucks on their bikes, has evolved into a grueling nocturnal marathon for low-income workers who toil almost invisibly on the edge of the economy.*
>
> *"Like many other newspaper delivery drivers, Juliani works 365 days a year and gets no vacation, overtime pay, or workers' compensation. He said he has not taken a day off in six years.*
>
> *"He delivers papers from 2 to 7 a.m., heads to a second job some days slinging weekly papers, and then a third dropping off Amazon packages until 8 p.m.*
>
> *"I have found myself so exhausted, literally sitting in someone's driveway, door open, and I'll wake up and say, 'Where the hell am I?'" he said. "I fell asleep right in my car. It might be 30 seconds and it might be 10 minutes."*

Second, if you read the *Globe* article headlined, "Globe delivery woes traced back to faulty routes,"[30] you will see that

---

[30] http://www.bostonglobe.com/metro/2016/01/15/globe-delivery-woes-traced-back-faulty-routes/vho07XxhtM8Ub8tALj7O6K/story.html

not only are the working class people who actually deliver the newspaper treated like dirt in the sense of being made to suffer, but they are also treated like dirt in the sense of being completely ignored regarding their knowledge of what the main problem was that caused the delivery catastrophe, even though these workers--and ONLY these workers--knew EXACTLY what the problem was--that the delivery routes they were given (by the new delivery company the *Globe* hired) were absurdly inefficient and stupid.

This entire debacle illustrates a fundamental fact about any society based on class inequality. The upper class must treat the lower class like dirt and in doing so it dares not respectfully ask working class people to participate as equals in figuring out how to get things done sensibly, and for that reason often does NOT get things done sensibly. One of the main reasons for abolishing class inequality is to abolish the treatment of ordinary people like dirt, which--and this is perhaps the worst thing about treating people like dirt--entails treating them like idiots and ignoramuses.

The main reason, therefore, for abolishing the class inequality of our society, for removing the rich from power to have no rich and no poor, is so that people will no longer be treated like dirt.

WHY NOT LET SOME PEOPLE BE JUST A LITTLE BIT WEALTHIER THAN OTHERS?

One of the reasons for making society egalitarian (*i.e.*, based not on money but rather on the principle of "From each according to ability, to each according to need," which is to say "No Rich and No Poor") is that if a society is based on money (*i.e.*, buying and selling) then the conditions exist for some people (because of luck or intention, as discussed below) to become a little bit wealthier than others. But with a little bit more wealth these people are a little bit more powerful. With a little bit more power (to influence politicians or other people) these people gain a little bit more wealth, which leads to more power, and so forth until eventually there is an upper class with far more wealth and power than other people, and this upper class will need to treat other people like dirt to keep them from making society more equal.

Mom and Pop Capitalism

There are two main ways that some people defend having "some rich and some poor." The first way I call "Mom and Pop Capitalism" and it stresses that some people can be a little bit wealthier than others, just not too much wealthier, as it is today.

Libertarians like Congressman Ron Paul, Justin Raimondo (of antiwar.com) and Alex Jones (of PrisonPlanet fame) say that what's needed is to restore America as "a republic, not an empire." They talk about the good old days when the Constitution was honored, when our foreign policy followed George Washington's advice to avoid meddling in the affairs of other nations, when we had "true capitalism" with small government, no military-industrial complex, and capitalism was about entrepreneurs producing good products, not bankers speculating as parasites on the productive economy.

Theirs is a vision of a "mom and pop" capitalist world that is very attractive. People are friendly and honest. The competition is about making "a better mouse trap," not "dog-eat-dog" competition to pit workers against each other in a race to the bottom. Nobody is extremely rich or poor. The needs of all are met for the most part. It is not hard to see why decent people are attracted to these ideas.

The problem, however, with "mom and pop" capitalism is the principles on which it is based and the kind of social relations that follow from those principles, and the dynamic that these set into motion. The principles are those of capitalism: capitalists own the means of production and their hired workers do not; people compete against each other instead of working for shared goals; instead of making the welfare of everybody the purpose of the economy, products and services are produced only to be sold for profit to those who can afford to buy them; it is considered natural and proper that some people are wealthier than others and should enjoy the benefits of socially produced wealth more than others.

When a society is organized around these capitalist principles, it inevitably enables some individuals, like the original John D. Rockefeller, to emerge and transform it eventually from a "mom and pop" world to a world of extreme inequality and corporate disregard for the values that decent people cherish. Mom and pop capitalism always and everywhere grows into corporate capitalism. This is the inevitable logic of the system that has landed us where we are today.

In the beginning of this process, the individuals like Rockefeller enjoy legitimacy and freedom of action because they operate within the principles of capitalism. But then they begin to grow wealthier. The competitive logic of capitalism cannot fail to produce winners and losers, and drive the winners to compete against each other resulting in ever larger and fewer winners. They buy up other companies until they dominate the industry, such as oil or railroads. With this economic power they gain power over the government like old John D. did, and like the railroad barons who had the government give them vast tracts of public land did. Soon the economic and political power of the biggest winners dominates the land. The rise to power of the Rockefellers and our present day plutocracy and their military-industrial complex and wars based on lies and vampire bankers like Goldman-Sachs are not flukes; they are the full development of the social dynamics of a long ago seemingly benign "mom and pop" capitalism.

Creating (or re-creating) "mom and pop" capitalism does not get to the root of the problem, which is capitalist social relations. Trying to make a truly better world based on equality and mutual aid by creating "mom and pop" capitalism is like trying to rid a lawn of crabgrass by merely mowing the weeds down instead of uprooting them entirely. It may produce a lawn that doesn't look too bad initially, but the roots of the weeds remain and will eventually make the lawn ugly again.

Capitalism itself needs to be replaced by something very different, and this will require a fundamental social revolution. A new kind of economic system needs to be created based on the principle that people contribute according to ability and take according to need, in a moneyless society in which things are shared, not bought and sold. And a new conception of democracy needs to emerge, in which lawmaking power exists only at the local level in assemblies that all who support equality and mutual aid may attend, with social order on a larger scale deriving from voluntary federation of local communities and workplaces.

As is becoming increasingly obvious to the American public, the problem in our society is a very big problem. And very big problems require very big solutions. Mom and pop capitalism is not a big enough solution to work.

Libertarianism

The second main way that "some rich and some poor" is defended is libertarianism, which says the problem in our present society is not class inequality but rather only the government's excessive power and interference in our lives. The following little tale illustrates the problem with the libertarian idea.

Libertaria: A Libertarian Paradise

Most people have never heard of Libertaria (not to be confused with Liberia), so let me tell you a little bit about this most interesting nation. It is a veritable libertarian paradise. With a population of fifty million people and plentiful natural resources, Libertaria is truly blessed.

There is a government in Libertaria, but it is so minimal that the Libertarians hardly notice it. The government is barely more than just the administration of a modest military force to protect Libertaria from foreign invasion, and the military consists entirely of volunteers--no draft or forced conscription whatsoever. The government also enforces private contractual agreements. The government does not censor speech, press, the media or the internet in any way.

There are no laws of any sort in Libertaria regarding sex for consenting adults. Sure, there's a law against adults having sex with minors too young to give informed consent, but that's all.

There are no laws prohibiting adult possession or use of drugs. People are free to smoke, inject, snort or otherwise enjoy whatever substance they wish. If somebody harms him or herself, well, it's their right to do so as long as they don't harm somebody else in the process.

It probably goes without saying that there is no national ID card; privacy is honored in Libertaria. The only time you tell another who you are is when you want to, period!

There is no "corporate welfare" or government handouts to business in Libertaria. Corporations and businesses either thrive because they are better than their competition, or they fail otherwise. Likewise, there are no government barriers to international trade, no tariffs or sanctioned foreign nations one cannot trade with.

People in Libertaria don't rely on the "government teat" to support them in their old age. There is no government-run Social Security. There are private companies that people can invest in if, and to the extent, they want to, to provide income if and when they may choose to retire. People are free to invest for their future, or not, as they see fit. If they regret their youthful failure to invest for their old age, well, that's nobody's fault but their own. In Libertaria people are expected to take responsibility for their lives.

Although the government has nothing to do with it, people in Libertaria are perfectly free to give to charity, and to create charitable organizations to do that on a large scale. Those who wish to donate to the charity of their choice are free to do so; those who don't wish are free not to.

As one can imagine, taxes and government spending in Libertaria are as minimal as one could possibly imagine, given the need to operate a defensive military and enforce very minimal legislation.[31]

The Constitution of the government in Libertaria is just like the one in the United States. The difference is that the government of Libertaria understands the importance of not making stupid, counter-productive and unnecessary laws-- something that the government prides itself on very much.

What's Life Like in Libertaria?

Describing what life is like in Libertaria is not simple, because it is very different depending on how much money one has. A small number of people in Libertaria have an enormous amount of money--many billions of dollars for a single person, in fact. (Their currency is dollars, and one of their dollars happens to be worth one U.S. dollar at the time of this writing.) It didn't used to be this way.

Many generations ago, in a distant past period that has been pretty much lost to the memory of most living people in Libertaria, everybody in Libertaria owned essentially the same amount of wealth and had essentially the same income. But you know how things are: some were luckier than others, some were more clever than others, some had no siblings and inherited all their parents' wealth and others had to divide it up among lots of siblings, and so forth; after a while some ended up being a little bit wealthier than others.

And, no surprise here, people with a little bit more wealth than others had a little bit more influence than others. They were able to acquire more property. They bought land that other

---

[31] Not surprisingly, the leaders of Libertaria score 100% libertarian on this little quiz at **https://www.theadvocates.org/quiz/quiz.php**

people owned. People who once were able to support themselves by working on their own land or working with their own tools or machines began to lose their property. Sometimes they were forced to sell it cheap because they farmed and bad weather destroyed their crop. Sometimes they had to sell their property cheap because they couldn't compete with a larger business selling the same commodity they did but at a lower price because economy of scale favored the larger business. Those who lost their property for one reason or another wondered if maybe something was unfair about what happened. But the transfer of their property to wealthier people didn't violate any of the laws of Libertaria, and it all seemed quite legitimate as far as the prevailing norms of the society went, so what could the poor losers do but resign themselves to their misfortune?

The wealthier, luckier, cleverer people were free to acquire wealth without any government interference. They came to own little businesses that were larger than the others, and they were able to employ more employees than the others. They were the most successful of the self-employed. The less fortunate, the ones who had to sell the land or tools or machines they had once used to make a living as a self-employed person, had to work for an employer, as an employee.

And, things being the way they are, some little businesses won out in the competition with others and became big businesses, employing lots and lots of people and owning vast tracts of land or mines or huge factories and skyscraper office buildings. The owners of these big businesses became wealthier and wealthier. The big businesses had more power than the small businesses, and began to order the small businesses around, telling little suppliers, for example, that they would only pay them a low price: take it or leave it. And the little businesses "took it" because "leaving it" meant going out of business and having to work as an employee for some business.

To work as an employee in Libertaria was something people

tried to avoid by being self-employed. But with the few extremely large corporations calling the shots, it just wasn't possible for very many people to succeed as a small businessperson; most ended up having to find work as an employee.

By the time we reach the present day in this brief history, there is extreme economic inequality in Libertaria. The vast majority of people are employees (or unemployed when, as often happens, they are laid off during economic downturns.) The few who own businesses are very well off; some are even billionaires. The economy works very well because there is no government interference messing it up with unintended consequences of well-intentioned legislation. Profits enrich the few. Businesses that make luxury items for the rich do very well.

At the same time, life is very hard now for the employees. The business owners pay their workers as little as possible, which is very little indeed because a worker has to take it or leave it, and leaving it means starving. People who can't find work receive, of course, no pay at all (although they might get some charity if they are lucky.) Wages might not be as low as they are if the workers had strong unions and could go on strike to win higher wages. But the culture in Libertaria is very much opposed to such collectivist solutions to problems. People are supposed to take responsibility for their own lives, and solve their own problems as individuals. Unions, it is felt, would take away from the freedom of the worker. If a union declared a strike, then a worker would be compelled to stay away from his or her job, against his or her own will: tyranny!

But even if the workers did have unions, what could they really accomplish? Unions don't object to capitalism, and in a free capitalist society if a business pays higher wages than its competition then it will eventually go out of business, and all of its workers will lose their jobs. If a union demanded substantially higher wages at one company, it would have to fight for higher wages in all of the other companies competing with it. But some of the competing companies are (or might become) located in nations other than Libertaria. The union would then have to organize workers all over the world.

Even then, however, the owners of the business could decide to just close shop, on the grounds that workers are demanding wages that make it impossible to make a profit. What could the union do then? The owners of the business own all of its productive wealth--its land and machines and buildings and intellectual property and so forth--and they are free (yes FREE, at least in Libertaria) to do with their property whatever they wish.

Alas, the workers in Libertaria live in abject poverty. They feel lucky to have any job at all, no matter how little it pays. The price and production of commodities is based on supply and demand. The impoverished workers have so little money that there is little demand (in terms of the number of purchasing dollars, that is) for the cheapest necessities of life, and therefore only the bare minimum required to keep the workers alive is produced. (No profit could be made producing any more than this.) The business owners with lots of money from their profits provide a large demand for luxuries. So workers are employed producing luxuries, from fancy watches to huge yachts and private jets (and some are employed, of course, as servants with fancy names like "personal trainer," *etc.)* The economy, as noted above, works fine; it's just geared to producing luxuries for the few and bare necessities for the many.

But Something's Not Quite Right

One of the troubling aspects of life in Libertaria is that now and then some workers get it into their heads that something isn't quite right. Yes, they are free, but something is missing. Yes, they are free to use any drugs they can afford to buy (not the pure high grade stuff of course, but the cheap stuff with sometimes poisonous adulterants), and they are free to have sex with their sibling or a same-sex person and even marry them if they both consent, and they don't have to serve in the military unless that's the only job available (which somehow seems to be the case for so many people), and they are free to buy whatever foreign product they want (if they can afford it, of course), and they are free to watch any TV show or internet site or listen to any radio station or read any newspaper they wish (funny how so many seem to be owned by a few of the richest people in Libertaria and promote ideas that legitimize the unequal status quo) and they are not taxed a lot by the government (not that they earn enough to pay taxes in the first place), and the government leaves them alone for the most part (although private security firms with armed police help the government make sure that property rights are strictly enforced) and the government doesn't invade their privacy, and yet...something's missing.

To make sure that such workers don't rock the boat and introduce any kind of tyranny into Libertaria, the business owners shrewdly decided to ensure that workers are indoctrinated with ideas that will make them accept their unpleasant lot as natural and inevitable. Various ways of doing this have been experimented with. The method that is now being used is to teach the workers, especially when they are young school children, that society is a meritocracy in which the best people rise to the top and the other ones fall where they belong, to the bottom. The children are taught that economic inequality is a good thing, a necessary thing in fact, because it is what motivates people to work hard and rise higher in society. Most of the children learn (it's set up to make this happen on purpose, of course) that they are meant to be at the bottom. They live lives of various forms of self-contempt and with feelings of inferiority. A bit sad, perhaps; but at least they are free from the tyranny of big government.

Teaching people about the wonders of Libertaria's meritocracy has been quite successful, but not quite successful enough to make the wealthy people of Libertaria feel sufficiently secure against the always-lurking threat of revolution. To deal with this problem, the leaders of Libertaria decided a while ago to use divide-and-rule against the poor people--the working class. The idea is simple. Pick some subset of the poor people, based on race or religion or ethnicity, and treat them much worse (or better) than the others. Make the ones treated worse blame the ones treated better as their enemy. And make the ones treated better fear the ones treated worse. Foment a little violence now and then; stir the pot; keep people divided against each other. It makes life brutally hellish for the workers, but it does the job of preserving the unequal status quo quite nicely.

Dear reader of this description of Libertaria, you might be thinking that Libertaria is not a great place to live for the majority of its population--the working class. But the leaders of Libertaria would caution you to avoid jumping to this rash conclusion. They would point out that things are not really that bad for the poor in Libertaria because people are free to give to charity, and many do. The leaders would also remind you that every single citizen of Libertaria is completely free to start a business and try to get rich. Doesn't that reassure you, dear reader, that Libertaria is actually a fine place to live, rich or poor?

Egalitarian Revolution in Libertaria

Just recently in Libertaria a revolution broke out. You might think that the revolutionaries wanted to set up a powerful central government that would make zillions of laws and take possession of people's property and tax them a whole lot and do all of the kind of things that the Libertarian government proudly does not do. Indeed, the leaders of Libertaria actually hoped that this is what the revolutionaries would say they wanted to do. Why? Because then it would have been very easy for the Libertarian leaders to turn the public against the revolutionaries, using well-known and persuasive arguments about the evils and stupidity of powerful and intrusive central governments. But no! The revolutionaries were opposed to having any central government with law-making powers at all.

Well then, what DID the revolutionaries want?[32] They wanted the following two things:

#1. A government based on voluntary federation of local assemblies of egalitarians. What's an egalitarian? An egalitarian is a person who believes in equality and mutual aid. What does "equality" mean in this context? Equality means that people who contribute reasonably to the economy have an equal right to enjoy the fruits of the economy according to need and reasonable desire. And "mutual aid"? Mutual aid means that people should help each other, regardless of race or religion or ethnicity or nationality. Voluntary federation means that the only bodies that can make laws are local assemblies, where all egalitarians, and only egalitarians, in the community have a right to participate as equals with all others in writing laws. It means that local assemblies can send delegates to meet with delegates from other assemblies to make proposals (not laws!) for the local assemblies to implement or not as they wish (typically doing so after back and forth negotiations to arrive at a proposal satisfactory to sufficient numbers of local assemblies to actually carry out the proposal.) These assemblies of delegates from local assemblies (or of delegates from assemblies of delegates, *etc.*) may encompass delegates from a large region, a nation or even the entire planet. There is no lack of large scale planning and coordination, but it is based on mutual agreement rather than commands (*i.e.,* laws) handed down from above by a central government.

#2. A sharing economy. What's a sharing economy? It's an economy in which people, by mutual agreement (using voluntary federation) share the fruits of their economic productivity with each other based on the principle of "From each according to reasonable ability, to each according to need and reasonable desire." Things that are not scarce are free for anybody in the sharing economy; scarce things are

---

[32] The following text about voluntary federation and a sharing economy briefly summarizes what is discussed in greater detail in Chapter Four and illustrated with real-life examples in Chapter Ten and Nine respectively.

rationed according to an equitable method determined by the voluntary federation government. People own all the personal property (houses, clothing, musical instruments, books, *etc.*) they reasonably should own; they just don't own what is properly owned by society: the means of social economic production such as vast tracts of land, mineral wealth in the earth, factories, *etc.* There is no buying and selling, and hence no money. Old people who have worked reasonably in the early years of their life, children too young to be expected to work, and people who are for some reason unable to work, can just take what they reasonably need and want for free. Those who don't contribute reasonably (lazy freeloaders and people who think that useful work is "beneath" them) have no right to enjoy the fruits of the economy.

The latest news from Libertaria is that the revolutionaries are gaining support from the poor people who, it turns out, support equality and mutual aid, making them egalitarians, not libertarians, it would seem. Apparently they think a sharing economy is better--morally and practically--than a capitalist one. They agree that big central governments are wrong, but they fail to see what's right, to take just one example, in telling old people who have worked all their lives, "Hope your privatized Social Security investments paid off because otherwise you'll have to work till you drop"--especially since workers are paid so little that they have practically nothing to invest.

If the egalitarians take over and make a revolution, the rich people in Libertaria will denounce it as "tyranny"--an attack on their freedom. And they will have a point! No longer will people in Libertaria be free to live in luxury at the expense of others. No longer will people with lots of money be free to enjoy the wealth and power and privilege that a billionaire has compared to an impoverished worker. No longer will a few be free to live in a society that praises them as a superior meritocracy while shaming the majority with lies about their "unworthiness." No longer will the few be free to use divide and rule against the many to create fear and mistrust amongst the many. Freedom is a concept that can be invoked by those who wish to oppress and dominate others (as discussed in Chapter Five).

In Libertaria, the wealthy few talk about "freedom." The rest are starting to talk about equality and mutual aid, and the freedom to live in an egalitarian society. If there is to be anything approaching paradise on earth for the many, it will be in an egalitarian, not a libertarian, world.

What about the arguments that say inequality (some rich and some poor) is better than equality (no rich and no poor)--even for the poorest?

Ludwig von Mises provides what is perhaps the most articulate defense of class inequality, *i.e.,* why there ought to be some rich and some poor, in his article titled "The Foundations of Liberal Policy"[33] which gives two faulty arguments.

First, von Mises argues that capitalism, which is indeed inherently based on economic inequality, produces more wealth than egalitarianism, and thereby provides a higher standard of living for the poorest people than they would have in an egalitarian society where all were economically equal. It turns out that this is just factually not true, as discussed in some detail in Chapter Nine. To the extent that we want to increase productivity (an important question, given important environmental concerns and the need for human life on the planet to be sustainable in the long term, and also that people may wish to work less and make do with less but have more leisure) an egalitarian society is far more capable of that than a capitalist one, and is far more likely to do it in a manner that is responsible rather than motivated by the greed of a few billionaires.

Second, von Mises argues that everybody benefits when just a few have luxuries. His claim is that what is considered a luxury ends up eventually being considered a necessity (von

---

[33] https://mises.org/library/foundations-liberal-policy

Mises cites the example of using a fork to eat--initially, he says, only the rich aristocrats used a fork and regular people used their fingers; he also cites indoor toilets enjoyed, initially, only by the rich but now considered a necessity by even the poorest in developed nations.) If such luxuries could not be initially enjoyed by the rich, he argues, then they would never be enjoyed by anybody.

This is a truly stupid argument. It uses the conclusion it aims to prove as a premise--totally illogical. It amounts to saying this: "**In a society that is organized in such a way that** novel things like forks and indoor toilets cannot be widely available to all unless they are first made available only to a few very rich people, then any novel thing not first made available only to a few rich people will never be widely available to all." But a pro-egalitarian argument would be just as logical. It would go like this: "**In a society organized in such a way that** novel things like forks and indoor toilets become widely available to all only after being made available to a few who enjoy them as a result of the rationing of scarce things in an equitable manner according to need or reasonable desire, then any novel thing not first made available only to a few who enjoy them as a result such rationing of scarce things will never be widely available to all."

People like von Mises argue from the premise that capitalism (or, more generally, class inequality) is the only way society can be organized, and idiotically conclude, therefore, that whatever good things appear in a capitalist (or class-inequality) society could only have appeared in a capitalist (or class-inequality) society in the manner that capitalism (or class inequality) causes them to appear. According to this "logic," if slaves ever got a decent meal it would prove that the only way a poor person could get a decent meal is by being a slave in a slave society.

We're always told by the defenders of inequality that the very rich--people like Bill Gates--produce jobs and if they weren't allowed to be very rich they would stop producing jobs. This argument, like the one above about how we need rich people to enjoy luxuries others don't get to enjoy, rests on the assumption that the only way the world can be is the way it presently is--a capitalist world. Sure, if a few rich capitalists personally own all of the things, like farmland and factories, *etc.*, that people need in order to produce the products and services they want (which is what capitalism means), and if the only way a regular person can obtain any of these products and services is by paying for them with money (which is what capitalism means), and if the only way a regular person can obtain money is by "having a job," *i.e.*, agreeing to work for a capitalist and do whatever he or she commands (which is what capitalism means), then yes, it is true that only a rich capitalist "produces" jobs and regular people need jobs: a lot of IFs!

But what if it is NOT a capitalist society but an egalitarian one? What if the farmland and factories, *etc.* are, like the air we breathe and the sunshine that warms us, not the personal property of a few rich capitalists but rather acknowledged to belong to all of society for the good of all? What if people in local communities democratically decided how the farmland and factories, *etc.* in their community should be used? What if they decided to let everybody who wanted to work reasonably on the farmland and in the factories, *etc.* do so, and then to let them take for free the products and services they needed or reasonably wanted (or have equal status when scarce things are equitably rationed according to need)? Then nobody would need or even want a "job" (meaning an agreement to work for a rich capitalist and do whatever he or she commanded). Here's a sort of parable about this:

No Jobs on this Island

Before you decide that we need rich people to provide jobs, please imagine this little story. Once upon a time a thousand passengers and crew members of an ocean liner cruise vessel became stranded on a remote, previously unknown, island when their ship sank after hitting a rock near it. They had no radio and knew that they would probably never be rescued. They knew that they would have to make as good a life for themselves on the island as they could, with nobody to rely on but themselves.

On their first day on the island they gathered at the beach to discuss what to do. First, let's think a moment about what did NOT happen. Here's what did NOT happen:

> First speaker: "Look everybody, we're doomed to die. Even though there are edible plants growing on this island that could be farmed, and wildlife that could be domesticated to provide food and milk and dairy products, and plants suitable for making clothing and trees suitable for making timbers to build houses, and plants good for medicinal purposes, and iron ore under the ground that could be made into all sorts of useful things, and so on and so forth, it matters not. The only way these natural resources could ever be turned into the things we need to survive is if there were somebody to provide jobs for us, so that we could be hired to plant crops and mine the iron and treat sick people with the medicinal plants and harvest the timber trees and build houses and so forth. But, alas! There is no rich person on this island to create these jobs. There is nobody to hire us. We shall surely perish.
>
> Second speaker: Sadly, the first speaker is correct.
>
> All the remaining speakers: Oh! Woe is us. We shall surely perish.

Why did this not happen? Because the stranded people were not stupid and crazy, obviously! Here's what DID happen.

They agreed among themselves to form groups to do things that needed to be done in order to survive and eventually make a comfortable life for each other. Some harvested edible plants and began farming them, others harvested timber from trees, others built homes with the timbers, some built boats and some used them to catch fish to eat, some treated the sick with the medicinal plants, some mined iron, others made iron tools, and so and so forth. They freely shared things according to need among all those who worked reasonably according to ability. (Yes, there was one jerk who thought work was beneath him and who insisted on having the others serve him as if he were a king, but when he discovered that nobody gave him so much as the time of day he began helping out with some of the work. And yes, there were some children and elderly people and sick people who were not expected to work and who were provided with the things they needed like everybody else.) Nobody hired anybody to do anything; people just did what they had to do to make a good life for themselves on the island. There were no jobs. And yet the people lived very well. They even discovered they could work much less than 40 hours per week to provide everything they really needed or wanted, and have lots more leisure time than they had when they worked back home.

Now you might wonder why this doesn't happen in our actual society. To help see why, imagine that one day on the island something like this happened.

One of the stranded passengers--let's say his name was Mr. Gates--had a pistol. And he knew he was the only person with a firearm. This gave him an idea. "I can be rich!" he said to himself. The next day, when everybody was on the beach discussing what needed to be done, Mr. Gates brandished his pistol and announced to the people of the island:

> "Listen up everybody! I own this island. I own the land and everything on it and under it. I own the plants and the trees. I own the wildlife. I own the minerals underground. You cannot take any of these things; they are my private property. If you touch any of these things without my permission, you are a criminal and will be punished.
>
> "Don't you ever forget, I have a pistol and you don't.
>
> "Now, I am a good person. I don't want you to starve. Here's what I'm going to do. I'm going to create jobs for

all of you. I'm going to hire you to harvest plants and timber and mine iron and grow food and build houses and produce all sorts of things and services with my island. Everything you produce will, of course, be my private property, not yours, because I am the owner of the island and you are just my employees.

"If you want food or a house or medical care and so on, then you will have to buy or rent those things from me because they are all--don't forget!--my private property. I will pay you wages in the form of suitable leaves from one of my trees, with numbers and my signature on them. The numbers will denote the value of the leaf in units I call dollars. I will pay you enough dollars for your labor so that most of you (but not all of you) will have enough to buy or rent as much of my private property as you need to just barely survive and keep working for me. Those of you whom I refuse to hire or to whom I pay too little to survive will serve me well--as an example to the others of what will happen to them if they don't go along with the way I'm arranging this island society.

"Don't worry! This island is going to be a wonderful economic success. Most of what I will pay you to produce, and most of the services I will pay you to perform, will be above and beyond what you will ever be able to buy or rent with your wages. These products and services will be for my personal comfort and amusement. I will need many houses, and very big ones. I will need lots of servants and personal attendants and entertainers. I will need people to carry me wherever I wish to be taken on the island. I will need a big yacht and a crew for it so I can enjoy the good life. And I will have all of these things.

"You may be thinking, 'That Mr. Gates wouldn't be getting away with this if he didn't have his pistol.' But listen carefully. I don't own the island because I possess a pistol. It's the other way around. I possess the pistol because I own the island. I own the island because I am better than all of you. I'm smarter. I work harder. I come from better stock. I deserve to own the island. You don't. Things are the way they are because that is how they ought to be. It is only natural that the superior person owns the island. If it weren't for me, nobody would know what to do. It would be chaos. Nobody would work because there'd be no motivation--no wages--to work. You'd all be living in much worse poverty. You'd perish of starvation and exposure to the elements. You are lucky I'm here to create jobs for you.

"Furthermore, if it weren't for me and the army that I'm going to hire and command to defend our island, then you'd be conquered and enslaved by your REAL ENEMY--the terrorist Muslim hordes who, I have been told by my secret sources, live on a nearby island, have weapons of mass destruction, and want to take away our freedom. You may not love me, but if you fail to obey me you'll suffer a far worse fate at the hands of the terrorist Muslims, and don't you forget it!"

What do you think the people on the island did when they heard Mr. Gates's announcement? Did they accept his new social arrangement? Or did they grab his pistol and tell him to go to hell?

The reason it is not known what the people on the island did is because they're still trying to decide. Really, you see, it's not a little island where this story is being played out. It's our very own society. We are the people on the island. We've got our Mr. Gateses to contend with. What are we going to do?

What About The Arguments That Say "Inequality Is Not Really So Bad"?

As economic inequality has become, for the first time in many decades, a topic of mainstream public discussion (thanks in large measure to Occupy Wall Street), the apologists for capitalism and economic inequality have felt it necessary to defend class inequality with every argument they can come up with. Here are some of their arguments of the "inequality is not so bad" variety:

> 1. So what if some are poor and others rich? The poorest people today are better off (with DVD players and washing machines, etc.) than most of the wealthiest people were in the past.
>
> 2. Yes, poor people rise up now and then in protest, and they have legitimate grievances. But their grievance is NOT that some are richer than others; their only complaint is that they want things like safer working conditions and higher pay and better benefits. They want a better life, which is not at all the same thing as wanting everybody to be equal.
>
> 3. Economic inequality is not such a bad thing when one takes into account that people are not necessarily stuck in their place in society their whole life. Poor people often become much richer later in life. Many of the richest people started out very poor, or were the children of rich people who started out very poor.
>
> 4. Economic inequality is not really as bad as many alarmists say it is; for example, the alarmists ignore the benefits that middle class homeowners enjoy from owning their home when these benefits aren't captured by money records.

The flaw in these arguments is that they are really all beside the point. The problem with class inequality is not merely that it is unjust (which it certainly is, because the child of a janitor deserves as good and fun and comfortable and secure and healthy and enjoyable a life and standard of living as the child of a doctor or anybody else). Nor is the problem with class inequality that nobody can rise from poor to rich (some do, but so what?); or that billionaires sometimes make their fortunes from scratch (so what?). And just because poor people often try to improve their condition without specifically demanding an end to class inequality doesn't mean that they wouldn't much prefer to live in an egalitarian society; the main reason people don't demand an end to class inequality is because they think it is an impossible demand to win.

No. The defenders of class inequality don't even mention the most important reasons to abolish it. **The top reason is that it means ordinary people are treated like dirt, as discussed above.**

The other big problem with class inequality, in addition to its fundamental injustice, is that it is the root cause of many evils, some of which are listed here in order from bad to even worse:

1. Class inequality is the root cause of crime (discussed further in Chapter Fifteen, which shows that class inequality and not something the matter with black people is the cause of crime) and corruption (discussed more in Chapter Thirteen.) A society based on class inequality provides a strong motive for people to do anything--no matter how evil--to get richer than others, because such a society tells people that a person's value is determined by how rich they are. This is why, in societies like ours that tolerate class inequality, people murder their spouse for the life insurance money, or they pay their workers the lowest wages they can get away with, or they sell products to the public that they know are unsafe, or they wage unjust wars, or a million other foul deeds we are all too familiar with, all for the love of money. Only in an egalitarian society will people be able to trust each other, knowing that the other person is not doing or saying something merely in order to get richer at the expense of others.

2. Class inequality makes genuine democracy impossible. In a society like ours in which money is power and some have a lot and most have little or none, there can be no real democracy. It will be one-dollar-one-vote, not one-person-one-vote, no matter what the law says it is. Money will buy people and influence one way or another, just as water flows to the ocean one way or another no matter what dams are built.

3. Class inequality gives power to people who use it for immoral purposes. In a society like ours based on money, power can (and inevitably will) be concentrated in the hands of a few, because money is something that can be concentrated in the hands of a few. Furthermore, the kind of power that money confers to its owner is morally very bad; it is the power to induce somebody do something that he or she knows is morally wrong, such as firing a worker who agitates on behalf of fellow workers or laying people off in order to increase profits for rich people or spreading a divide-and-rule lie in a newspaper or covering up an important truth. Money gives its owner the power to make people do bad things they would not otherwise do. In contrast, the power that accrues to a person because of his or her ability to persuade others to do something because it would be good for them or for others-- this kind of good power is undermined by the power of money, which in turn enjoys its power because of class inequality (when class inequality is abolished, there is no longer any role for money because the economy is a sharing economy.)

4. Class inequality makes science for the people impossible. In a society like ours based on class inequality, everybody knows that Big Money calls the shots in every area of life, including science. Everybody knows that scientists and doctors[34] are influenced[35] by Big Money[36]. We hear about how medical journals print articles that purport to be independent of any pharmaceutical company but that are actually secretly written by "ghost-authors of papers written by drug companies or their agents"[37] to get doctors to prescribe a drug that they wouldn't prescribe if they new the truth about

---

[34]　http://www.nybooks.com/articles/2009/01/15/drug-companies-doctorsa-story-of-corruption/

[35] http://www.nejm.org/doi/full/10.1056/NEJM200410073511522

[36]　http://e-patients.net/archives/2012/03/former-nejm-editors-on-the-corruption-of-american-medicine-ny-times.html

[37]　http://www.nybooks.com/articles/2009/01/15/drug-companies-doctorsa-story-of-corruption/

how bad or unproven it really was. The poisoning of the drinking water in Flint, MI, required[38] this corruption of science.

Many people are therefore, quite understandably, extremely skeptical about anything scientists tell them. Even when what the scientists say is true, many don't believe it. Does HIV cause AIDS? Does smoking cause lung cancer? Is fracking safe for our environment? Are people causing catastrophic global warming? Anybody who knows how much Big Money controls scientific research cannot help but be skeptical of all such claims.

When there is so much distrust of scientists, people will not do the things that scientists say would be good for them to do. Under these circumstances, science cannot serve the people, as most scientists want it to. Only in an egalitarian society will scientists be able to avoid ever doing the bidding of the very rich at the expense of others and gain the trust of the public so that their scientific knowledge can truly serve the people.

5. The mistrust by the public of scientists who may be acting in the interests of Big Money is just one small example of the enormous mistrust that pervades our entire society. When a society is, like ours, based on class inequality then people have a strong motive to lie to others, to cheat them and take advantage of them, in order to acquire great wealth and power at the expense of others. In such a society parents teach their children to distrust others so as not to be taken advantage of by the proverbial "used car salesman"; except it isn't just used car salesmen, it's virtually any stranger that one has to deal with in life. Only in an egalitarian society will this wealth-and-power motive for lying and cheating others be eliminated. Only in an egalitarian society will there be a true basis for trusting strangers that one deals with. The advantages--emotionally!-- of living in such a society are beyond calculation.

---

[38] https://www.commondreams.org/news/2016/02/03/professor-who-exposed-flint-crisis-says-greed-has-killed-public-science

6. When society is divided into the haves and the have-nots, then inevitably have-nots tend to resent, and be angry at, the haves. Knowing this, the haves tend to fear the have-nots. Fear, anger and resentment pervade all of society--all because it is not egalitarian.

WHAT THE RICH DO TO ENFORCE INEQUALITY IS WORSE THAN THE INEQUALITY ITSELF!

7. In a society based on class inequality the rich and powerful few must somehow persuade the many at least to tolerate the inequality. The ways that ruling elites do this often involve, in one way or another, inculcating in the many the notion that they are inferior and less deserving than the few. Thus the American public school system does exactly this with high stakes standardized tests designed to have a substantial failure rate no matter how well students learn their lessons[39]. Making people feel inferior and less deserving is a profound attack on their humanity, and it is an essential part of any society based on class inequality. For this reason alone we would be justified in abolishing class inequality.

8. Perhaps the worst thing that ruling elites do to make people tolerate inequality is to foment divide-and-rule conflict between people along national, race, religious or ethnic lines, using lies and manipulation. Ruling elites want the people they rule over to think that their rulers are protecting them from some bogeyman "real enemy" so they will obey their rulers. To accomplish this, ruling elites lie about ordinary people and manipulate things to create intense fear, distrust and resentment among people.

Thus America's rulers want whites to perceive all blacks as criminals; our rulers go to great lengths to make that happen (as discussed in Chapter Fifteen.)

---

[39] http://www.ckollars.org/mcas.html

Often ruling elites orchestrate false flag violence against "their own" people--violence that is designed to appear to be by the bogeyman enemy. 9/11 was evidently[40] an inside job intended to launch the Orwellian war of social control known as the War on Terror; the FBI has notoriously instigated[41] Muslims in the United States to carry out terrorist[42] violence in order to make Americans fear Muslims so that the War on Terror will continue to be effective in making Americans believe that our rulers are protecting us from the "real enemy."

Most of the horrible ethnic, racial and religious violence in the world is caused this way. Whenever violence against one group of people is carried out in the name of another group it is invariably the case that ruling elites are orchestrating the violence in order to control and dominate people with divide-and-rule. This doesn't happen in an egalitarian society.

Some Rich People ARE Good

Yes, despite everything said above about the ruling class's terrible deeds, some rich people are good people. Just as some poor people are bad people. Likewise, in the course of human history no doubt some kings and queens were good and well-intentioned people. But monarchism means the king or queen rules, whether well-intentioned or not. Likewise, our present society based on class inequality in which money is power means that the richest people have the real power no matter if they are well-intentioned or not. The reason for removing the rich from power is the same as for abolishing monarchism. It's not because there have never been good kings or that there are no good rich people. It's because

---

[40] http://newdemocracyworld.org/world_911.html

[41] http://www.nytimes.com/2012/04/29/opinion/sunday/terrorist-plots-helped-along-by-the-fbi.html?pagewanted=all&_r=0

[42] http://www.salon.com/2011/09/29/fbi_terror/

ordinary people should have an equal say in making important social decisions.

A good person, no matter if rich or poor, wants society to be based on the Golden Rule, which is what egalitarianism is all about. A good person therefore wants the economy of society to be based on "From each according to reasonable ability, to each according to need or reasonable desire, with scarce things equitably rationed according to need." This is what "no rich and no poor" means. It is what an egalitarian economy is based on.

Two articles about rich people doing good recently appeared: One[43] is about the owner of the Chobani Yogurt company making his employees co-owners of part of the business. The other[44] is about an anonymous wealthy person who donated money to make it possible for two poor families to own their own homes.

Some philanthropy, such as that of Bill Gates, is for the purpose of maintaining[45] class inequality so that the rich will remain richer than most people with vast privileges and power. But let us take the above articles at face value. These two wealthy persons apparently wanted to do the morally right thing, and they did. Good for them!

Here are two different and not necessarily conflicting thoughts about these generous acts.

---

[43] https://www.usatoday.com/story/money/2016/04/27/chobani-employees-get-surprise-ownership-stake/83585844/

[44] http://www.bostonglobe.com/metro/2016/04/29/two-roxbury-families-have-new-homes-thanks-habitat-for-humanity-benefactor/959cd5sgzOeV2GKT7sM7QJ/story.html

[45] See https://educatingthegatesfoundation.com/2014/06/09/the-almost-outrageous-opposition-to-bill-gates-market-based-ed-reform/ and http://www.globalresearch.ca/big-pharma-and-the-gates-foundation-guinea-pigs-for-the-drugmakers/5384374?print=1 regarding Bill Gates's philanthropy.

#1. These acts are evidence that at least some rich people--capitalists--want to share their wealth in an essentially egalitarian spirit. This shows that an egalitarian revolutionary movement can reasonably expect to have some support from some rich people. And it shows that some rich people probably would rather be equals in a just and egalitarian society than be rich in an unjust one. Note that this doesn't conflict with the fact that if they have to choose between being poor in an unjust society or rich in an unjust society they'd rather be rich. This is why pro-egalitarian rich people don't give ALL their money away!

Very few people respond to the PDR button by disagreeing with the idea of removing the rich from power, but of these few, many of them say something like, "But not all rich people are bad people." It wouldn't be polite to respond, "So what?" but that would be the most logical response. The good rich people want to be removed from the kind of power that comes from being richer than practically everybody else.

#2. How come these rich benefactors don't try to help people abolish class inequality? I can't read their minds, but it is of course possible that they think there is no point in doing that because they think it is impossible to abolish class inequality, which would make them the same in this regard as most people today, rich or poor.

What Will Happen To The Rich Who Are Removed From Power?

Removing the rich from power means that they become like everybody else. If they contribute reasonably to the economy then they can take, for free, the products and services from it that they reasonably need or desire (or, in the case of scarce things, have the same chance as anybody else to have them when they are rationed equitably according to need.) It means that if they support equality (no rich and no poor) and mutual aid, then they can participate in their Local Assembly and have an equal say with others who support equality and mutual aid in determining the laws and policies that people in their local community must obey. It means they can enjoy all of the rights and freedoms that people enjoy in an egalitarian society and that are discussed in the next chapters of this book. But it also means that they can no longer have the special privileges and power that they formerly had from being rich. Those who try to maintain such privileges and power are prohibited—by force if necessary—from doing so.

Most people would consider having this "equal with everybody else" status in society to be wonderful. People who think they deserve to hog most of the socially produced wealth for themselves, however, would feel "oppressed." And those who think that they--but not most other people--should have the real say in important decisions would feel "oppressed." Only the kind of people who rule America today would say it's morally wrong to make them be just like everybody else with respect to being able to enjoy the wealth of society and having a say in social decisions.

This disagreement about what is morally right and wrong is a disagreement between the values of egalitarianism and the values of capitalism, between the values of most people and the values of a small but powerful ruling elite.

Egalitarian revolution is the shaping of society on a large scale by the same values with which millions of ordinary people everyday try to shape the little corner of the world over which they have any real control. Egalitarian revolution is when ordinary people finally succeed in making the world be the way they think it ought to be, and the way they have been trying to make it be for a very long time. To succeed in this effort we need to remove the rich from power.

The Rich Have A Very Different Morality From Ordinary People

The very rich (the ones who are the problem, at least, although some are good people, as discussed above) have a morality, embedded in a culture, that is very different from that of most ordinary people. The morality and culture of most ordinary people is based on the Golden Rule[46], and the values of equality and mutual aid. In contrast, the morality of the very rich is the morality of a ruling class. It is a morality that says they *must* rule over society or else society will go to hell in a hand basket. It is a morality that says their dominance over the bulk of humanity and their wealth and privilege is required in order for the best of humanity--the human race's creation and appreciation of fine literature, art and culture, civilized refinement and elegance, exploration and scientific achievement, *etc.*--to flourish, even to exist. To allow the common masses, the riff-raff, the mob, to take over would be a sin, according to this morality.

This is why the very rich, with only rare individual exceptions, feel no guilt or remorse when, in the course of enforcing their dominance and protecting their wealth and privilege, they inflict brutality and violence and oppression on ordinary people. The very rich are trained from childhood to hold the values of their ruling class culture.

Slave owners in the slavery years of the United States, for example, virtually never exhibited any remorse or guilt for enslaving people. One reads in the book *Southern History Across the Color Line* by Nell Irvin Painter[47] that,

> *"In 1839 a Virginian named John M. Nelson described his shift from painful childhood sympathy to manly callousness. As a child, he would try to stop the beating of slave children and, he said, 'mingle my cries with theirs, and feel almost willing to take a part of the punishment.' After his father severely and repeatedly rebuked him for this kind of compassion, he 'became so blunted that I could not only witness their stripes*

---

[46] https://www.pdrboston.org/the-golden-rule

[47] A Google search for: Thomas Jefferson slavery remorse , to see the book's link

[whippings] with composure, but myself inflict them, and that without remorse."

The same book in the next paragraphs goes on to talk about the views on slavery of a slave owner thought by many to be the most remorseful about being a slave owner: Thomas Jefferson.

> *"Jefferson found African Americans stupid and ugly, a people more or less well suited to the low estate they occupied in eighteenth-century Virginia...[A]s a gentleman whose entire material existence depended on the produce of his slaves, he was never an abolitionist. In fact, his reluctance to interfere with slavery hardened as he aged. By 1819, as the Missouri Compromise was being forged, Jefferson was warning American politicians not, under any circumstances, to tamper with slavery."*

Today one looks in vain to discover evidence that any but very rare individual members of America's ruling plutocracy, or the politicians and corporate managers or top-level academic advisors who serve them, feel any remorse or guilt for waging unjust wars of social control or violently oppressing pro-democracy and pro-equality movements. Robert McNamara, the Secretary of Defense who waged the Vietnam War, famously "apologized" for it in his old age, but his apology was not for waging an unjust war but, on the contrary, for his mistake in thinking that that JUST war was winnable. Former Secretary of State in the Bill Clinton administration, Madeleine Albright, famously told Leslie Stahl that she thought the killing of 500,000 Iraqi children by the U.S. imposed sanctions "was worth it."[48]

The reason America's ruling elite exhibits the self-assurance and conviction and confidence that we naturally associate with having a clear conscience is because the members of this

---

[48] https://www.youtube.com/watch?v=4V44qDIs_II

elite class do indeed have a clear conscience. They think what they do is morally right. These are not storybook villains who know they are the "bad guys" and who know they are committing immoral deeds for which they should feel shame. These people feel no guilt or shame or remorse for doing what we know is disgustingly immoral, because in their culture and morality what they are doing is noble and perfectly moral.

This is why we need to remove the ruling class--the plutocracy and its obedient servants--from power. We'll never persuade them, as a class, to ditch their elitist morality any more than one can persuade a tiger to ditch its stripes.

CHAPTER THREE: WHAT EQUALITY DOES NOT MEAN

This is a short chapter, the only purpose of which is to avoid a common misunderstanding about what egalitarian equality means. There are two things that egalitarians are commonly-- and wrongly!--accused of wanting or believing when using the word "equality." Here they are.

#1.

When egalitarians talk about how people are equal we do NOT mean that people are identical. We do not mean that people have the same talents or skills or integrity of character. We know full well that people vary from one another in all sorts of ways, physically and mentally.

Egalitarians do not advocate making people equal, in the sense of identical. We're not concerned that some people are different from others. Indeed these differences are often a positive thing that makes life more interesting!

For egalitarians, equality (meaning "equality of outcome" as opposed merely to "equal opportunity" to get richer than others) most certainly does **NOT** mean anything at all like what the novelist, Kurt Vonnegut, portrayed it to be in his satirical story titled "Harrison Bergeron[49]" in which:

> "It is the year 2081. Because of amendments to the Constitution, all Americans are fully equal, meaning that no one is allowed to be smarter, better-looking, or more physically able than anyone else. The Handicapper General's agents enforce the equality laws, forcing

---
[49] https://en.wikipedia.org/wiki/Harrison_Bergeron

> citizens to wear 'handicaps': a mask if they are too beautiful, radio earphones with shrill noise to disrupt the thinking of intelligent people, and heavy weights to burden the strong or athletic."

Apologists for social/economic inequality want people to believe that egalitarians are crazy people aiming to make everybody exactly the same. Asserting that egalitarians hold such a stupid view is just a cheap debater's trick. Thus Ayn Rand[50], the champion of inequality, writes[51]:

> "To understand the meaning and motives of egalitarianism, project it into the field of medicine. Suppose a doctor is called to help a man with a broken leg and, instead of setting it, proceeds to break the legs of ten other men, explaining that this would make the patient feel better; when all these men become crippled for life, the doctor advocates the passage of a law compelling everyone to walk on crutches—in order to make the cripples feel better and equalize the 'unfairness' of nature."

The fact that the critics of egalitarianism have to resort to flat out lying about what egalitarians believe shows how incapable they are of making a persuasive argument against what egalitarians *actually* believe.

So what do egalitarians mean by "equality?" We mean equality in the sense of no rich and no poor. We mean that people--despite their very real differences--nonetheless have an equal right to enjoy the benefits made possible by naturally occurring and socially produced wealth according to **need** and reasonable desire if they contribute reasonably according to ability. It's that simple.

---

[50] https://en.wikipedia.org/wiki/Ayn_Rand

[51] http://aynrandlexicon.com/lexicon/egalitarianism.html

Sure, people have different needs. So a sick person needs more medical care than a healthy person; a large family needs a larger house than a small family; one person may need to eat more than another, *etc*. People have all sorts of different needs. So what? The point is that, among those who contribute reasonably, there should be **equality of status** with respect to being able to take (for free) products and services from the economy according to need and reasonable desire (or in the case of scarcity to have equal status when things are rationed equitably according to need). THIS is what it means to have "no rich and no poor."

Yes, of course, some people have greater or different abilities than others; and some people have greater or different needs and desires than others. We know that, and have no problem with that. We believe, however, that the differences between people are not a reason for some being richer than others. We believe, for example, that the children of a janitor and the children of a physician should enjoy the same standards of education, healthy food, quality health care, comfortable living space, quality clothing, leisure time, fun vacations, and healthy and attractive environment.

#2.

Egalitarian equality does NOT mean Equal Opportunity. Equal Opportunity means an equal opportunity to get rich in a society in which some are rich and some are poor. Egalitarian equality means there are no rich and no poor because all who contribute reasonably according to ability have the same right to take for free products and services from the economy according to need or reasonable desire (or, in the case of scarcity, to have things that are equitably rationed according to need.)

To repeat from the #1 discussion above, the children of a janitor and the children of a physician should enjoy the same standards of education, healthy food, quality health care, comfortable living space, quality clothing, leisure time, fun vacations, and healthy and attractive environment. This is the kind of equality egalitarians aim for.

Apologists for class inequality (*i.e.*, those who approve of having some rich and some poor) such as Robert Reich[52], call for Equal Opportunity in order to divert people from even thinking about, never mind fighting for, what most people ACTUALLY want, which is egalitarian equality.

---

[52] http://robertreich.org/post/80717261549 with further discussion of Reich's role at http://newdemocracyworld.org/revolution/reich.html

CHAPTER FOUR: WHAT IS AN EGALITARIAN SOCIETY?[53]

Egalitarian Values

Egalitarianism is the idea that society should be based on the Golden Rule, and hence on the following two egalitarian values:

1) Equality (in the "no rich and no poor" and "from each according to ability, to each according to need or reasonable desire" sense, not the "equal opportunity" sense that means an equal opportunity to get richer than others, and not in the sense of people being identical either)

2) Mutual Aid (also known as Solidarity, meaning helping each other, not being pitted against others in competition by an oppressor to control us)

Egalitarians are people who share these values, in other words the *vast majority of people*.

Egalitarianism Is *Not* Utopia!

Egalitarianism is NOT a utopia; it is not a perfect society in which all problems have disappeared. It is, however, a whole lot better (see Chapter Two) than any society based on class inequality, such as our present one.

---

[53] In 2011, before we used the word "egalitarianism," Dave Stratman and I co-authored a pamphlet laying out the key ideas about what we later referred to by that word. The pamphlet is titled "Thinking about Revolution," is online at http://newdemocracyworld.org/revolution/Thinking.pdf, and is still very much worth reading.

In an egalitarian society people with egalitarian values have gained the upper hand and have the real power in society, but this doesn't mean they are perfect people. There will still be problems stemming from the fact that people are not saints. There will still be individuals sometimes doing nasty things to other people. Selfishness will not disappear.

The difference is this. In a society based on class inequality there is official approval for some people to have extreme power to dominate others and to act in extreme opposition to the Golden Rule. In contrast, an egalitarian society is based on principles that promote rather than impede egalitarians' ability to oppose any individual or group of people attempting to gain the power to dominate and oppress others or act in flagrant opposition to the Golden Rule. (See Chapter Thirteen.)

It's not utopia. But egalitarianism is much better than our present unequal society, and worth fighting for.

Egalitarian principles of government and the economy are ways of implementing egalitarian values. These principles are:

1. Social order--including, in particular, democratic government--should be based on mutual agreements among egalitarians, not on the anti-democratic authoritarian principle that egalitarians must obey laws that they have no equal say in writing and that are written by other people (such as so-called "representatives").

2. People who work reasonably according to ability share (not buy and sell) freely the fruits of the economy among themselves according to need and reasonable desire, where what is reasonable is determined by democratic government.

Not a Blueprint, But Here are Ideas about How Egalitarianism Could Work

I do not have a blueprint for how an egalitarian society will be--that is impossible because people will have all sorts of ideas for how to implement egalitarian values and might experiment (trial and error) with different approaches or use different methods in different places. But some of us have thought about one way that an egalitarian society might work, because it is important to be confident that there is at least one way it could work. Otherwise how could we persuade other people--or even ourselves--to fight for egalitarianism? The two most important ideas are voluntary federation and a sharing economy, which are ways of ensuring genuine democracy and genuine equality (as discussed in Chapters Seven and Eight), and are the only ways I know of that do this:

Voluntary Federation. The **only** law-making bodies are local assemblies at which all of the egalitarians in the local community (*i.e.,* residing in the community or, in the case of a person who resides outside the community, working reasonably in an enterprise located in the community) and only they have the *right* to partake, as equals, in making, and deciding how to enforce, the laws for that community. Social and economic and all other kinds of order or coordination on a larger-than-local scale are accomplished by local assemblies sending delegates (re-callable any time) to meet with delegates from other local assemblies (in what I call non-local assemblies). Non-local assemblies do not write laws; instead they craft proposals that the local assemblies implement or not as they wish. In practice, there is back and forth negotiation between local assemblies and non-local assemblies (*i.e.,* assemblies composed of delegates) in an attempt to arrive at a proposal that is acceptable to enough local assemblies to be actually implemented.

Non-local assemblies can, in turn, send delegates to form a non-local assembly corresponding to an even larger region, and these non-local assemblies can, in turn, do likewise so that regional planning and coordination can be achieved on as large a scale as desired, even globally if people wish. Still, non-local assemblies do not write laws; they only craft proposals for consideration by the assemblies from which their members were sent as delegates. Back and forth consultation and negotiation between assemblies at lower and higher levels either results eventually in a proposal that meets the approval of a sufficient number of *local* assemblies to be implemented, or else no new plan or policy is implemented. This is how large-scale order is achieved by mutual agreement, rather than by the anti-democratic authoritarian principle that says "you must obey the highest level governmental body, no matter what." Also there can be non-local assemblies for different purposes, say sports events in one case, economic coordination in another, and scientific research in yet another.

Nothing about voluntary federation, however, prevents local assemblies from mutually agreeing to form a militia (or army) to forcibly prevent other people from attacking egalitarian values. Thus if a local assembly or even a region decided (no matter how "democratically"), for example, to enslave all the [fill in the blank] people or engage in, say, child abuse, then other local assemblies of true egalitarians would be entirely within their rights in forcibly preventing people elsewhere from enslaving or abusing people this way. The principle is that voluntary federation is the way for egalitarians to democratically shape society by egalitarian values; it is also the way for egalitarians to democratically (among themselves) prevent (violently if necessary) the enemies of egalitarian values from shaping society by anti-egalitarian values.

How, it may be asked, can egalitarians form a militia or an army? A military force, to be effective, relies on the principle that soldiers of a lower rank must obey officers of a higher rank. Isn't this the very authoritarian principle that egalitarians reject, by denying that egalitarians are obliged to obey laws they have no equal say in writing and that are written by other people? The answer would be "yes" if the soldiers were conscripted against their will. But an egalitarian militia or army is composed of volunteers who agree to obey appropriate military orders and commands from officers a) whom they elect and whom they can recall and b) who enjoy no special privileges or insignia. The authority of the officers, in other words, is entirely based on the trust that is accorded to them by the soldiers, based on the officers' reputations for integrity and judgment in defense of egalitarianism. The militia or army, in turn, depends for its supply of weapons and ammunition and clothing and food, *etc.*, on the workers in the sharing economy (described below) who voluntarily agree to supply it with these material needs. Furthermore the entire membership of the militia, as equals, democratically determines fundamental goals.[54]

The authority of the officers in an egalitarian militia or army is essentially the same as the authority of a surgeon in an operating room with nurses and attendants, or of a pilot in a passenger jet plane: it is the authority that people respect and obey because of their trust and respect for the person exercising that authority. Almost any time that people work together for a common purpose there will be some who are more respected for their integrity and judgment and knowledge related to achieving the common purpose than others, and who will, for that reason alone, be accorded greater authority. This kind of authority is a positively good thing. It is very different from the bad kind of authority that egalitarians reject, which is based on the authoritarian principle: "You must obey the higher authority whether you want to or not, whether you think the authority is aimed at goals that you support or not, whether you respect the motive and judgment and integrity of the authority or not; you must obey simply because it is the higher authority, period."

---

[54] These principles, in whole or in part, were applied by peasants in the German Peasant War of 1525, by peasants and other working class people in England in their New Model Army in the 1640s, by the American revolutionaries in the Minuteman militia in the 1760s, and by workers and peasants in the anarchist militias of Spain in 1936-9.

Sharing Economy. *[Note, this has nothing whatsoever to do with the "sharing economy" phrase that has lately been used in the mass media to refer to things such as people renting out parts of their private homes to make some extra money, or driving people somewhere in one's own car for a payment.]*

A sharing economy is one in which all the people in it mutually agree to work reasonably according to ability and to share among themselves the products and services they produce, for free, according to need or reasonable desire, with scarce things rationed according to need in an equitable manner. The local assembly decides what is reasonable, and how scarce things are to be equitably rationed. (See Chapter Nine for further discussion of rationing and current real-life examples of it.) **Money is not used at all inside a sharing economy or between distinct sharing economies;** Chapter Six explains why.

Local assemblies, by mutual agreement, join in a sharing economy, with as many or as few local communities in a given sharing economy as mutually agree to be in it. (The advantages of being in a very large sharing economy are so great that it is likely that sharing economies--or a single sharing economy--would be almost, or even actually, global at some point.) Those who do not work reasonably according to ability--people who would normally be expected to do some work but who just refuse--are not members of the sharing economy and cannot take anything from it for free. Egalitarians, being reasonable people, will no doubt count children and retired elderly and people unable to work as "working reasonably according to ability" even though they do no work, and likewise deem it "reasonable work" when people care for their own or other children or for other sick adults or attend school or apprentice programs to learn skills so as to be able to work in the future.

A local assembly may determine if an individual person is working reasonably and taking products or using services reasonably and is therefore a member in good standing of the sharing economy, but more typically the local assembly determines whether an entire economic enterprise itself (consisting of people who work together or do similar kinds of work) is working reasonably and taking products and services from the economy reasonably and is, therefore--as an entire enterprise--a member in good standing of the sharing economy. If the enterprise provides a useful or desired product or service of reasonable quality and makes it available to appropriate people in a reasonable way and does all this with a reasonable number of workers who take products and use services reasonably then the local assembly will determine that the enterprise is a member in good standing of the sharing economy. This means that the enterprise may freely take products or use services from the sharing economy that the enterprise needs to operate, and each of its workers (except any specific individual the local assembly may judge to be taking more than reasonable) may freely take products and services for personal or family use according to need or reasonable desire.

The people in each economic enterprise know that the enterprise's membership, as well as their own personal membership, in the sharing economy depends on the enterprise and its workers having a good reputation for reasonableness in contributing to the sharing economy and reasonableness in taking from it. Rather than profit, the indicator of the enterprise's success is the strength of its good reputation. This is discussed more fully in Chapter Nine.

Within an economic enterprise (including, in this context, organizations such as a school or hospital, as well as non-economic neighborhood associations, *etc.*) at the local community level, the workers (or members) are all formally equals, although some, as discussed above, may provide leadership based on respect for their greater experience, knowledge, integrity or commitment to the purpose of the enterprise. All of the workers democratically determine all of the policies relating to the enterprise, consistent with all policies and decisions and laws of the local assembly. Among other things, the workers of the enterprise decide how, exactly, they will democratically make decisions (majority rule, consensus, elected "officers" or otherwise), who is or may become a member of the enterprise or organization and the general and individual-specific conditions of their membership, and all decisions formerly considered the responsibility of "management." A worker in any enterprise is always free to quit working for the enterprise and look for a different way of "contributing according to ability."

Economic enterprises at the local level may use voluntary federation, parallel to that discussed above for local assemblies, to achieve order and coordination and cooperation on as large a scale--even global--as is mutually agreed upon by the local economic enterprises. Still, a local economic enterprise must obey the laws of the local assembly for the community in which it is located.

What about a person or family or group of people who want to work on their own land or in their own workshop (or equivalent) and be self-sufficient and not be a member of the sharing economy? That's perfectly fine if that's what they want to do, and they can own, in addition to personal items, as much land or other things related to economic production as they can put to productive use by their own, and only their own, labor; they cannot hire other workers or in general use another person in a relationship of status inequality such as employer-employee or master-slave. What they do with the fruits of their labor is up to them; but since society is no longer based on money and they have chosen not to be in the sharing economy, they might decide to barter some of the fruits of their labor with individual members or economic enterprises in the sharing economy, which is fine.

In this kind of egalitarian society, people are as free as the realities of human existence permit to do wonderful things to enrich their own lives and the lives of others, both in formal economic enterprises that they democratically run and on their own individual "off work" time. Aside from the laws of nature and the limits imposed by physical reality, the only limits to what people can do to make the world better and better are the limits of their imaginations and creativity, and the limits of their ability to obtain the support of others who may be affected by a given project or whose help may be required by it.

Is this Utopia? No. Is it enormously better than a society based on class inequality such as ours today? Absolutely yes! Chapters Five and Six are about some important freedoms and benefits to people in general that only an egalitarian society can provide. Here I want to discuss the benefits of egalitarianism to specific groups of people, including small businesspersons, people who are today relatively well off financially such as professionals and managers, and manual workers.

Small Business Persons And Egalitarianism

Small businesspersons have every reason in the world to desire an egalitarian revolution in the United States. Their lives in an egalitarian society would be improved in terms of both their material standard of living and their emotional well-being. Here's why.

First, let's see who exactly we're talking about with the phrase "small businessperson." A *Forbes Magazine* article[55], "16 Surprising Statistics about Small Businesses," reports that while the Small Business Administration defines a small business as one having fewer than 500 employees, of the 28 million such small businesses in the United States, a whopping 22.5 million (80%) are run by self-employed persons with no additional payroll or employees.

A U.S. Census report for 2013[56] shows that of 5,726,160 firms of any size, 5,130,348 (or about 90%) employed fewer than 20 employees and 3,543,991 (or about 62%) employed only zero to four employees. I'm not sure why the total number of firms

---

[55] https://www.forbes.com/sites/jasonnazar/2013/09/09/16-surprising-statistics-about-small-businesses/#5d9f5f15ec88

[56] Table 1 at https://www.sba.gov/advocacy/firm-size-data

in the U.S. Census report is much smaller than the number of small businesses in the *Forbes* article; perhaps it involves using different definitions. But the general picture seems to be that the overwhelming majority of small businesspersons are either self-employed with no employees (80%) or with only one to four employees.

How much money do small business owners make? Most don't make very much. One source[57] states that, "In 2008, the average nonfarm sole proprietorship had revenues of only $58,256 and net income of only $11,696." According to the *Forbes* article, the average annual revenue of self-employed (no employees) businesses was only $44,000, of which the business person's take home income was necessarily only the part remaining after costs of running the business were covered by this revenue. 80% of these "nonemployer" businesses had annual revenues less than $50,000.

Another source[58] reports on the incomes of what most people have in mind by the phrase "small business owners"; it describes these "everyday" small business owners this way:

> "These are the everyday businesses that don't interest VCs [venture capitalists] and other investors who look for big paydays. They have fewer than 20 employees, and for the most part have fewer than 10 employees.
>
> "These everyday businesses are software developers, electrical contractors, freelance writers, salvage companies, bagel store owners, consultants, automotive parts dealers, pet store owners, Internet publishers, accountants, small manufacturers, and well, the list goes on. They are the small businesses in your town or at the local strip mall. They are the home-based businesses in

---

[57] https://smallbiztrends.com/2010/11/how-much-money-do-small-business-owners-make.html

[58] http://www.businessknowhow.com/money/earn.htm

your neighborhood or maybe your own basement. And they are the businesses in the local industrial park or office building downtown. They generate income, but not big bucks.

"For the most part, these small businesses have few employees. According to US Census Bureau statistics, while there are more than 27 million businesses operating in the United States, only 655,587 of them employ 20 or more employees.

"In fact, the majority of US small businesses are very small. A whopping 21 million are "nonemployers." In other words, they are self-employed individuals who pay taxes, but are not counted in the monthly jobs reports that are based on payroll data because they do not have a payroll.

"Another 3.7 million have 1 to 4 employees."

A Better Standard of Living

The pie chart in this article cited above gives the 2010 household annual incomes of these "everyday" small business owners. It shows that 91% of them made less than $150,000 and 59% made less than $75,000. To put this in perspective, consider that the total U.S. personal income in 2010 was $12.5 trillion[59] and the U.S. population that year was 308.7 million[60]. Doing the division yields a per capita (what every person--man, woman and child--would have if each had exactly the same) income of approximately $40,000. This means that had there been an egalitarian distribution of income in 2010, a family of four would have had an income of $160,000 that year, $10,000 more than the income of 91% of the households of the "everyday" small business owners described above.

---

[59] https://www.statista.com/statistics/216756/us-personal-income/

[60] https://en.wikipedia.org/wiki/2010_United_States_Census

In terms of very narrowly defined (*i.e.*, income) material standard of living we see that the great majority of small business owners would actually be better off in an egalitarian society than they are in the present one. But their lives would be better in even more important respects, because of the fundamental difference between an egalitarian society and our present one.

Small business owners--especially when there are no other employees--often work far more hours per week (and per year) than most people would consider reasonable. In an egalitarian society they would share equally in the wealth of society while only being expected to work a reasonable amount.

Greater Emotional Happiness

Many small business owners today try to make the business one in which the employees are treated fairly and feel "part of the family." But the need to turn a profit and compete with other businesses makes this very difficult. The owner is caught between a rock and a hard place: provide good health insurance to the employees and go out of business, or deny good health insurance in order to stay in business. What a choice! What a recipe for emotional distress to the owner, not to mention the employees. This dilemma would vanish in an egalitarian society.

In an egalitarian society, in contrast, former small business owners who had hired employees would enjoy a much more friendly relationship with the other workers in the business. Why? Because the workers in any enterprise would be equals with respect to formal status in decision-making and standard of living. (Informally, those with greater knowledge and experience and skill would command greater respect for their opinions, of course.) All of the workers would share a common desire for their enterprise to have a good reputation in the larger society so they can maintain their membership in the sharing economy (which enables them to take what they need from stores for free or, in the case of scarcity, have the same chance as others to obtain what is rationed according to need.) The business would be about providing a service to the society, and its workers enjoying, in consequence, the right to share in the wealth of society according to need or reasonable desire. No longer would a particular person--the former owner--need to get the other workers to work more for less pay in order to make the business turn a profit. All of the old antagonism and resentment that was generated by this conflict of interest would vanish. This gain in emotional happiness is priceless.

These words about small businesspersons first appeared on the PDRBoston.org website and elicited the following comment on January 13, 2014:

"John, I spent 30 years as owner of a small contracting business with up to twenty employees. You hit the nail on the head regarding small business life. I thought very often over the years about the false perceptions that are perpetrated regarding the efficiency of the competitive, dog eat dog system I operated within. There is a huge regulatory (policing) apparatus required to attempt to rein in the actions businesses take in their attempts to compete and survive. HR conflicts are constant, struggling to find affordable health care each year. Attempting to navigate federal, state, local and private rules and regulations and bidding requirements required a staff of employees in itself - and this is all tied to competition. I often wondered what a true accounting of the overhead burden of a company would reveal about just how efficiently products and services are produced and delivered in our capitalist system. As much profit driven regulation as there already is, much more is needed to attempt to protect the environment and for many other reasons - all because of the profit motive. Replacing the narrowly focused, profit driven system with a resource based, non-monetary one is critical to the future of the whole planet. Many small business persons become consumed in an unhealthy way, in their attempts survive while being fair with employees, customers and themselves."

Egalitarianism Creates Trust Among People, Which Improves The Lives Even Of Those Who Are Today Relatively Well Off Financially

Cooperation and mutual aid are the source of the material and emotional well being in society. This cooperation requires trust among people. Treating others as you would like to be treated is a behavior pattern that makes it possible for human beings to survive and thrive. An intuitive understanding of the Golden Rule is part of our very makeup as human beings, as important for our survival as our opposable thumb and large brain. Only in a society based on this principle will people have maximum trust in one another.

When a society is not based on economic equality, the Golden Rule is broken: there is less trust, less cooperation and mutual aid, and hence less material and less emotional well being for all. The more unequal a society, the more anxious people feel about their place in the hierarchy of wealth. The more equal and supportive a society, the more happy and fulfilled people can be.

Making society economically equal will improve the lives not only of the poorest but also of many people who are financially better off than most people today. Professionals, intellectuals, managers and small business owners will all benefit.

They will not bear the constant stress of scrambling to save for their children's education or their own retirement or "keeping up with the Joneses." Their marriages will not break up over disputes about money, the leading cause of divorce today. They will wake up each morning in a world where people trust each other and are friendly towards each other. It will no longer be a world of Orwellian wars of social control designed to make us live in fear of other people.

They will no longer feel threatened by the good fortune and creativity of others, as is the case today when every business owner must fear his competitor.

Managers will no longer experience work as battling with workers under their supervision. They will not experience social isolation, but will be part of a group of equals working toward a common purpose.

Egalitarian Equality Is Emotionally Beneficial Particularly For Manual (Blue Collar) Workers

In an egalitarian society manual workers have an equal status with everybody else; they are no longer wrongly treated as if they contributed less to society than mental workers. Furthermore the distinction between manual and mental work, and the division of people into exclusively manual workers and exclusively mental workers, is greatly reduced.

Virtually all manual work naturally involves both mental and manual aspects simultaneously. Carpenters and cooks think about how to build or cook more efficiently and creatively. An American slave invented the first cotton scraper. The most regulated assembly line workers today invent ways to make their work safer. In an egalitarian society there will no longer be capitalists trying to separate the mental and manual aspects of work as a way of controlling people. People will be free to study every aspect of their work and apply their creativity to it. No longer will they fear losing their job because somebody figured out how to make the work more efficient; instead work will become easier and more enjoyable for all.

The mental aspects of manual work, involving the theory behind it and its relation to the larger society, will no longer be the concern only of exclusively mental workers. At the same time, when mental workers are no longer considered "better" than manual workers, they will be called upon to share equally in manual work that nobody wants to do.

Egalitarianism Levels Up, Not Down

Egalitarianism, whenever possible, levels people's standard of living up, not down.

The U.S. economy today produces such gigantic wealth that much of it has to be wasted, even literally blown up. The military budget, for example, exceeds 1.2 trillion dollars per year, without counting the costs of its multiple wars; the Middle East wars were estimated by Nobel laureate economist Joseph Stiglitz already to have cost 4 trillion dollars in direct costs and in funds committed to caring for disabled veterans.

Why must so much wealth be wasted? Because the ruling class learned to its horror in the "radical 1960s" (when U.S. economic equality and economic security was at a peak, and when the Civil Rights Movement and the Anti-Vietnam War Movement and the Welfare Rights Movement and other similar movements scared the hell out of the ruling class) that the more economically secure people feel, the more rebellious they are prepared to act. The past fifty years have witnessed an enormous redistribution of wealth in the U.S., all of it upward, into the pockets of the rich. Their motive in snapping up all the wealth is not simple greed but a keen interest in controlling people by making them economically insecure. Imagine what could be done with all that wealth if there were no ruling elite.

CHAPTER FIVE: INDIVIDUAL FREEDOM AND AN EGALITARIAN BILL OF RIGHTS

This chapter addresses the question of individual rights in an egalitarian society, by a) offering a possible egalitarian Bill of Rights, b) discussing the right to private property in an egalitarian society, c) examining what freedom means and how this relates to egalitarianism, d) discussing the enormous freedom to be an entrepreneur in an egalitarian society, and e) showing that the U.S. Constitution does not protect egalitarian rights and freedom.

An Egalitarian Bill of Rights

In every local community (typically a region with, very loosely, about 40,000 residents) the egalitarians in that community, meeting in their Local Assembly (to which all resident egalitarians have a right to belong, as equals with all others) are the sovereign power. There is no "higher" body of government or document that they are obliged to obey.

Egalitarians want society to be based on equality (no rich and no poor) and mutual aid (people help each other). Such people usually want society to be arranged so that people are happy too. To accomplish all of these goals, egalitarians may very well create a document they intend to obey, a document that identifies the rights of individuals relative to the sovereign Local Assembly of egalitarians. These documents may vary from one local community to another.

There is no single "correct" egalitarian document to replace the Bill of Rights or the United Nation's Universal Declaration of Human Rights or the French Revolution's Declaration of the Rights of Man and of the Citizen. The principles and rights stated in these documents are certainly very important for egalitarians to study and evaluate with respect to their value and appropriateness in a society ruled by egalitarians aiming to abolish class inequality. But it is important also to recognize that the rulers who wrote these documents, unlike egalitarians, accepted the rightness of class inequality (some rich and some poor).

Here is a possibly incomplete list of principles that I, personally, think should be honored in an egalitarian society.

1. All human beings have the same rights.
2. People have the right to join their Local Assembly and be an equal with all other members of it, but only for the purpose of shaping society by the egalitarian values of equality (no rich and no poor) and mutual aid (people helping each other); any person clearly motivated by a contrary aim may be excluded from membership in the Local Assembly.
3. Nobody in a local community is obliged to obey any authority other than that community's Local Assembly or authorities derived from delegation by that Local Assembly.
4. People have the right to leave (if not lawfully incarcerated) any local community and the right to return to their local community of birth.
5. No one shall be subjected to arbitrary arrest or detention, *i.e.*, in a manner that is not in compliance with formal explicit policies determined by and made public by the Local Assembly.
6. People have the right, when accused of a crime, to be considered innocent until proven guilty beyond a reasonable doubt in a formal public court of law using fair rules of evidence in which a randomly selected jury of egalitarians decides (however they wish) if the defendant is guilty or not guilty, and the defendant may not be compelled to be a witness against himself or herself.

7. No one shall be subjected to torture or to cruel, inhuman or degrading treatment or punishment.
8. People have the right of freedom (*e.g.*, to speak and publish by any technical mode, associate with others [or not, as they wish], choose and practice a religion [or not, as they wish], own personal property and use it as they wish, have personal privacy, marry and found a family [or not, as they wish], *etc.*) so long as the exercise of that freedom does not unjustly harm another person or promote the emergence, or strengthen the reality, of class inequality relations contrary to equality and mutual aid.
9. People have the right to contribute to the sharing economy according to reasonable ability and in return to take--for free--products and services from the sharing economy according to need or reasonable desire or, in the case of scarce things, to have equal status when such things are equitably rationed according to need. People also have the right not to contribute to the sharing economy and thus forfeit permission to take from it for free. Everybody has the right to barter. Nobody has the right to use another person in a relationship of status inequality such as employer-employee or master-slave.
10. People have the right to contest a decision by the Local Assembly that they are not contributing according to reasonable ability or that they are taking from the sharing economy more than according to need or reasonable desire (*i.e.*, a decision that results in exclusion from the sharing economy), by presenting their case to the full Local Assembly (or relevant subcommittee if they prefer) and having it vote on the matter.
11. People have the right to refuse to be in a militia or military organization in which they are required to obey militarily justified orders of elected superior officers.

The Right to Private Property in an Egalitarian Society

Yes, people own private property in an egalitarian society. The egalitarian principle of "From each according to ability, to each according to need" (which is short for "From each according to *reasonable* ability, to each according to need or *reasonable* desire, with scarce things rationed equitably according to need") is perfectly consistent with, and in agreement with, people owning private property.

What distinguishes private property ownership in an egalitarian society from private property ownership in a non-egalitarian society based on class inequality (such as our present capitalist one) is this: in an egalitarian society egalitarians--those who support the principle of "From each according to ability, to each according to need," who are the **vast majority** of people in most communities--democratically decide in their local assembly which claims to private property ownership are reasonable and which are not.

The private property that most ordinary people own today--their house[61] (if they're lucky enough to actually own it!), the land their house and back yard or garden are on, the things that are inside their house (and garage if they're lucky enough to have one), a small boat (again, if they're lucky enough to have one), *etc.*--would most likely be considered by the egalitarians in their community's local assembly to be reasonably owned as private property. Why?

Because these are things that an individual (or family), by themselves, make proper and reasonable *personal* use of. Also, things that an individual (or family) create with ONLY their own labor (or with tools and machines and raw materials obtained in trade for things made only with their own labor) would most likely be considered by the local assembly of egalitarians to be reasonably owned by the individual (or family) as their private property. Also, things that are of sentimental value to a particular person but not otherwise of great value would likely be considered reasonably owned by the individual for whom they are of sentimental value.

---

[61] In connection with housing, see, in Appendix I, the egalitarian law passed in the imaginary town of Somewhereville, making squatting legal.

Things, and only things, that are reasonable for an individual or family to own as private property are also reasonable for them to inherit as private property.

Some things, however, would likely NOT be considered reasonable to be owned as the private property of a single individual or small group of people, and would be considered instead to be under the control of the local assembly. What kind of things are we talking about? Things like this:

- A large tract of land that should reasonably be enjoyed by lots of people for recreation
- Natural resources needed by many people
- The "air waves" for communication
- Streets for transportation
- A large tract of land that is suitable for agriculture and which would require the labor of very many people
- Things or places where many people work, such as a factory, warehouse, skyscraper, office building, mine, hospital or university
- Things the production of which requires the labor, directly or indirectly, of many people, essentially of society (such as highways and railroads)
- Other similar things that an individual or family does not, by themselves, make proper and reasonable *personal* use of, such as multiple mansions or homes in which *other* people or families live, or a home in which nobody lives.

What about luxury items, such as a huge yacht, a personal jet, extremely valuable artwork, and so forth? Local assemblies will have to decide on a case-by-case basis. The guiding principle is that scarce things should be equitably rationed according to need, and if nobody really needs something but many desire it, then it can be rationed with something like a lottery (rationing is discussed further in Chapter Nine). There could also be a time limit on how long somebody owns something, such as a piece of artwork or a yacht--whatever egalitarians in the local assembly decide is reasonable.

In some parts of the world, including the United States, there is a long tradition that defines freedom as the right to own private property. Egalitarianism is in agreement with this tradition in so far as this tradition is stated as the "right to own private property *reasonably*"--with "reasonably" defined as above and determined in specific cases by the local assembly of egalitarians in the relevant community.

There is, however, a big difference between the "right of *reasonable* private property" versus the "right of private property." For example, the American Revolution took property away--without compensation--from some people who claimed (with perfectly "legal" documents) to own extremely unreasonable amounts of land. "The largest estate confiscation in all colonies was that of the Penn family, which at 21.5 million acres was worth a million pounds. Under the Divesting Act of 1779, Pennsylvania's Assembly took control of these vast holdings of the proprietor's family [the Penn family.] Virginia confiscated the six-million-acre Fairfax estate. In Massachusetts, a law was passed confiscating the property of everyone who had fought against the colonies; the aristocratic William Pepperel lost his lands, which stretched for thirty miles along the coast of Maine (then part of Massachusetts)...Nor did the provincial and state committees and governments simply resell confiscated lands to wealthy bourgeois...By and large, in what amounted to a virtual land redistribution, the broken-up estates were sold in small parcels to ordinary farmers and agricultural workers. To sell tracts of land in excess of 500 acres was viewed with opprobrium." [from *The Third Revolution*, vol. 1, pg. 222, by Murray Bookchin]

Anti-egalitarians defend class inequality by arguing that "The right to private property is sacred, and the basis for freedom." Egalitarians know that this is a specious argument that only sounds true when people forget about the huge difference between "*reasonable* private property" and "*unreasonable* private property."

103

There were conflicting aims by opposing groups of people inside the American Revolution. Many of the revolutionaries had egalitarian values and aims, but these values and aims were not stated explicitly, at least not nearly as often and as effectively as the contrary values and aims espoused and advocated by the upper class that came to dominate post-revolutionary American society and create what became the thoroughly capitalist society of class inequality that exists today. This underscores the crucial importance of building an ***explicitly*** egalitarian revolutionary movement.

Freedom in an Egalitarian Society

Egalitarianism is a society without class inequality. In an egalitarian society people are free to do whatever they want so long as it doesn't mean oppressing other people or hogging wealth unfairly. And yes, people still own private property, as discussed above.

Only in an egalitarian society are people free to enjoy the benefits of living in a society where people trust and help each other in a way that is simply impossible when there is class inequality and the upper class needs to pit people against each other to control them to make them accept their position at the bottom of an unequal society.

Only in an egalitarian society are entrepreneurs free to propose a new idea for an economic enterprise (discussed further below) and have it actually happen merely because it seems like a good idea to one's fellow citizens.

Only in an egalitarian society are people free to live where they want and work where they want and not have to worry about being economically insecure--unemployed or without medical care or without whatever else they need when they need it.

Only in an egalitarian society are people who support equality and mutual aid free to live under no laws other than ones they, as equals with all others like them in their community, are able to partake in writing themselves (this is what voluntary federation is all about). **Only in an egalitarian society are people free from the dictatorship of so-called "representatives."**

Only in an egalitarian society are people free not to be treated like dirt (as Chapter Two shows they always will be in a non-egalitarian society of class inequality).

Of course there will be a small number of people who will oppose egalitarianism on the grounds that it makes people less free. These are the kinds of people who say that the abolition of slavery made people less free because it denied them the freedom to own slaves. Such people use the word "freedom" in a way designed to pull the wool over our eyes. This deserves some focused discussion.

Freedom. Everybody says freedom is such a very good thing that it's worth fighting for. But something so good and important deserves a clear meaning, no? Well, what is it?

The word "freedom" has been hijacked by all sorts of unsavory characters to mean freedom for them to do unsavory things. Slave owners in the American Civil War fought for their freedom to be slave owners. Adolph Hitler fought for what he called "freedom," saying[62], "If freedom is short of weapons, we must compensate with willpower." No matter what is the true purpose of a war, the rulers of a nation waging it invariably say the purpose is to defend freedom. Millions of people have died in wars fighting each other even though both sides were supposedly fighting for the same thing--freedom. Is freedom just a dangerous bogus concept?

Yes, at least in its present deliberately vague sense, it is. The word "freedom" is used more often than not for a bad purpose: as a way for rulers to get the ruled to do what they want them to do. In World War II, for example, the Nazis told Germans

---

[62] http://www.goodreads.com/author/quotes/30691.Adolf_Hitler

that Nazism was about defending "freiheit" (freedom) just as the American government told Americans that the fight against Nazism was about defending freedom. (See four such typical wartime posters below.) Both the German and American ruling classes used warfare to strengthen their domination over working class people, and this is what they actually had in mind behind the rhetoric of "Freedom" and "Freiheit." (See an online summary[63] of my book, *The People as Enemy: The Leaders' Hidden Agenda in World War II*[64], for a full discussion of this.)

---

[63] http://www.newdemocracyworld.org/old/War/good-war-myth.htm

[64] https://www.amazon.com/People-As-Enemy-Leaders-Hidden/dp/1551642166/ref=sr_1_3?s=books&ie=UTF8&qid=1494177288&sr=1-3&keywords=spritzler

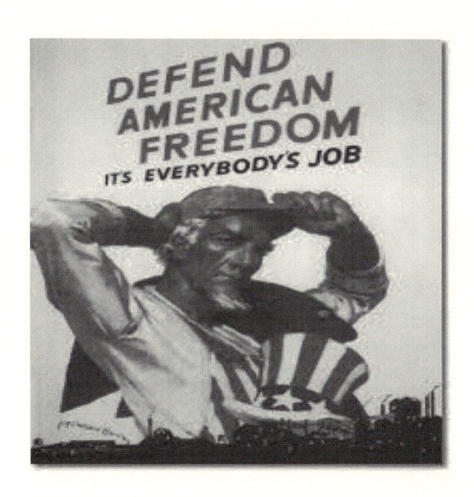

If we're going to fight for freedom and make great sacrifices to defend (or obtain) it, shouldn't we know what we're fighting for? Let's first list some things that we don't think people should be free to do.

Nobody should be free to:

- Own a slave
- Own a serf
- Exploit an employee, *i.e.*, claim to privately own socially produced wealth such as a factory, or wealth belonging to society such as mineral deposits in the earth or vast tracts of land, and then tell the worker that he or she can only have access to these means of production to produce wealth (with which to provide for all the things his or her family needs) if he or she agrees to labor for the employer--who will then own what is produced--and accept in return wages worth less than the value contributed by his or her labor
- Be a hog, *i.e.*, unfairly make some people suffer as a result of taking for oneself more of the socially owned wealth [such as land] or socially produced wealth [economic products and services] than is reasonable in the eyes of egalitarians. Egalitarians are the majority of people, people who believe in equality and mutual aid, specifically that people should help one another and that all who contribute reasonably have an equal right to share in the fruits of the economy according to need and reasonable desire, and those who don't contribute reasonably have no such right.
- Do things to make people accept being exploited and being treated unfairly by hogs, such as teaching them that they are inferior in some way and less deserving, or telling them lies to make them fear a boogieman enemy and making them think their safety requires obeying exploiters and hogs

- Make egalitarians (defined above) obey laws that they did not have an opportunity, as equals, to democratically write for themselves
- Prevent egalitarians from a) meeting as they see fit, b) freely discussing anything and everything, c) making and enforcing laws in their local communities, and d) reaching mutual agreements with egalitarians in other communities regarding large scale planning (economic and otherwise), coordination and policies
- Prevent egalitarians from forcibly preventing anybody from doing anything on this list

Some people (Bill Gates, David Rockefeller (when he was alive), the Koch brothers, the entire Walton family, Barack Obama, Donald Trump, Fidel Castro (when he was alive), the entire Chinese Communist Party Central Committee, King Faisal, the Supreme Ruler of Iran, Vladimir Putin, Benjamin Netanyahu, and a host of others) would, to put it mildly, not agree with this entire list of NO-NOs. Most of them would go along with the first two items, but balk at the ones after that. But to disguise the venality and utter selfishness (or perhaps just arrogance) of their view, they would probably try to change the subject by talking about things that people should be free to do; they might offer up a list of such things as the following, and hope that endorsing this list would make people perceive them as "good guys"--defenders of "freedom."

Freedoms that ruling elites want us to be grateful for, if and when they grant them:

- Worship as you please
- Quit your job whenever you want to
- Move to a different part of the country whenever you want to
- Read whatever newspaper, listen to whatever radio station, watch whatever television station, and view whatever web page you want to

- Express any opinion you wish, as long as it's not during work hours, to whomever you wish, if you have the means to do so
- Vote for any politician you wish
- Own a gun
- Buy or not buy whatever commodity you wish as long as you have the money
- Marry whomever you want (unless he or she is a close relative) and have as many children as you want
- Meet with whomever you wish, write petitions and demonstrate publicly
- Send your children to whatever school you can afford
- Do almost anything you want on your private property if you own any
- Have your guilt or innocence of a crime determined by a jury of your peers, not be required to testify against yourself, and not be tried for a crime after once being found not guilty of it

It's a very nice list of freedoms, at least in so far as none of them are interpreted as allowing anybody do to anything on the first list of NO-NOs. The problem with this list of freedoms, however, is that it is used to make us forget about the first list of NO-NOs. It is used by people who do bad things on the first list to make us feel grateful to them for allowing us to do things on the second list, instead of feeling angry with them for doing things on the NO-NOs list.

This is how the slippery and ill-defined notion of "freedom" is typically used to attack the most important freedom of all--the freedom to live in a society where people are not allowed to do the no-no's on the first list, and thus the freedom to create a really wonderful world to live in, where people are free--in all sorts of different and unique ways--to make it a great world for each other: an egalitarian world.

Entrepreneurship, Egalitarian Style

One important difference (between an egalitarian sharing economy and a Socialist or Communist centrally planned economy) concerns entrepreneurship; it is suppressed in a centrally planned economy but promoted in a sharing economy. The reason for this stems from the difference between voluntary federation versus an authoritative central government. In the sharing economy (with voluntary federation) there is no central government, certainly not one making the zillions of economic decisions that a centralized planned economy entails. Unlike a centralized planned economy, people in the sharing economy, as individuals or larger groups, are free, in fact encouraged, to be entrepreneurs, in the good sense of the word. Entrepreneurship, in the good sense (the "better mousetrap" sense), means thinking creatively about how to provide a much-loved new product or service, or a traditional one much more efficiently. The motive is not to get richer than others (as in capitalism), but the satisfaction of doing something wonderful and the enjoyment of the consequent respect and admiration from others for doing it.

In the sharing economy, a person or group of people with an entrepreneurial idea can "pitch" their idea as a proposal to the local community assembly, say Assembly A. If the proposal is approved then the enterprise and its workers individually are granted membership in the sharing economy. This means the enterprise can take (for free) from the sharing economy everything it needs, and the workers, as members of the sharing economy, can take for free everything they need or reasonably desire, as described above.

Before objecting that this process for an entrepreneur to get the green light to start his/her new enterprise is too restrictive or cumbersome, compare it to what a would-be entrepreneur must do in our current capitalist society. Unless a would-be entrepreneur is very wealthy, he or she needs to get wealthy people to loan or invest the big bucks required to start the new enterprise. This means going to venture capitalists or banks or appearing before the "sharks" on that T.V. show. It means trying to persuade rich people that they can get even richer by investing in or loaning money to one's proposed business. This too can be a restrictive or cumbersome process. Even worse is the fact that instead of having to persuade people that one's proposed enterprise will be good for ordinary people (as in egalitarianism), one must persuade rich people that it will make them even richer.

U.S. Constitution: Help Or Hindrance?

Even if the U.S. Constitution were obeyed 100%, it would not prevent some people from becoming enormously rich compared to most others. It would not stop our society from being one in which money is power. It would not prevent a very wealthy upper class from having far more power--over both the private sector and the government--than ordinary people have, despite the fact that ordinary people have "one man one vote" and the rights in the Bill of Rights. It would not, therefore, prevent class inequality. And class inequality is the root of our worst problems.

As is acknowledged by academics who study the question rigorously and even by the business press, the United States presently is an oligarchy (or plutocracy--same idea), not a republic or a democracy. In other words a small number of very rich people make the important government decisions and ordinary people have virtually no say in the matter either directly or even indirectly by means of representatives that truly represent them (as some people say would be the case in a republic).

This is the conclusion of a widely cited academic paper reporting on a study with an enormous data base, online[65] and reported on by *Business Insider*: "Major Study Finds the US is

---

65 https://www.cambridge.org/core/journals/perspectives-on-politics/article/testing-theories-of-american-politics-elites-interest-groups-and-average-citizens/62327F513959D0A304D4893B382B992B

an Oligarchy"[66] and *TPM*: "Princeton Study: US No Longer an Actual Democracy"[67] and *BBC*: "Study: US Is an Oligarchy, Not a Democracy"[68]. Additional proof is provided at the PDRBoston website[69].

Some people say that yes, this is the case today, and it is the source of many of our worst problems, including Orwellian wars of social control based on lies (wars that also enrich the plutocracy) and much suffering by the many for the benefit of the few. In order to make things right, they say, we need to make things be the way the U.S. Constitution, which is unfortunately being ignored, says things should be: a "representative democracy" otherwise known as a republic.

The problem with this "solution" is that it doesn't eliminate the root of the problem, which is class inequality. Class inequality in our present United States takes the form of some people being very rich compared to most people, and our society being one in which money is power. Billionaires thus have the power to shape society by their values; regular people do not. The power of money makes one-man-one-vote a meaningless right. Big Money dominates the decisions the government makes. Elected representatives are influenced by Big Money, not their constituents. This is a fact that is plain to see.

Why is it that the poorest people do the hardest work and enjoy the benefits of socially produced wealth the least, while the richest do the easiest work in great luxury or do no work at all, and enjoy the lion's share of these benefits? It's not because poor people don't have "one man one vote"; it's not

---

[66] http://www.businessinsider.com/major-study-finds-that-the-us-is-an-oligarchy-2014-4

[67] http://talkingpointsmemo.com/livewire/princeton-experts-say-us-no-longer-democracy

[68] http://www.bbc.com/news/blogs-echochambers-27074746

[69] https://www.pdrboston.org/proof-we-have-a-fake-democracy

because poor people are not "represented" by congresspersons and senators the way that the Constitution spells out (for what it's worth, which obviously is not very much!); it's not because poor people lack the rights of free speech and freedom to assemble, *etc.* in the Bill of Rights. It's because these rights count for diddly-squat in any contest between people with billions of dollars versus people whose net worth (assets minus debts) is close to zero--less than zero for one in five families!

Why is it that when the rich want to wage a war, they do it regardless of the majority of the population opposing it? This was the case with the Vietnam War, which went on until the refusal of GIs to fight it forced Nixon to withdraw in 1975, seven bloody years after a majority of Americans came to oppose that war. It's because when the Billionaire class wants to do something, their Big Money gives them the power to do it regardless of the fact that the vast majority who disagree have all of the useless rights in the Constitution.

There is nothing in the U.S. Constitution or the Bill of Rights or the Declaration of Independence that prohibits some people from being extremely rich and, thus, having far more actual power (over government decisions as well as private sector decisions) than other people despite the fact that everybody gets only one vote.

In fact, the Constitution protects the right of the very rich to remain very rich. Here is how it does it, as reported by PBS[70]:

> *"The Fifth Amendment protects the right to private property in two ways. First, it states that a person may not be deprived of property by the government without "due process of law," or fair procedures. In addition, it sets limits on the traditional practice of eminent domain, such as when the government takes private property to*

---

[70] http://www.pbs.org/tpt/constitution-usa-peter-sagal/rights/privacy-and-property-rights/

> *build a public road. Under the Fifth Amendment, such takings must be for a "public use" and require "just compensation" at market value for the property seized. But in Kelo v. City of New London (2005), the Supreme Court interpreted public use broadly to include a "public purpose" of economic development that might directly benefit private parties. In response, many state legislatures passed laws limiting the scope of eminent domain for public use."*

The reason that the rich can ignore the Constitution when they feel like it is because they are powerful, and nothing in the Constitution prevented them from becoming powerful or prevents them from being MUCH more powerful than regular people. **Honoring the Constitution to the letter would be, at most, a nuisance and an inconvenience for the rich. It would not prevent billionaires from running the show; it would simply mean they would have to be more careful and creative about how they used the power of money to get what they wanted.**

The U.S. Constitution HELPS the Rich Dominate the Rest of US

Indeed the U.S. Constitution, far from being an impediment to the power of the rich, makes the U.S. government one that is extremely *useful* for the rich to dominate the entire American population. How so? It does this by making the government one that is based on the authoritarian principle. The authoritarian principle is that one must obey the highest body of government no matter what. In our republic (which is what the United States Constitution makes the United States) when the members of Congress write a law and the President signs it, everybody in the United States must obey it. Ditto when the members of a state legislature write and the Governor signs a law, everybody in the state must obey it, no matter what.

The authoritarian principle (if the population accepts it as legitimate, which is unfortunately often the case) is a veritable "welcome mat" for rich people to dominate the entire population merely by using the power of their money to control a relatively small number of individuals who constitute the highest body of the government. (The authoritarian principle was also a "welcome mat" for the Bolshevik Party leaders to dominate the entire population of the Soviet Union by controlling--by hook or by crook--the relatively few people at the top of the Soviet government.) **Oppressive ruling elites LOVE the authoritarian principle, and the U.S. Constitution is pure authoritarian principle!**

Why do people accept the authoritarian principle? (They sometimes don't, as you can read about in Chapter Eight.) In the United States a big part of the reason why people accept the authoritarian principle is that people have a misunderstanding about democracy (including representative government, a.k.a. republics.) The misunderstanding is the false belief that there can exist today in the United States a democracy (or a republic, if you will, and now I'll just use the word "democracy" if you don't mind, OK?) of ALL the people. By a democracy of all the people I mean a system of government in which all conflicts and disagreements among the entire population of citizens are resolved peaceably by mutual agreements and compromises according to some agreed-upon method of decision-making (such as the principle of a majority vote of elected representatives) *without the use of violence or even the credible threat of violence by either side* when there is a conflict.

The fact is that there CANNOT exist today in the United States such a democracy of ALL the people, for the reason discussed in the following paragraphs. What purports to be a democracy of ALL the people is in fact a fake democracy that is really an oligarchy. The authoritarian principle derives its legitimacy from the idea that we really have a democracy of ALL the people, in which the laws written by the government reflect peacefully made mutual agreements and compromises among ALL Americans, and should therefore be obeyed.

Why can't there be a democracy of ALL the people? Because there is a conflict in the United States today that is what I call a "fundamental conflict," meaning a conflict in which neither side will agree to any compromise or make any mutual agreement with the other side no matter what the decision-making method is and what decision it produces; this fundamental conflict is one that can only be resolved by one side prevailing over the other side by using superior force--actual violence or the credible threat of violence. What is this fundamental conflict?

The fundamental conflict is this: Should there be class inequality or not?

The only reason the vast majority of people who do not think there should be class inequality (meaning they think there should be no rich and no poor) accept class inequality is because the rich use violence or the credible threat of violence to prevail over the vast majority. It is not because there was ever an election where people were permitted to vote for or against class inequality and the pro-class-inequality side got more votes and then regular people said, "OK, we lost the election so we'll accept class inequality now."

Whether to have class inequality or not is a question that can ONLY be resolved by violence or its credible threat, and never by any so-called "democratic" decision-making procedure. This was also true in the past for the question of whether slavery should exist or be abolished, and that is why there was a violent Civil War over the question despite the fact that there was--officially--a perfectly adequate representative government of ALL the people (at least all the white males on both sides of the slavery/abolition question) based on the U.S. Constitution in effect for resolving things peaceably.

The alternative to the false notion that there can be a democracy of ALL the people today in the United States, and likewise the alternative to the authoritarian principle, is egalitarianism. Specifically, it is the Voluntary Federation aspect of egalitarianism (as described in Chapter Four). Egalitarianism is about how people who don't want class inequality can ensure that it won't come into existence. This is why in an egalitarian society only egalitarians in local assemblies have the right to make laws (as discussed more in Chapters Seven and Eight). Enemies of egalitarian values have no right to make laws and participate in the government. This is simply the flip side of the coin, on one side of which is the fact that today advocates of egalitarian values have no ACTUAL right to make laws or meaningfully participate in government.

Constitutions that were written by slave-owning upper classes (or modeled on such constitutions, *i.e.* republics) are definitely NOT the answer! All the talk by the Founding Fathers known as the Federalists about protecting against the "tyranny of the majority" was actually about protecting the upper class from the lower class. As soon as the Founding Fathers had their Republic, what did they do? They violently attacked lower class people when they tried to make things more democratic (in the sense of ordinary people having a real say) and equal. Read (just use Google) about the way this new government violently attacked the Shays Rebellion[71] and the Whiskey Rebellion[72], not to mention the way it attacked runaway slaves[73]. ("In 1793, Washington signed the first fugitive slave law, which allowed fugitives to be seized in any state, tried and returned to their owners. Anyone who harbored or assisted a fugitive faced a $500 penalty and possible imprisonment."[74])

What most Americans want, even if they don't know its name yet, is egalitarianism. "Honoring the U.S. Constitution" sounds good when it's used as a slogan to oppose what the rich are doing to the rest of us, but it's a very misleading slogan that

---

[71] http://www.history.com/topics/shays-rebellion

[72] https://en.wikipedia.org/wiki/Whiskey_Rebellion

[73] https://classroom.monticello.org/media-item/runaway-ad/

[74] https://www.nytimes.com/2015/02/16/opinion/george-washington-slave-catcher.html

doesn't lead to what most people really want--an end to class inequality.

CHAPTER SIX: WHY ABOLISH THE USE OF MONEY?[75]

"Money is a new form of slavery, and distinguishable from the old simply by the fact that it is impersonal—that there is no human relation between master and slave."— Leo Tolstoy, Russian writer

"It is well enough that people of the nation do not understand our banking and money system, for if they did, I believe there would be a revolution before tomorrow morning."—Henry Ford, founder, Ford Motor Company

"We may have democracy in this country, or we may have wealth concentrated in the hands of a few, but we cannot have both."--US Supreme Court Justice Louis Brandeis

For hundreds of years economists have told themselves and anybody else who cared to listen a little fairy tale myth about the origin of money. According to the tale, human beings a long time ago before they invented money suffered enormous inconvenience when they exchanged things by barter. We've all heard the story about how hard it was to exchange your pig for some clothing when the person with the extra clothing didn't want a pig, and how you had to find somebody who wanted a pig who would give you in exchange for it something that you could then trade with the person who had the extra

---

[75] Much of this chapter comes from the 2011 pamphlet, "Thinking about Revolution," co-authored by Dave Stratman and myself, online at http://newdemocracyworld.org/revolution/Thinking.pdf

clothing. What a headache! But then, so the tale goes, money was invented and anybody could then exchange things with anybody. And so, the economists love to assure us, money is a truly wonderful thing that we never want to live without.

The only problem with this tale is that there is no evidence for its veracity. Those annoying anthropologists all say this. What there is evidence for is this. Before money people just shared things. As Ilana Strauss writes in "The Myth of the Barter Economy"[76]:

> *But various anthropologists have pointed out that this barter economy has never been witnessed as researchers have traveled to undeveloped parts of the globe. "No example of a barter economy, pure and simple, has ever been described, let alone the emergence from it of money," wrote the Cambridge anthropology professor Caroline Humphrey in a 1985 paper. "All available ethnography suggests that there never has been such a thing."*
>
> *So if barter never existed, what did? Anthropologists describe a wide variety of methods of exchange—none of which are of the "two-cows-for-10-bushels-of-wheat" variety.*
>
> *Communities of Iroquois Native Americans, for instance, stockpiled their goods in longhouses. Female councils then allocated the goods, explains Graeber. Other indigenous communities relied on "gift economies," which went something like this: If you were a baker who needed meat, you didn't offer your bagels for the butcher's steaks. Instead, you got your wife to hint to the butcher's wife that you two were low on iron, and she'd say something like "Oh really? Have a hamburger, we've got plenty!" Down the line, the*

---

[76] https://www.theatlantic.com/business/archive/2016/02/barter-society-myth/471051/

butcher might want a birthday cake, or help moving to a new apartment, and you'd help him out.

On paper, this sounds a bit like delayed barter, but it bears some significant differences. For one thing, it's much more efficient than Smith's idea of a barter system, since it doesn't depend on each person simultaneously having what the other wants. It's also not tit for tat: No one ever assigns a specific value to the meat or cake or house-building labor, meaning debts can't be transferred.

In his book, *Debt, the First 5000 Years*[77], anthropologist David Graeber shows that, contrary to economists who tell us that money was invented by ordinary people to make their lives easier, it was actually invented by Kings to make life harder for peasants. Kings introduced money as a better (for the king) way of forcing peasants to provide food to soldiers. It worked like this. The king created some kind of money (coins typically) and paid the soldiers with this money. Then the king declared that the peasants had to pay him a tax, payable only with money. The only way peasants could get the money they needed to pay the tax was by selling food to the soldiers.

No Money in an Egalitarian Society

Perhaps the most surprising feature of an egalitarian society is that money (of all kinds, from cash to checks to credit cards) is abolished. Why is this necessary and how does it make sense?

The economy of egalitarianism is based on the principle of "From each according to ability, to each according to need." It is a "Contribute what you can and take what you need" economy (sometimes called a "gift economy" or a "sharing

---

[77] https://www.amazon.com/Debt-Updated-Expanded-First-Years-ebook/dp/B00Q1HZMCW/ref=sr_1_1?s=books&ie=UTF8&qid=1473865049&sr=1-1&keywords=debt+the+first+5000+years

economy") not a 'If you give me this I will give you that" economy (sometimes called an "exchange economy.") This means people provide products or services for free according to their reasonable ability and in turn take what they need or reasonably desire for free. Money, which is indeed a means of exchanging things more conveniently than barter in an "exchange economy," is therefore not necessary in an egalitarian society because it is not an "exchange economy."

Furthermore, buying and selling is not an equitable way for the wealth of society to be distributed. Goods ought to be shared on the basis of need. If someone who contributes to society is in need of food or shelter, he should receive them, whether he has money or not. (Most homeless[78] adults in the U.S. have at least part time work and are looking for steady full time work; but many fulltime workers have jobs that pay too little to afford them a home.) If somebody is sick and needs care, it is immoral that she should only receive as much health care as she can buy. The Golden Rule is to share, not buy and sell.

Money may not be necessary in a good society but it is extremely important for a society based on inequality. In a society based on money a single individual can accumulate a great deal of money and use it to buy many things and pay many people, and thus control the use of things and the behavior of people on a vastly greater scale than would otherwise be possible.

Money thus makes inequality easy to impose because it makes it easy to concentrate power in the hands of a few, even in a society like ours today that purports to be a democracy. Money enables wealthy people to buy the votes of politicians, make laws to benefit themselves at the cost of society and sway public opinion through their corporate media. A society based on money is incompatible with genuine democracy and equality. As long as a society is based on money and buying and selling things to make a profit instead

---

[78] http://www.lcchousing.org/about-homelessness

of sharing them according to need among those who contribute according to ability, that society will eventually become unequal like ours today. This is discussed further in Chapters Two (how people with just a little bit more money have a little bit more power and use it to get more money and so on) and Thirteen (how money and class inequality makes corruption much easier to get away with, which in turn increases inequality further.)

Without Money, How Can New Enterprises Get Start-Up Capital?

On the surface it might seem that without money there would be no way to accumulate capital for investing in new enterprises. But if we look closely at what "capital" is, we see that capital accumulation for new enterprises does not require money in a society based on sharing.

Today, when a businessman wants to start a new enterprise, he needs money to buy or rent the necessary equipment and to pay wages for the necessary labor. In an egalitarian society, when people decide to start a new enterprise and the larger society democratically approves of it, then the people who carry out the enterprise may freely use the required land and natural resources and machinery, and the workers may freely take what they need to live on. The point is that in a money-based society, money is indeed important, but in a moneyless society it is not.

There remain two additional major reasons for not using money: money is an instrument of elite social control, and money poisons social relationships.

Money Is an Instrument of Elite Social Control

In an earlier time in America, the rich landowner or bank would extend credit to the tenant or farmer for seeds and fertilizer and food to sustain his family till harvest. At harvest the farmer would often find that his debt combined with the interest owed exceeded the value of his crop; with each passing year he would sink further into debt peonage. In current times in the United States, a young person graduates from college saddled with gigantic loans, which by law she can never escape, not even through personal bankruptcy. She is in debt peonage to the bank. She is forced by his debt to seek out the highest paying job she can find, no matter what career she would prefer. Economic pressures make her work at an unfulfilling job for a boss she may despise. The more successful she is at finding that high-paying job, the more pressure she is under to conform to capitalist values and keep her mouth shut.

At the same time her parents may carry a mortgage on a home worth perhaps half of what they paid for it. They are in debt peonage to the bank. Someone with a car loan or needing health insurance is under similar pressure to find and keep a job and make the daily compromises necessary to stay employed in a corporate dictatorship. Young people under economic stress join the military and are trained to kill their class brothers and sisters on command. As the rulers crank up the economic pressure on families, more parents are forced to work two or three jobs and barely have time to share with their children. Money reduces life to a rat race.

The banks gain and exercise their power in society through the power of money. The power of the banks looms over all our life choices. They hold our lives in their hands. A society based on money enables the few who are wealthy to control the many who are not.

Money Poisons Social Relationships

In a society based on money, many human interactions are mediated by money, with one person using money to exert power over another. The more money plays a role in society, the less of a role is played by the Golden Rule: moral persuasion, mutual agreement, or reciprocity of good deeds among equals. Money suppresses the role of positive human values and replaces it with greed and domination. In a money society, money confers on its possessor an almost magical power. If the owners of a corporation want a manager to fire long time employees in order to increase profits, they just pay the manager to do the nasty deed. No need to persuade the manager that it is a morally good thing to do. The owners of the corporation have a perverse power over the manager.

In the absence of money, social power comes from one's ability to persuade others that doing this or that is morally right or at least that it benefits them. It also comes from having relationships of mutual support: because one has helped others in the past, they want to return the favor. In the absence of money, social power is not power over people but power to act with people to accomplish goals that are shared.

It has long been said that the love of money is the root of all evil. Only in the absence of the power of money will people's moral feelings and their best values truly be able to shape all of society.

CHAPTER SEVEN: WHY SHOULD ONLY EGALITARIANS MAKE THE LAWS?

One of the main features of voluntary federation as a principle of democratic government is that only egalitarians (those who support equality and mutual aid) have a *right* to be members of a local assembly and only local assemblies can make the laws that all people in the community must obey. Is this feature consistent with the idea of democracy, or not?

At first it may seem inconsistent. After all, in the United States laws are made by representatives elected by all eligible voters and, except for having to be at least a certain age and having to be a citizen (and in some places having to be a non-felon), there are no other restrictions on who can vote. Democracy, as we have all been taught in school, means that EVERYBODY can vote because EVERYBODY--rich and poor alike--should have an equal say in determining government laws and policies.

The standard conception of the meaning of democracy is that it is a way for everybody--rich and poor alike--to resolve their differences (by agreeing on what government laws and policies should be) peaceably with everybody having an equal say. (Whether the method of resolving these differences is by a system of majority-rule or consensus or some hybrid, and whether the method is by electing representatives or direct democracy with town meetings is all secondary to the core, standard, meaning of democracy.)

The problem is that this standard meaning of democracy is based on a big misunderstanding. In real life, when there is a fundamental conflict of values among people in a society (such as whether there should be slavery or not, or whether there should be class inequality or not) then the way the decision is made is always by a contest of force. The side that prevails is the side that brings to bear the greatest force (including violence) or the credible threat of such force against the other side.

A fundamental conflict of values is, by definition, a conflict in which neither side will willingly surrender to the other no matter who has a majority or wins the most votes, *etc*. The question of slavery in the United States was not settled by a vote in Congress, and was only settled by the Civil War's outcome, precisely because neither side would willingly surrender to the other on this question. There was no lack of democratic procedure available to resolve the conflict--there were elections and a fully functioning representative democracy. But the conflict was a fundamental one, and hence could not be resolved peaceably no matter how perfectly the U.S. Constitution purported to make the United States a representative democracy (a.k.a. a republic). When it comes to resolving a fundamental conflict, there is no such thing as a "democracy of all the people." The standard meaning of democracy (being of "all the people") has no relation to the real world and is simply misleading.

In the United States today we have extreme class inequality. The conflict between those who want class inequality and those who don't is a fundamental conflict. The minority who want class inequality have prevailed, but not because they won a vote. When was the last time anybody was even able to vote on this question? The majority, who oppose class inequality, never agreed to accept the outcome of class inequality. On the contrary, the majority who don't want class inequality have accepted it only because the minority has brought to bear overwhelming force or the credible threat of force against people who try to reduce the harshness of class inequality: police attack striking workers if they actually try to block scabs from crossing their picket lines; police drag a fired worker away from the worksite if he or she does not leave willingly; the national guard or the 82nd Airborne Division will, if it should ever be necessary, be ordered to attack working class people who dare to lay claim to own the vast industrial and agricultural property that the rich claim to own; *etc., etc.*

The violence inherent in routine everyday economic coercion—the violence at the other end of the chain of coercion—is only apparent when one considers what would happen to a person who refuses to be fired. What if a fired person continues to show up for work? She would be arrested for trespassing and hauled away forcibly by police. If she resisted she would risk being shot. If a large number of workers behaved this way then the National Guard or, if necessary, the Army would be called in to use whatever violence was needed to suppress the disobedience.

The police, National Guard and military virtually never receive orders to support disobedient workers; they only receive orders to suppress them. Why is this? It is because the American upper class of billionaires uses their money to control the electoral process and the government. They use the trappings of democracy to make the reality of their upper class dictatorship less visible and to persuade people that when the government enforces class inequality it is legitimate force because it is 'of, by and for the people.'

The reality, in other words, in the United States today is that only those who support class inequality are permitted to make the laws. Politicians who don't support class inequality are not permitted to enter the legislature in numbers sufficient to pass legislation making class inequality illegal. Big Money is confident today that by controlling the mass media and by bankrolling the political parties (and by rigging votes and threatening individuals with violence when necessary) it can prevent the electoral process from making class inequality illegal, even though most Americans would LOVE it to be illegal. But if Big Money ever felt that it could no longer control the outcome of the electoral process sufficiently to prevent it from making class inequality illegal, then Big Money would change the "rules of the game" and, if necessary, impose its dictatorship of the rich without any longer trying to make it seem as if it was "the will of the people."

Most people in the United State oppose class inequality. If we had a democracy in the United States that actually resolved fundamental conflicts peaceably by majority-rule or consensus, then the government would not enforce class inequality and the billionaire class would lose its wealth, power and privilege. The fact that this has clearly not happened proves that we do not have such a democracy. The fact that billionaires—or slave-owners or any class of people who aim to exploit, dominate and oppress others—will use force and violence to do so means that there cannot exist a democracy that resolves such fundamental conflicts peaceably. Whenever the claim is made that such a democracy exists, it is false.

WHAT IS GENUINE DEMOCRACY?

Democracy, in reality, can only have meaning if it is understood to be a means by which people **with shared fundamental values** peaceably resolve their conflicts over NON-fundamental disagreements with everyone having an equal say. This is the meaning of democracy that is not based on a misunderstanding.

The democracy that egalitarians need is one that enables us to cooperate in shaping society by our shared egalitarian values of equality and mutual aid. This is genuine democracy. There will, for a certain amount of time at least, be people in society who strongly disagree with these egalitarian values and who will do whatever they can to prevent society from being shaped by them. (Recall that the slave owners after the Civil War continued to fight violently against the Reconstruction laws that gave blacks the right to vote and hold office, and in the end they overturned those laws and made Jim Crow the law in the South.)

There is no good reason to invite the declared enemies of egalitarianism to partake in writing laws that egalitarians (and others) must obey. If, because of a misunderstanding about democracy, we did invite the enemies of egalitarians into the local assemblies, then we would have debates in these assemblies about WHETHER we should shape society by egalitarian values, not HOW. This would open the door to legitimizing the view that we should NOT shape society by egalitarian values. And this in turn would make it easier for the enemies of egalitarians--the proponents of class inequality--to impose on society a fake democracy like the one that we have today--a fake democracy that is actually a dictatorship of the rich.

In practice, very likely in most communities the overt enemies of egalitarian values, if any, would be well known and not allowed membership in the local assembly. All others would be welcome in the assembly. If it became clear that an individual in the assembly was strongly opposed to egalitarian values, however, the egalitarians in the assembly--for the reasons discussed above--would have every right to tell that person to leave the assembly, and this would be perfectly consistent with the principles of genuine democracy.

CHAPTER EIGHT: WHY SHOULD LAWS ONLY BE MADE BY LOCAL ASSEMBLIES?

One of the novel things about egalitarianism is that laws are only made by local assemblies of egalitarians (as discussed in Chapter Two and illustrated by the online eyewitness account of an actual local assembly of egalitarians in revolutionary Spain around 1937 introduced in Appendix II). This idea of local community sovereignty may seen novel to us, but it has a long historical tradition of being fought for by people including the "Levelers" in England in the 1640s, Americans who fought in the American Revolution against King George III, and some of the French who fought in the French Revolution.

The reason local community sovereignty seems novel and strange today is because the contrary principle, which I call the "authoritarian principle," is so widely accepted.

History Of People Rejecting The "Authoritarian Principle"

The "authoritarian principle" is the (wrong, as discussed below) notion that one must obey the highest level of government, no matter what. Often this principle is defended on the grounds that the government, typically a nation's central government, is "legitimate" because it was directly or indirectly elected, or because its leaders are special for some reason (closer to God than are regular people, divine, experts in the "science" of Marxism-Leninism, or whatever.)

If one knows only what we're taught in school and what we read in the newspaper, then it would seem that pretty much everybody throughout history has accepted the authoritarian principle without question. History, so we are led to believe, has been about conflicts over WHO should be in control of the central government, but never about whether one is obliged to OBEY it no matter what.

But people in the past HAVE, to their great credit, rejected the authoritarian principle. They knew that blind obedience to a far-away handful of people is a recipe for domination by an oppressive elite.

In England in the 1640s there was a revolutionary movement, known as the "Levellers," that aimed to abolish the monarchy and the House of Lords. There was also a popular and anti-Monarchist army called The New Model Army that was strongly influenced by Leveller ideas. "They expressly opposed blind obedience to unjust civil law. **'I confess to me this principle [of obedience] is very dangerous,'** declared John Wildman, one of the civilian Levellers. '...It is contrary to what the army first declared' in the June 14 declaration: 'that they stood upon such principles of right and freedom, and the laws of nature and nations, whereby men were to preserve themselves though the persons to whom authority belonged should fail in it.'" [*bracket in, but emphasis not in, the original: The Third Revolution*, vol. 1, pg. 113, by Murray Bookchin]

In France at the outbreak of the Revolution in 1789, after people in the streets of Paris stormed the royal Bastille prison and took it over, similar events took place throughout the nation. "When existing municipal corporations failed to meet the townspeople's demands for price controls on food, they would invade the Hotel de Ville [*i.e.*, City Hall] and forcibly expel the old authorities, replacing traditional institutions and their officeholders with more democratic forms and personnel. Once again, the unreliability of the army made these changes possible. At Strasbourg, for example, royal troops looked on passively as the Hotel de Ville was sacked by demonstrators. By such various means did the vast local officialdom of the ancien regime--from the loftiest intendant to the lowliest bureaucrat--withdraw from the places they had occupied, causing the collapse of the central authority. Effectively, France was now decentralized: the new municipal governments agreed to accept the decisions of the Assembly [*i.e.*, the central governmental body], **but only with the proviso that those decisions accorded with the wishes of the local population.**" [*emphasis not in the original: The Third Revolution*, vol. 1, pg. 286, by Murray Bookchin]

Laws Only Made By Local Assemblies Of Egalitarians

The two main concerns that people have about local community sovereignty are: 1) Does it mean that people can enact terrible laws somewhere and good people elsewhere are prevented from stopping that? 2) Does this mean that there is no large-scale order, no large scale planning and coordination and cooperation? The answer to both questions is "No."

What If Bad People Make Terrible Laws In A Local Community?

Does local community sovereignty in an egalitarian society mean that people can enact terrible laws somewhere and good people elsewhere are prevented from stopping that? No. Here's why.

As stated in Chapter Two in the description of voluntary federation, nothing about voluntary federation prevents local assemblies from mutually agreeing to form a militia (or army) to forcibly prevent other people from attacking egalitarian values. Thus if a local assembly or even a region decided (no matter how "democratically"), for example, to enslave all the [fill in the blank] people or engage in, say, child abuse, then other local assemblies of true egalitarians would be entirely within their rights in forcibly preventing people elsewhere from enslaving or abusing people this way. (See Chapter Seven for more on this point.) The principle is that voluntary federation is the way for egalitarians to democratically shape society by egalitarian values; it is also the way for egalitarians to democratically (among themselves) prevent (violently if necessary) the enemies of egalitarian values from shaping society by anti-egalitarian values.

Local Community Sovereignty And Large-Scale Cooperation And Planning

There is nothing about egalitarianism that prevents or discourages large-scale--even planetary--cooperation and planning. On the contrary, egalitarianism (rule by those who value mutual aid) encourages it. The question is not whether there should be large-scale social order, but rather upon what should this large-scale order be based.

There are two ways to achieve large-scale order. The way that exists today is to base it on the "authoritarian principle." This principle says that a legitimate central authority or highest level governmental body (such as the American Federal government or the World Trade Organization or the International Bank, *etc.*) has the right to make laws (or policies) that everybody in its jurisdiction must obey whether they agree with the law or not, simply because it IS the highest level legitimate authority.

The source of legitimacy for the highest level governing body can be whatever persuades most people of its legitimacy. In some cases the individuals comprising the highest level governing body claim they have the right to make laws that others must obey because they were elected. In other cases these individuals claim to be the representatives of God. In yet other cases they claim to have the greatest grasp of Marxism-Leninism. Regardless of the source of their claim to legitimacy, these individuals (or in some cases a single individual) act as a dictator: their will (called laws) must be unquestioningly obeyed by everybody--like it or not.

Once the population accepts the authoritarian principle, all that an oppressive class of people must do to dominate and oppress the population is to gain control of the highest level governing body. Once in control of this relatively small governing body, the oppressive class of people has total control over the entire population.

No matter how reasonable the source of legitimacy of the highest level governing body, such a body can often be taken over by a determined class of oppressors and used for its oppressive purposes. We see how this has happened in the United States, where government that is legitimized by elections as being of, by and for the people has been effectively taken over by Big Money. Now Americans feel obliged to obey laws that are written, in effect, by Big Money.

This illustrates the fact that the authoritarian principle is the friend of oppressors. Until people reject the authoritarian principle they will be sitting ducks at the mercy of any oppressor who gains control of the highest level governing body.

The way to avoid this problem is to reject the authoritarian principle by deciding to create large-scale social order on a very different principle: voluntary federation of local assemblies of egalitarians, each in a different local community[79]. Voluntary federation of local assemblies

---

[79] How large is a local community? The local community would need to be small enough so that everybody in it who supports the values of equality and mutual aid and who wishes to attend its local-assembly-of-egalitarians meeting can fit in the same room (or interact with each other satisfactorily in a "virtual online room" if people choose to meet that way.)

Today many conventions take place with plenary meetings of more than 5,000 people. In a community of 40,000 people (including children) it is likely that fewer than 1 out of 8 people would attend a given community's local assembly meeting, which would mean 5000 or fewer people at the meeting. There is no need for all 40,000 people in the local community to know each other personally, because what the local assembly

achieves order on a large scale by having higher-level bodies (formed of delegates from lower level bodies) craft proposals (**not laws!**) for the lower-level bodies to accept or reject as they wish. Back and forth negotiations between lower-level bodies and the proposal-writing higher-level bodies seeks to reach a mutual agreement among however many lower-level bodies are required to implement a given proposal.

Local assemblies of egalitarians thus send delegates (whom they may recall whenever they wish) to meet with delegates from other nearby local assemblies as a one-step-higher level assembly of delegates. These assemblies of delegates in turn send delegates (whom they may recall whenever they wish) to meet with other such assemblies of delegates. This process continues as much as people desire, possibly to national assemblies of delegates sending delegates to a global assembly of delegates. This process can exist in parallel for different kinds of things with some assemblies of delegates focused, for example, on economic or transportation order and others, say, on organizing events like the World Olympics.

At every level, when an assembly of delegates has accepted a proposal from a higher-level assembly, it then offers this proposal to the lower level assemblies from which its

---

meeting does is establish general principles (*i.e.*, laws) and appoint committees to implement them.

If people wish to limit the size of a local community to much smaller than 40,000 people, that would be easy to do. If a community with 40,000 people wanted to, it could divide into, say, ten smaller communities of 4,000 people each, and each local assembly meeting would then consist of only around 500 people. Then these small assemblies would each send a delegate to a "regional" assembly of delegates and voluntary federation would be used to achieve order for the larger region of 40,000 people. Even much smaller assemblies are possible if people so desire.

delegates come. Back and forth negotiations again take place to try to reach a mutual agreement among the lower level assemblies on a proposal. Eventually the local assemblies of egalitarians are presented with a proposal and at this local level they either accept or reject the proposal. If they reject it then negotiations may continue. If and when enough local assemblies agree with a proposal to make its implementation possible, it is implemented. This is how people can develop mutually agreed upon proposals, on the scale of a region of any size no matter how large, even on a planetary scale if so desired. This is genuine democracy. And this is how egalitarians can make it extremely difficult for any oppressive power to end up ordering them to do what they don't wish to do.

Sounds nice, but can it <u>really</u> work? See Chapter Ten **for real-life examples showing that the answer is "Yes," even on a global scale.**

CHAPTER NINE: IS EGALITARIANISM'S SHARING ECONOMY PRACTICAL ON A LARGE SCALE?

The egalitarian principle, described in Chapter Four, of a sharing economy is based not on money and buying and selling things but rather sharing products and services on the basis of "From each according to reasonable ability, to each according to need or reasonable desire, with scarce things equitably rationed according to need." The question is, can this work? Is it practical? Would it result in an economy that produces what people want and desire, or would it lead to mass (and perhaps equally shared) poverty? Would it require some kind of central planning that would inevitably be dictatorial and oppressive? These are all important questions that will be addressed in this chapter.

Egalitarianism Out-Produced Capitalism In Revolutionary Spain 1936-9

One often hears capitalism defended on the grounds that it is the economic system that best improves the standard of living of all people. Pro-capitalists cite three facts[80]: 1) that the proportion of people in the world living in poverty has been declining, especially in China after the decision of the Chinese

---

[80] I am not sure whether or not these three "facts" are true, but I am willing to accept them as true for the sake of argument, because they are irrelevant to any consideration of the relative merits of capitalism versus egalitarianism.

Communist Party to embrace capitalism; 2) that the number of years of life expectancy is rising globally; and 3) that the standard of living and life expectancy of the English population improved during the Industrial Revolution, despite the bad image of that period created by writers such as Charles Dickens.

What the pro-capitalists choose not to mention, however, is that the relevant way to evaluate the merits of capitalism is not by comparing it to the feudalism that preceded it or by seeing whether or not some things are getting better in recent decades, but by comparing capitalism to egalitarianism. Egalitarianism is the alternative to both feudalism and capitalism that people in different parts of the world, at least as early as the English Peasant Rebellion of 1381[81], have fought to implement; their efforts were defeated by violence from the wealthiest people, whose objections to egalitarianism had nothing to do with whether it was better or worse than capitalism for improving people's standard of living.

In fact, the evidence, to be discussed below, is that egalitarianism is far better than capitalism even if compared only on the basis of economic productivity and standard of living. Equally important, although not the focus here, is the fact that everybody[82] is seriously harmed by inequality (no matter how big the "pie" is overall) and benefits from equality; on this basis the extreme inequality generated by capitalism, in China[83] as well as the United States[84], only

---

[81] http://newdemocracyworld.org/revolution/john.html

[82] See "Why inequality is bad for you -- and everyone else" at http://www.cnn.com/2011/11/06/opinion/wilkinson-inequality-harm/
and "Income inequality hurts economic growth, researchers say" at https://www.washingtonpost.com/business/economy/income-inequality-hurts-economic-growth-researchers-say/2014/01/24/cb6e02a0-83b0-11e3-9dd4-e7278db80d86_story.html?utm_term=.6d943bf006c9 for starters.

[83] https://cip.cornell.edu/DPubS?service=UI&version=1.0&verb=Display&handle=dns.gfs/1200428169

[84] http://www.vanityfair.com/news/2011/05/top-one-percent-201105

further weakens the case for capitalism when compared to egalitarianism.

To compare economic productivity in capitalism to egalitarianism I will compare a) productivity in the parts of Spain where the egalitarian revolution (sometimes called the Spanish Civil War) of 1936-9 saw wholesale reorganization of productivity with voluntary egalitarian collectives inspired by anarchist ideas, to b) productivity in the same place just prior to the revolution when capitalism (even if some of the capitalists still retained their feudal titles, such as "Count") prevailed.

In several provinces of Spain an egalitarian revolution either eliminated money altogether or made its use secondary while making primary the principle of "from each according to ability, to each according to need." Thus where money remained at all, a person's wage was based on how much he or she needed (how big was their family, *etc.*), quite unlike in our present capitalist society.

The following are excerpts from *The Anarchist Collectives*, edited by Sam Dolgoff, online[85]. The collectives varied from region to region, but what they all shared in common was a dramatic increase in economic equality and cooperative ways of doing economic work. As a result, productivity increased.

"In the village of Magdalena de Pulpis a visitor asked a resident, 'How do you organize without money? Do you use barter, a coupon book, or anything else?' He replied, 'Nothing. Everyone works and everyone has a right to what he needs free of charge. He simply goes to the store where provisions and all other necessities are supplied. Everything is distributed free with only a notation of what he took.'" [pg. 73.]

"[During the revolution peasants collectivized the land

---

[85] https://www.scribd.com/document/25020337/The-Anarchist-Collective-Sam-Dolgoff

properties of Count Romanones:] The peasants altered the topography of the district by diverting the course of the river to irrigate new land, thus tremendously increasing cultivated areas. They constructed a mill, schools, collective dining halls, and new housing for the collectivists. A few days after the close of the Civil War, Count Romanones reclaimed his domains, expecting the worst, certain that the revolutionary vandals had totally ruined his property. He was amazed to behold the wonderful improvements made by the departed peasant collectivists.

"When asked their names, the Count was told that the work was performed by the peasants in line with plans drawn up by a member of the CNT Building Workers' Union, Gomez Abril, an excellent organizer chosen by the Regional Peasant Federation. As soon as Abril finished his work he left and the peasants continued to manage the collective.

"Learning that Gomez Abril was jailed in Guadalajara and that he was in a very precarious situation, the count succeeded in securing his release from jail and offered to appoint him manager of all his properties. Gomez declined, explaining that a page of history had been written and his work finished." [pg. 150]

This next excerpt is an eyewitness account of Graus, a "district situated in the mountainous northern part of the province of Huesca."

"As in the collectivization of industry, similar procedures were applied to agriculture. In Graus, as in many other places in Aragon, the first step toward socialization was organization of the agricultural collective. The Revolutionary Committee first tackled the most urgent problems: harvesting planting, overcoming the shortage of young workers (many were away fighting on the Aragon front), and still getting maximum yields from the land. Thanks to the strenuous effort and initiative of the comrades of the CNT and UGT, better ploughs and stronger horses were procured, and other improvements were made. The land was cleared and fields sown with corn. The agricultural collective was established on October 16th, 1936, 3 months after the fascist assault was repulsed. On the same day transportation was collectivized and other new collectivizations were scheduled by the two unions, the CNT (libertarian) and the UGT (socialist). Printshops were socialized on Nov. 24th, followed 2 days later by shoe stores and bakeries. Commerce, medicine, pharmacies, horseshoers' and blacksmiths' establishments were all collectivized December 1st, and cabinet makers and carpenters on December 11th. Thus all social economic activities were gradually integrated into the new social order.

"There was no forced collectivization. Membership in the collectives was entirely voluntary, and groups could secede from the collective if they so desired. But even if isolation were possible, the obvious benefits of the collective were so great that the right to secede was seldom, if ever, invoked.

"Ninety percent of all production, including exchange and distribution, was collectively owned. (The remaining 10% was produced by petty peasant landholders.)

"The collective modernized industry, increased production, turned out better products, and improved public services. For example, the collective installed up-to-date machinery for the extraction of olive oil and conversion of the residue into soap. It purchased two big electric washing machines, one for the hospital and the other for the collectivized hotel...Through more efficient cultivation and the use of better fertilizers, production of potatoes increased 50% ... and the production of sugar beets and feed for livestock doubled. Previously uncultivated smaller plots of ground were used to plant 400 fruit trees, ...and there were a host of other interesting innovations. Through this use of better machinery and chemical fertilizers and, by no means least, through the introduction of voluntary collective labor, the yield per hectare was 50% greater on collective property than on individually worked land." [Pg. 135-9]

The collectives improved production in urban industries too.

Here is an account of the metal and munitions industry:

"One of the most impressive achievements of the Catalonian metal workers was to rebuild the industry from scratch. Toward the close of the Civil War, 80,000 workers were supplying the anti-fascist troops with war materiel. At the outbreak of the Civil War the Catalonian metal industry was very poorly developed. The largest installation, Hispano-Suiza Automobile Company, employed only 1,100 workers. A few days after July 19th this plant was already converted to the manufacture of armored cars, hand grenades, machine gun carriages, ambulances, etc., for the fighting front. ... In Barcelona during the Civil War, four hundred metal factories were built, most of them manufacturing war material...

"Very few machines were imported. In a short time, two hundred different hydraulic presses of up to 250 tons pressure, one hundred seventy-eight revolving lathes, and hundreds of milling machines and boring machines were built. A year after the beginning of the Civil War, production of ammunition increased to one million 155-millimeter projectiles, fifty thousand aerial bombs and millions of cartridges. In these last three months of 1937 alone, fifteen million other war materials were produced." [Pg. 96]

Adding to the evidence for the economic superiority of the egalitarian collectives is the fact that production during the revolution was seriously hampered by the facts that a) so many men were prevented from doing economic work because they had to be in the militias fighting to defend the revolution from the fascist attack on it and b) so much productivity had to be for war material rather than for things to make life better for people. People's standard of living would no doubt have been even greater were it not for this problem, a problem caused by capitalists and not by egalitarians.

Apologists for capitalism might argue something such as, "Oh sure, these egalitarians produced a lot in wartime when they knew their survival depended on it, but in peacetime they'd probably revert to being lazy and mass poverty would result."

This argument, when one thinks about it, defeats itself. It admits that when people have a good reason (such as military defense) to produce a lot in a sharing economy, then they will. Presumably when people have a different reason for wanting to produce a lot, they would then as well. And by the same token, if people do not have a reason for wanting to produce a lot, and decide not to, what's wrong with that? This choice is a freedom that people have in an egalitarian society, but don't have in a capitalist one.

What Replaces The "Free Market" In A Sharing Economy? Is It **Practical**?

The sharing economy as described in Chapter Four is based on sharing, according to need, among those who contribute to the economy reasonably according to ability. Critics of this kind of economy argue that it is either a Soviet-style centrally planned economy or, at any rate, it suffers from the same fatal faults as a centrally planned economy. They assert that when it comes to making an economy work properly, nothing can replace the discipline imposed by the free market in a capitalist economy.

Defenders of capitalism argue that the only way to ensure that the economic activity of people actually provides the products and services that consumers want, in an efficient manner, is by allowing the free market to guide economic decision-making by disciplining businesses with the threat that if they don't provide what customers want, at a price customers are willing to pay, efficiently enough to make a profit while doing this, then they will go out of business.

The beauty of discipline imposed by the free market, in this view, is that it requires no central planning board to determine if a business is providing what customers actually want, or if it is doing it efficiently enough to be permitted to operate. The problem with a centrally planned economy, according to this view, is that it is impossible for any central body to possess all of the vast information required to make all of the zillions of decisions that must be made in operating the economy of a nation rationally. This criticism of centrally planned economies is perfectly valid. The question then is whether there is a way for an economy based on sharing and equality (no rich and no poor) that is neither centrally planned nor disciplined by a capitalist free market to "deliver the goods." What follows is an argument for the "Yes" answer to this question.

The Political Context Of A Sharing Economy: Egalitarianism

First, we need to recall what the political context is for a sharing economy. Egalitarianism means that the people who support the principles of equality and mutual aid ("egalitarians") hold power in society, and the people who oppose those principles do not. Furthermore, it means that egalitarians use voluntary federation to achieve social order and coordinate things and cooperate with each other on a large scale, rather than authorizing a central government to dictate laws, as is the practice of today's so-called "democracies" as well as Communist governments. (The so-called "democracies" of today legitimize the dictatorial power of the central government by arguing "they were elected"; the Communist regimes (China and Cuba) argue that the Party must rule for the good of the people until some time in the far distant future when people will be socially engineered in such a manner as to make society classless and cause the state to "whither away" as discussed in Chapter Twelve.)

Voluntary federation means that the only laws that people in a local community must obey are laws made by its local assembly, at which all egalitarians (but not people who oppose egalitarianism) in that community[86] are able to participate as equals. Local assemblies send delegates to meet with delegates from other local assemblies (forming a

---

[86] Here, in the context of who can participate in a local assembly, the phrase "in the community" means residing in the community or, in the case of a person who resides outside the community, working reasonably in an enterprise located in the community.

non-local assembly of delegates), and these delegates craft proposals (not laws!) that are only implemented when sufficient numbers of local assemblies voluntarily agree to implement them, typically after a process of amendments being suggested by local assemblies and amendments being made by the assembly of their delegates. Likewise, non-local assemblies (of delegates) send delegates in turn to meet with others like them from other regions to craft proposals for larger regions. And these assemblies may send delegates to yet "higher" level assemblies, *etc*. In this manner there can even be assemblies of delegates from all over the planet making proposals for globally coordinated efforts. But local assemblies (of egalitarian people living in the same community) only implement a proposal if they voluntarily wish to. There is no central government making laws that everybody is required to obey.[87]

One of the most important ways for local assemblies to cooperate with each other is to mutually agree to form a single sharing economy. In a sharing economy, there is no money; one is either a member of the sharing economy or not. If one is a member of the sharing economy then one enjoys the right, equal to all other members, to take (for free--there is no money) products and services that one needs or reasonably desires, or--in the case of things that are in short supply--to have a chance, equal to others with a similar need, to obtain these by an equitable rationing method determined by the local assembly. If one is not a member of the sharing economy, then one then one may barter with individuals or economic enterprises that are in the sharing economy. The ultimate authority that determines if one is or is not a member of the sharing economy is the local assembly for the community in which one resides.

---

[87] Local assemblies can, however, cooperate to defend people who are attacked by anti-egalitarians. If, for example, people somewhere decided (democratically or not) to enslave others, then local assemblies of egalitarians would have every right to form a militia and forcibly prevent them from enslaving anybody. From the point of view of the would-be slave owners, they would essentially be ordered by a "central government" to cease enslaving people. It is the egalitarians, not anti-egalitarians, who should enjoy the absence of a law-making central government.

The local assembly may, if it wishes, allow somebody to be a member of the sharing economy for any reason it wishes, but it also has the right to deny membership to a person who does not contribute to the economy reasonably according to ability, as judged by the local assembly. Obviously, what constitutes a reasonable contribution according to ability would take into account a person's age and health and everything else that reasonable people would consider relevant.

Replace Profit With Reputation

Now we can address the question of what, in a sharing economy, takes the place of the free market in a capitalist economy. What, in other words, ensures that economically sensible activity is promoted and economically nonsensical activity is discouraged? In a free market capitalist economy it is profitability (or the lack thereof) that supposedly does this job. It does indeed discipline people in the economy, and it does indeed drive some businesses out of business that, from a reasonable point of view, ought to be driven out of business.

But a business can be profitable by catering to the very rich, thus directing economic resources towards producing things or services (*e.g.*, psychiatry[88] for a rich person's pet dog, a twenty-million dollar mansion[89] for one small family) that are not terribly important at the cost of depriving others of things that are (*e.g.*, health care, housing.) Profit is the reason why landowners don't grow food for people too poor to buy it, and instead grow crops that get made into luxury items that wealthy people can afford to buy. This is one reason capitalism is not good. In particular, this shows that in looking for something to replace profitability in a free market we are looking to replace something that is far from perfect to begin with. It is not necessary, therefore, for the replacement to be

---

[88] http://content.time.com/time/health/article/0,8599,2079795,00.html

[89] http://articles.latimes.com/2013/may/05/business/la-fi-ellison-malibu-20130505

perfect, just better, as judged by criteria we think are important.

What are these important criteria? The following seem reasonable objectives for whatever replaces profitability in a free market: 1) Promote economic activity that provides for the needs and desires of people living as equals in an egalitarian society. 2) Motivate people to contribute reasonably to the economy according to ability. 3) Promote efficient (with respect to the previous criteria) use of human and material resources.

The sensible replacement for profitability in a free market capitalist economy is reputation (with respect to the above criteria, as described below) in a sharing economy. Here is how reputation plays this key role.

A local assembly, call it Assembly A, has the option of saying, "We won't agree to our community being in a sharing economy that includes local community X." If X has a reputation for admitting lots of people into the sharing economy who don't actually contribute and share reasonably according to ability in the opinion of Assembly A, or if, in Assembly A's opinion, local community X contributes things that are unreasonably useless compared to things that they could otherwise contribute, then Assembly A may exercise this option. If other local assemblies also share Assembly A's opinion, then Assembly X, if it wishes to remain in and enjoy the great benefits of membership in a larger sharing economy, will have a strong motivation for making changes to ensure that it has a good reputation.

Having a good reputation (for contributing to the economy reasonably and efficiently) plays a role in a sharing economy analogous to having a high rate of profit in a capitalist economy. A decline in reputation /profit leads eventually to exclusion from the sharing economy / bankruptcy.

Like profitability in a capitalist economy, reputation in a sharing economy operates at all scales, from that of a hot dog vendor on the sidewalk to a multi-national corporation. Here is why.

A local community assembly would typically oversee a committee it appoints to decide if economic enterprises in the community should be members of the sharing economy. The decision would be about the enterprise as a single entity, not about each individual worker in it. And the decision would be based on the overall reputation of the enterprise. A hospital, for example, would be judged on the basis of its overall reputation, not a close inspection of every person who works in it, much as today when a sick person decides on what hospital to use he or she goes by overall reputation of the hospital, which might include things such as whether the hospital is certified by the appropriate organization, *etc*.

In order to maintain its good reputation, a hospital (to take that as an example, but we could be talking about any other economic enterprise), would in turn want to ensure that its component entities (the emergency room, the intensive care unit, *etc*.) have good reputations. The hospital (meaning the hospital workers, acting democratically as equals, in a "hospital assembly", or more generally a "workplace assembly") decides who can be a worker at the hospital. If the hospital is a member of the sharing economy, then so are all of its workers. If, however, a section within the hospital, say the ER, has a sufficiently bad reputation, then the hospital would be motivated to dismiss the workers who are responsible for the bad reputation, in order to maintain the reputation of the hospital and its membership in the sharing economy. Thus the role of reputation extends downward from the level of the local community assembly to the economic enterprises within the community and even to the individual workers in those enterprises.

In a community there may be economic enterprises of varying sizes, from a one-person hot dog vendor on the sidewalk to a large hospital or local branch of a multinational organization. In the case of hot dog vendors, it would be likely that all of them would join an association of hot dog vendors (or something similar) and this association would, as a single entity, seek membership in the sharing economy based on its reputation; it would also be concerned with the reputation of individual hot dog vendors for the same reason as discussed above in the case of a hospital.

In the case of a local branch of a multi-national organization, the local branch could gain membership in the sharing economy for itself alone the same way any other economic enterprise does, or it could obtain membership in the sharing economy by virtue of being part of the larger multi-national organization if that organization itself is a member. The multi-national organization could seek membership in a sharing economy by having a "higher level" assembly of delegates, one that contained as members all of the local assemblies in the sharing economy, grant it membership. (An assembly, A, is a member of a "higher level" assembly, B, if it sends a delegate to assembly B, or it is a member of an assembly that, in turn, is a member of assembly B. Thus there may be many "steps" between a local assembly and a national or even global assembly that it is a member of.)

As discussed above in the case of a local assembly not agreeing to remain in a sharing economy that included local assembly X with a bad reputation, local assemblies have the option of not agreeing to remain in a sharing economy that includes a multi-national organization whose reputation they don't like. If only local assembly A objects to multi-national organization X then A's choice, in practice, is to leave the sharing economy or remain in it with X. But if lots of local assemblies object to X, then one or more relatively high-level assemblies could threaten to leave the larger sharing economy and establish a smaller one of their own unless X was denied membership in the larger sharing economy. To avoid this, X would of course be motivated to ensure that it has a good reputation among as many local assemblies as possible; otherwise it would risk exclusion from a large sharing economy--the equivalent of going out of business in a capitalist economy.

Consider Assembly A's decision whether or not to approve of a new economic enterprise in its local community. Assembly A's decision would take into account the availability of relevant raw materials and manufactured items. If these things must come from other communities, then Assembly A would need to determine that their reputation will not be adversely affected by taking these things for the proposed project. To do this they might simply use their knowledge about how other people felt. But this runs the risk that they approve a project only to discover that other local assemblies object to it, adversely affecting Assembly A's reputation. Instead, Assembly A might have their delegate to the appropriate "higher-level" assembly introduce a proposal for sharing the things that the new project requires. This proposal would go through the process of being amended by other delegates. Then, in the course of seeing if the local assemblies agreed there might be suggested amendments from them, and back and forth negotiations until there was a proposal that sufficient assemblies agreed with to make the new project possible.

Reputation thus plays an extremely important role in the sharing economy, a role similar to that played by profitability in a capitalist economy. Reputation in a sharing economy would be so important that some economic enterprises in a sharing economy would specialize in performing the function of deciding whether or not to grant their version of the "Good Housekeeping Seal of Approval" or their version of what is today called "certification" for colleges, *etc*. Others might be more like newspapers that investigate wrongdoing (and excellence as well) and report it. It is impossible to anticipate all of the creative ways that reputations might be established for various kinds of economic enterprises. Who, for example, could have anticipated a few decades ago Facebook's "like" system? But one way or another, in a society in which reputation plays such an important role, ways will be invented for establishing reputations sensibly.

The striking advantage of reputation driving economic decision making in a sharing economy, in contrast to profit in a capitalist one, is that reputation is based on the most important criteria, whereas profit is not. Only when reputation, and not profit, drives decision-making is it possible for a local community assembly to make reasonableness prevail over unreasonableness, by, for example, denying membership in the sharing economy to a person or enterprise whose "contribution" is providing psychiatry for pet dogs, or constructing twenty-million dollar mansions for small families when this is at the expense of some people having far more important things, such as good health care or shelter.

But how would economic decisions actually be made based on reputation? How is it possible, practically speaking? Letting individual consumers make decisions by choosing how to spend their money has resulted in the remarkable entrepreneurship, creativity and productivity that capitalism claims for itself and for itself alone. Because the only sustained (at least more than a few years) modern challenge to free market capitalism--Soviet style central planning--has clearly failed, capitalism claims that, as Margaret Thatcher famously put it, There Is No Alternative. Doesn't decision-making by reputation instead of profit entail the same problems that make a centrally planned economy fail? Doesn't a reputation-based sharing economy suffer from the same two defects as a centrally planned economy: a) stifling entrepreneurship creativity and b) failing to make use of information scattered among huge numbers of people, information that is incorporated in the price of things in the market place? How is a reputation-based sharing economy, with respect to these key questions, any different from a centrally planned economy?

(How Entrepreneurship Works Fine In The Sharing Economy is Described in Chapter Five**)**

Reputation Embodies More Important Information Than Market Place Price

Economic decision making as described above, which applies to both entrepreneurial and well-established enterprises, involves a huge number of people--possessing an enormous amount of information collectively---contributing directly or indirectly to the decision whether to give an economic project a green light. The knowledge of the entrepreneurs is made use of far more than in a centrally planned economy that is hostile to creative ideas arising outside the central planning body. Additionally, the knowledge and opinions of every person in any way affected by the decision to give or not give a green light to the project is tapped in one way or another because the actual economic decisions are always made with great consideration paid to not damaging one's reputation in the eyes of all others affected by the decision. Furthermore, the criteria for a good reputation are the right criteria--the things that egalitarians (the only ones who can be members of a local community assembly) care about most, whereas the criterion of profit is a deeply flawed one. This means that the information gathered from large numbers of people for economic decision-making is not only vast in quantity but also better in quality than the information incorporated into mere price in the market place. The sharing economy based on reputation for decision-making is thus both superior to a centrally planned economy and a market place capitalist economy based on profit.

A reputation-based sharing economy will certainly not be perfect. Perfection is an impossible goal. There is not, and never could be, a profit-based capitalist society in which every worker worked 100% efficiently and every business derived the maximum conceivable profit that the laws permit. Look closely anywhere today and one will find what, from the point of view of profitability, is inefficiency. From the point of view of human happiness and decency, however, what a capitalist calls inefficiency might often better be called reasonableness. Basing economic decisions on reputation (for reasonableness) is, arguably, the best way for reasonable people to make society reasonably good, which is to say a whole lot better than our present capitalist society.

"Rationing Scarce Things Equitably According To Need": Is This Really Desirable?

Most people would love to live in an egalitarian society in which the economy was based on the principle, "From each according to reasonable ability, to each according to need or reasonable desire." But when people hear the last phrase of this egalitarian principle, "with scarce things rationed according to need in an equitable manner" they wonder if this would really be desirable.

The word "rationing" conjures up negative images sometimes. Perhaps it's because rationing is only necessary when there is scarcity, and who likes scarcity? Perhaps it's because we think of wartime rationing during WWII, which was unpleasant.

Rationing, however, is something that goes on today in ways that we often don't even think of as "rationing" and to which we have no objection.

For example, a popular fancy restaurant very likely rations its tables because there are more people who want to eat there on a given evening than the restaurant can serve. There is thus a scarcity of served meals at the restaurant. How are the meals rationed? Typically the rationing is by either first-come-first-served or by reservations according to first-call-first-priority. This is, in a sense, rationing according to need but with the assumption that everybody's need for a fancy restaurant meal is the same.

Library books are similarly rationed: first-come-first-priority.

We also ration donated human organs for transplant, such as kidneys and livers and hearts. Here the rationing is according to need, where one component of need is the ability to make use of the transplant (*e.g.,* how long one may be expected to live with it) and we know that people are not all the same in this regard.

Most people think these examples of rationing are entirely proper and more desirable than any alternative. So let's not dismiss rationing as something necessarily undesirable.

Today Almost Everything Is Rationed, But We Don't Notice It

On the other hand, there is a terribly undesirable kind of rationing that takes place in our present society so frequently and ubiquitously that we don't even perceive it as "rationing." This is rationing according to wealth: the more scarce a product or service is, the greater its price and only people who can afford to buy it get it. The more that a product or service is needed, the more obviously unjust it is to ration it this way, according to wealth instead of need. This is why virtually everybody would be outraged if donated organs were sold to the highest bidder.

In today's society the only things that are not rationed, one way or another (according to need or wealth), are things that are freely available to anybody any time: the air we breathe, the use of non-toll roads (ignoring the cost of one's vehicle), enjoyment of "the great outdoors" (ignoring the cost of getting there and having what it takes to enjoy it), the radio and T.V. and web content that is available "for free" (ignoring the cost of one's T.V. or radio or computer or internet provider), *etc*.

Most products and services in an economy--any kind of economy, capitalist or Communist or egalitarian--are inevitably rationed in the sense that the economy can only produce so much of anything, and so to have more of this entails a rationing decision to have less of that. Whatever the manner (be it the free market, or a dictator or egalitarian equitable rationing according to need) by which it is decided how much of this or that to produce and who will receive it, the result is rationing. When, for example, the decision is made to produce more multi-million dollar luxury yachts and mansions, and fewer inexpensive but nice homes, this is rationing according to wealth because the desires of multi-millionaires trump the needs of poor people.

Most things are thus rationed at the production end (where a decision is made how much or little of it to produce) and also, if they are at all scarce, at the receiving end (where the decision is made who can have some of what is produced.)

This is why we do indeed need to ration even something so necessary as health care. If, in attempting to avoid rationing health care, we had every single person engaged in providing health care, then we would not have schools, or food production and distribution, or shelters constructed and so forth. The limitation to the amount of health care that any society can provide means that the question is not whether to ration it, but how to ration it: according to wealth? Or need? Or some other criterion?

Egalitarianism says that scarce things should be equitably rationed--to those who contribute according to reasonable ability--according to their need, in a reasonable manner decided by the Local Assembly of egalitarians. For things such as seating at a fancy restaurant this would likely mean rationing it the same way it's rationed today (but with everybody being equally able to "afford"[90] the meal.) For things such as donated organs it would also likely mean rationing them the same way as today (minus the corruption that money may introduce today.)

But for most things the rationing--at both the production end and the receiving end--would be according to need or reasonable desire of those who contribute reasonably according to ability. Because of this rationing at the production end many things will be abundant enough (construction labor won't be diverted to making huge luxury yachts and mansions when lots of people still lack decent homes to live in) so that no explicit rationing is required at the receiving end. These are the products and services that are free for the reasonable taking by those in the sharing economy that produced them

---

[90] People wouldn't pay for the meal; they would be equal in the sense of having an equal right to enjoy the meal if they got a reservation. If they hogged such reservations, however, they might risk gaining a reputation as a hog and eventually losing their membership in the sharing economy.

(*i.e.*, by those who have contributed reasonably to that sharing economy.)

For things that, despite rationing according to need at the production end, are still too scarce for everybody (who contributes reasonably) to have as much as they want or reasonably desire, there will be rationing at the receiving end also. This rationing will be according to need and by a reasonable equitable manner determined by the Local Assembly of egalitarians. If there is a more desirable way to handle inevitable scarcity of some things, I do not know what it is.

CHAPTER TEN: IS EGALITARIANISM'S VOLUNTARY FEDERATION PRACTICAL FOR A LARGE COUNTRY-SIZED REGION?

Many people wrongly believe that honoring the authoritarian principle ("You must obey the highest governmental or organizational body no matter what") is the only way to achieve--on a large scale such as nationally--the kind of order in society that we need in our extremely complex modern world. The fact, however, is that there is another basis on which to achieve order on a large scale that is better: voluntary federation. Voluntary federation, described in Chapter Four, is a way of achieving order among many relatively small organizations by enabling them to reach a consensus (mutual agreement) on an overall plan they agree to carry out. There is no "highest authority" that every small organization must obey no matter what. Any small organization that remains in disagreement with the plan the others mutually agree on is free not to carry out the plan and leave the federation (and, of course, forfeit the advantages of being in a mutual agreement with the others.)

First I will demonstrate the practicality of voluntary federation by giving real-life examples of how it has worked in a non-revolutionary context, even up to a global scale. Lastly, I will discuss how, in the social revolutions of the 20th century in Europe, local groups much like what I call a local or workplace assembly, spontaneously formed and, by sending delegates to "higher" regional, then provincial, and ultimately national bodies, achieved order on a national scale, within mere weeks.

Examples of Real-Life Voluntary Federation

Here are some examples of order achieved by what is essentially voluntary federation. Example #1 is national is scope; example #2 is continental in scope; example #3 is global in scope.

Example #1: The National Football League (NFL). The NFL website[91] describes how the League achieves its high degree of order:

> "The NFL pays meticulous attention to every detail that goes into putting on a professional football game — crafting the rules, training the officials, implementing the technology and more — to make sure that games are fair and entertaining.
>
> "The league does this by leading through consensus, but acting decisively when it's in the best interest of the game.
>
> "It starts at the top, with the Executive Committee and the commissioner. The Executive Committee includes one representative — an owner or top officer — from each of the league's 32 clubs. **Any change in game rules, league policy or club ownership or other modification to the game must be approved by at least three-fourths of the committee. Without consensus, nothing will pass.**" [bold not in the original]

---

[91] http://operations.nfl.com/football-ops/league-governance/

A football team may apply to join the NFL, or decide not to join it. If it does not join it, then the NFL has no authority over it. If it does join it, it is entering into a form of voluntary federation, with the Executive Committee playing the role of facilitating mutual agreements between the membership teams. If a team cannot reach a mutual agreement on something it considers important, then the team is free to leave the NFL and do things as it wishes on its own or with other teams that it can find mutual agreement with. There is no "Football Czar" who can command all football teams how to operate whether they want to or not. And yet, the fans of the NFL teams do not complain that the League is characterized by chaos or annoying disorder, do they?

Example #2: In his *The Conquest of Bread*, written in 1892, Peter Kropotkin writes about how the European railroad system achieved its very high degree of continent-wide order:

> "We know that Europe has a system of railways, 175,000 miles long, and that on this network you can nowadays travel from north to south, from east to west, from Madrid to Petersburg, and from Calais to Constantinople, without stoppages, without even changing carriages (when you travel by express). More than that: a parcel thrown into a station will find its addressee anywhere, in Turkey or in Central Asia, without more formality needed for sending it than writing its destination on a bit of paper.

> "This result might have been obtained in two ways. A Napolean, a Bismarck, or some potentate having conquered Europe, would from Paris, Berlin, or Rome, draw a railway map and regulate the hours of trains. The Russian Tsar Nicholas I dreamt of taking such action. When he was shown rough drafts of railways between Moscow and Petersburg, he seized a ruler and drew on the map of Russia a straight line between these two capitals, saying, "Here is the plan." And the road was built in a straight line, filling in deep ravines, building bridges of a giddy height, which had to

be abandoned a few years later, at a cost of about £120,000 to £150,000 per English mile.

"This is one way, but happily things were managed differently. Railways were constructed piece by piece, the pieces were joined together, and the hundred divers companies, to whom these pieces belonged, came to an understanding concerning the arrival and departure of their trains, and the running of carriages on their rails, from all countries, without unloading merchandise as it passes from one network to another.

"All this was done by free agreement, by exchange of letters and proposals, by congresses at which delegates met to discuss certain special subjects, but not to make laws; after the congress, the delegates returned to their companies, not with a law, but with the draft of a contract to be accepted or rejected.

"There were certainly obstinate men who would not be convinced. But a common interest compelled them to agree without invoking the help of armies against the refractory members.

"This immense network of railways connected together, and the enormous traffic it has given rise to, no doubt constitutes the most striking trait of our century, and it is the result of free agreement. If a man had foreseen or predicted it fifty years ago, our grandfathers would have thought him idiotic or mad. They would have said: 'Never will you be able to make the shareholders of a hundred companies listen to reason! It is a Utopia, a fairy tale. A central Government, with an 'iron' director, can alone enforce it.'

"And the most interesting thing in this organization is, that there is no European Central Government of Railways! Nothing! No minister of railways, no dictator, not even a continental parliament, not even a directing committee! Everything is done by contract."

Example #3: The Universal Postal Union[92] is the reason that one can send a letter or parcel by mail from any one of 192 countries to any other of those countries and be fairly confident it will be delivered successfully and efficiently. The UPU's website states:

> "Established in 1874, the Universal Postal Union (UPU), with its headquarters in the Swiss capital Berne, is the second oldest international organization worldwide.
>
> "With its 192 member countries, the UPU is the primary forum for cooperation between postal sector players. It helps to ensure a truly universal network of up-to-date products and services.
>
> "In this way, the organization fulfills an advisory, mediating and liaison role, and provides technical assistance where needed. It sets the rules for international mail exchanges and makes recommendations to stimulate growth in mail, parcel and financial services volumes and improve quality of service for customers.
>
> "The Congress is the supreme authority of the Union and meets every four years. Plenipotentiaries from the UPU's 192 member countries gather on this occasion to decide on a new world postal strategy and set the future rules for international mail exchanges."

Nations are free to join (or apply for admission in the case of non UN nations) or not join the UPU as they wish. If they do not join, the UPU Congress has no say in how they handle mail. The UPU *"fulfills an advisory, mediating and liaison role,"* which is to say that it facilitates mutual agreements among the nations that voluntarily join it; it does not command

---

[92] http://www.upu.int/en/the-upu/the-upu.html

all nations on the planet what they must do--whether they want to or not--regarding postal-related issues. The UPU is thus a kind of voluntary federation and it is not at all based on the authoritarian principle. And yet, as you and your foreign pen pals no doubt know, the UPU has achieved a high level of order for international mail.

In 20th Century European Social Revolutions, Voluntary Federation Spontaneously Self-Organized Even To A National Scale

The political scientist, Hannah Arendt (famous for her book, *The Origins of Totalitarianism*), wrote a book especially relevant to the question of the practicality of voluntary federation. In *On Revolution*[93], Arendt describes how, in the 20th century, voluntary federation, or at least something very similar to it, spread rapidly in revolutionary Germany, Russia and Hungary. Referring specifically to Russia and Hungary Arendt wrote:

> *"In both instances councils of* soviets *had sprung up everywhere, completely independent of one another, workers', soldiers', and peasants' councils in the case of Russia, the most disparate kinds of councils in the case of Hungary: neighbourhood councils that emerged in all residential districts, so-called revolutionary councils that grew out of fighting together in the streets, councils of writers and artists born in the coffee houses of Budapest, students' and youths' councils at the universities, workers' councils in the factories, councils in the army, among the civil servants, and so on. The formation of a council in each of these disparate groups turned a more or less accidental proximity into a political institution. The most striking aspect of these spontaneous developments is that in both instances it took these independent and highly disparate organs no*

---

[93] https://www.amazon.com/Revolution-Penguin-Classics-Hannah-Arendt/dp/0143039903

more than a few weeks, in the case of Russia, or a few days, in the case of Hungary, to begin a process of co-ordination and integration through the formation of higher councils of a regional or provincial character, from which finally the delegates to an assembly representing the whole country could be chosen." [Pg. 266-7]

CHAPTER ELEVEN: IS EGALITARIANISM COMPATIBLE WITH HUMAN NATURE?

Yes, egalitarianism is compatible with human nature. The claim that it is not is a capitalist Big Lie about human nature, one that legitimizes the ugly class inequality we have today in which ordinary people (as discussed in Chapter Two) are necessarily treated like dirt.

Capitalism is a social system that tries to legitimize itself as one that, unlike all others, is based on what human nature really is, not what we'd like it to be. Capitalist ideologues claim that it is human nature to place self-interest above all other concerns. Adam Smith, capitalism's early and perhaps most well-known ideological defender, famously argued that only the capitalist system allows an "invisible hand" to ensure that the net result of everybody acting just in their own self-interest results in the betterment of society for all. The baker makes bread just to make a profit; ditto the shoemaker and the candlestick maker. And, behold!, it results in people having the bread and shoes and candlesticks they need.

Greed is good, say the defenders of capitalism. Were it not for greed, we're told, the baker and shoemaker and candlestick maker would have no incentive to make their wares, and we'd all go shoeless and hungry in an unlit world.

Economic inequality is also good, in fact necessary, we're told, because the only reason people work hard and smart is to get richer than others. In a society where everybody who contributed reasonably to the economy shared with each other according to need as equals there would, according to the capitalist view, be no reason for people to work and hence the economy would stop producing things.

The belief that greed is human nature, that it is good for society, and that inequality is natural and necessary are the beliefs that make our present social structure seem legitimate. It is a social structure in which money is power. Economic inequality inevitably means political inequality too. One person, one vote may be the theory, but in real life it ends up being one dollar one vote, as politicians respond less to the concerns of their constituents and far more to the concerns of Big Money. It is Big Money that funds politicians' campaigns, decides how the mass media will treat them, and provides them with cushy jobs when they leave office. Also, it is Big Money that can relocate a business that is a major employer if it doesn't get legislation that it wants.

'You May Not Like It, But It's Just Human Nature'

Those who rule our world, whose chief aim in life is the greedy pursuit of money, and who enjoy power and privileges that money makes possible for the very rich in an economically unequal society--this capitalist class of people justify it all with a Big Lie. The Big Lie is that selfishness is the primary human motivation, always has been and always will be because it is simply human nature. Capitalists argue that there is no difference between the motives and values of ordinary people and those of the richest families in society. The only difference is that the rich ones were more successful than the others.

Defenders of capitalism use the Big Lie about human nature when they tell us that there is no point in trying to create a better world that is more equal and democratic. Even if we succeeded initially, they say, it would just revert back to the same inequality we have today because human nature would remain the same. People would compete against each other, there would be winners and losers, and inequality would re-emerge. Greed, inequality, and competition for self-interest: it's all just human nature. The wisest thing to do, say the defenders of capitalism, is to recognize the fact, and turn it to the best advantage by letting Adam Smith's invisible hand work its wonders in a capitalist society.

Big Facts Refute The Big Lie About 'Human Nature'

Human nature is not the same as capitalist nature, no matter what the capitalists want us to believe. Human beings create cultures. Cultures embody values about how relations between people ought to be. Being selfish or sharing is a behavioral choice determined in large part by one's culture.

Conflicting cultures have developed, especially conflicting class cultures. Classes of human beings have arisen that dominate, oppress and exploit other human beings, and they have created a culture that legitimizes and even glorifies their oppressive relation to others. But these oppressive classes that survive by taking economic wealth from those who actually produce it are numerically small. The majority of human beings whose labor produces all the wealth of society have developed a very different culture.

The culture of the people who produce the wealth of society is different because we are a social species; we produce the things and services we need for survival and for our comfort and enjoyment only by cooperating with others. Cooperation requires mutual trust. The reason why the Golden Rule is universally honored as the basis of morality, and the reason why it is therefore incorporated into every major religion, is because it is the basis for establishing the trust that cooperation and hence human survival requires[94].

There is a class culture that says to be selfish. And there is a

---

[94] See http://newdemocracyworld.org/culture/worshipping_a_strange_god.html

conflicting class culture, enshrined in the Golden Rule, that says to share.

It is well known by anthropologists that hunter-gatherer societies are extremely egalitarian. For example in the journal, Current Anthropology, Vol 35, No 2 (April 1994) online[95], on page 176 one reads, "Yet the universality of egalitarianism in hunter-gatherers suggests that it is an ancient, evolved human pattern." This Big Fact contradicts the Big Lie that human nature is innately selfish and that inequality is simply what human nature inevitably produces.

In this regard it is worth reading a passage from Peter Kropotkin's *Mutual Aid: A Factor of Evolution*. In his chapter, "Mutual Aid Among Savages," he writes about the "Hottentots, who are but a little more developed than the bushmen":

> *"Lubbock describes them as 'the filthiest animals.' and filthy they really are. A fur suspended to the neck and worn till it falls to pieces is all their dress; their huts are a few sticks assembled together and covered with mats, with no kind of furniture within. And though they kept oxen and sheep, and seem to have known the use of iron before they made acquaintance with the Europeans, they still occupy one of the lowest degrees of the human scale. And yet those who knew them highly praised their sociability and readiness to aid each other. If anything is given to a Hottentot, he at once divides it among all present--a habit which, as is known, so much struck Darwin among all Fuegians. He cannot eat alone, and, however hungry, he calls those who pass by to share his food. And when Kolben expressed his astonishment thereat, he received the answer: 'That is Hottentot manner.' But this is not Hottentot manner only: it is an all but universal habit among the 'savages.' Kolben, who knew the Hottentots well and did not pass by their defects in silence, could*

---

[95] http://www.unl.edu/rhames/courses/current/readings/erdal.pdf

> *not praise their tribal morality highly enough.*
>
> *"'Their word is sacred,' he wrote. They know 'nothing of the corruptness and faithless arts of Europe.,' 'They live in great tranquility and are seldom at war with their neighbors.' They are 'all kindness and goodwill to one another.... One of the greatest pleasures of the Hottentots certainly lies in their gifts and good offices to one another,' 'The integrity of the Hottentots, their strictness and celerity in the exercise of justice, and their chastity, are things to which they excel all or most nations in the world.'"*

The Hottentots are, of course, the same species as us. Their innate human nature enabled them to develop an extremely egalitarian culture. That means that our innate human nature (whatever it may be) enables us to do the same, contrary to the Big Lie of capitalism.

Some defend the Big Lie by arguing that human nature may permit egalitarianism within a tribe, but it also causes tribes to wage war against each other. But the anthropological evidence does not support the assertion, made by the Nobel Peace Prize laureate and (former) Warmonger in Chief, Barack Obama, that "war appeared with the first man." As John Horgan writes in his *The End of War*[96]:

> *"The Homo genus emerged about 2 million years ago and Homo sapiens about two hundred thousand years ago. But the oldest clear-cut relic of lethal group aggression is not millions or hundreds of thousands of years old. It is a 13,000-year-old gravesite along the Nile River in the Jebel Sahaba region of Sudan. Excavated in the 1960s, the site contains fifty-nine skeletons, twenty-four of which bear marks of violence, such as embedded projectile points.*

---

[96] **https://www.amazon.com/End-War-John-Horgan/dp/1938073126**

> "What's more, the Jebel Sahaba site is an outlier. Most of the other evidence for warfare dates back no more than 10,000 years. The oldest known homicide victim--as opposed to war casualty--was a young man who lived 20,000 years ago along the Nile...
>
> "Sarah Blaffer Hrdy, an anthropologist and authority on both primates and early humans, believes that our human and proto-human ancestors were at least occasionally violent. Given how often fights occur among virtually all primates, including humans, 'we can be fairly certain that lethal aggression occasionally broke out' in the Paleolithic era, she says. 'It would be amazing if it did not.' But Hrdy sees no persuasive evidence that war--which she defines as 'organized aggression between groups with the intent of killing those in other groups'--is either ancient or innate." [pg. 30-31]

Nor does it require living in primitive conditions for egalitarianism to arise. The modern labor movement, with all its strikes and campaigns for things like the Eight Hour Day, and the social movements against racial discrimination (*e.g.,* the U.S. Civil Rights Movement and the Global Anti-Apartheid Movement) are all examples of the mass support for making the world more equal.

The fact that when polled, most Americans[97] say they want health care to be a right of all people, and furthermore say they would agree to paying higher taxes to make it so, cannot be explained by any theory that includes the capitalist Big Lie about human nature being mainly motivated by self-interest.

Workers often continue their labor strikes far beyond the point when they have any chance at all of making up in higher wages all of the wages they have already lost during the

---

[97] https://www.washingtonpost.com/news/the-fix/wp/2016/05/16/most-americans-want-to-replace-obamacare-with-a-single-payer-system-including-a-lot-of-republicans/?utm_term=.932e1d25f89d

strike, not to mention homes foreclosed for lack of money to make the mortgage payments and cars repossessed. This was the case in the Hormel meatpackers strike in the 1980s in Minnesota. Why do they do this? A striker explained why this way, as recounted by Dave Stratman in his online *We CAN Change the World* (pdf)[98]:

> *"Like the British miners, the striking meatpackers understood that far more was at stake than their specific demands. In a speech to supporters in Boston in February, 1986, Pete Winkels, business agent of Local P-9, made this clear: 'Our people are never going to get back what we've already lost financially. We know that. But we're fighting for our families and for the next generation. And we're not going to give up.'*
>
> *"Since it was precisely the strikers and their families who suffered the economic and emotional costs of the strike, the explanation that "we're fighting for our families and for the next generation" has to be interpreted in a class context. "For the next generation" was a phrase the strikers used again and again to describe why they were fighting, as if these words encapsulated their feelings about creating a future very different from where things seem headed, not just for their immediate families, but for other people like themselves."*

The Hormel strike, and many others like it, was a struggle to make the world more equal; as a fight for merely personal self-interest it would have been crazy to continue the strike, as the strikers well knew.

During the Spanish Revolution that involved millions of people in almost half of Spain in 1936-9 peasants expropriated the land from the rich landowners. They invariably decided to own

---

[98] http://www.newdemocracyworld.org/old/Revolution/We%20Can%20Change%20the%20World%20book.pdf

it collectively instead of dividing it up into parcels to be owned individually. Some collectives abolished money altogether and those that didn't made changes in the direction of economic equality, such as paying people according to the size of their family instead of their education or job type. If the Big Lie of human nature were true it would be very difficult to explain how this could have happened. But it did happen.

From the most common everyday acts of kindness, such as people I see everyday getting up and giving their seat on the subway to an elderly person, to epic struggles for equality, there is abundant proof that the capitalist assertion about human nature being the same as capitalist nature is flat out false. There are countless Big Facts that refute it.

What Are Scientists Finding Out About Human Infants' and Toddlers' Nature?

Here are some examples of scientific studies about the human nature of infants and toddlers.

A *New York Times* article[99] of June 21, 2015 titled, "Toddlers Have Sense of Justice, Puppet Study Shows" reports:

> *Children as young as age 3 will intervene on behalf of a victim, reacting as if victimized themselves, scientists have found.*
>
> *With toys, cookies and puppets, Keith Jensen, a psychologist at the University of Manchester in England, and his colleagues tried to judge how much concern 3- and 5-year-olds had for others, and whether they had a sense of so-called restorative justice.*

---

[99] https://www.nytimes.com/2015/06/23/science/toddlers-have-sense-of-justice-puppet-study-shows.html?mabReward=A5&moduleDetail=recommendations-0&action=click&contentCollection=Science&region=Footer&module=WhatsNext&version=WhatsNext&contentID=WhatsNext&configSection=article&isLoggedIn=false&src=recg&pgtype=article

> *In one experiment, when one puppet took toys or cookies from another puppet, children responded by pulling a string that locked the objects in an inaccessible cave. When puppets took objects directly from the children themselves, they responded in the same way.*
>
> *"The children treated these two violations equally," said Dr. Jensen, a co-author of the study published in the journal Current Biology.*

In a July 26, 2015 report of a scientific study, in PLOS[100] (Public Library of Science) the authors conclude:

> *"We investigated 15-month-old infants' sensitivity to fairness, and their altruistic behavior, assessed via infants' reactions to a third-party resource distribution task, and via a sharing task. Our results challenge current models of the development of fairness and altruism in two ways. First, in contrast to past work suggesting that fairness and altruism may not emerge until early to mid-childhood, 15-month-old infants are sensitive to fairness and can engage in altruistic sharing. Second, infants' degree of sensitivity to fairness as a third-party observer was related to whether they shared toys altruistically or selfishly, indicating that moral evaluations and prosocial behavior are heavily interconnected from early in development. Our results present the first evidence that the roots of a basic sense of fairness and altruism can be found in infancy, and that these other-regarding preferences develop in a parallel and interwoven fashion. These findings support arguments for an evolutionary basis – most likely in dialectical manner including both biological and cultural mechanisms – of human*

---

[100] **http://journals.plos.org/plosone/article?id=10.1371/journal.pone.0023223**

egalitarianism given the rapidly developing nature of other-regarding preferences and their role in the evolution of human-specific forms of cooperation."

In this 2011 report of a study in the journal *Child Development*[101], the authors conclude:

"In sum, the findings of the current study reveal an important developmental transition at the end of the second year of life when toddlers' helping behavior expands to include empathic as well as instrumental helping. The results point as well to the late emergence of altruistic helping, after other-oriented helping first becomes evident, inasmuch as even two-year-olds find costly helping especially difficult. This suggests that changes in social understanding and prosocial motivation may be closely linked, with other-oriented concern developing in concert with growth in children's ability to represent and understand others' subjective internal states, and altruistic helping developing later, in concert with understanding of social and moral norms. It would be productive in future research to investigate these links more directly, possibly by including additional measures of self- and other-understanding and empathy, as well as by testing older children in situations that require various types of helping."

George Monbiot has an article in *The Guardian* titled, "We're not as selfish as we think we are. Here's the proof."[102] He reports on a recent scientific study:

A study by the Common Cause Foundation, due to be published next month, reveals two transformative findings. The first is that a large majority of the 1,000 people they surveyed – 74% – identifies more strongly

---

[101] https://www.ncbi.nlm.nih.gov/pmc/articles/PMC3088085/

[102] https://www.theguardian.com/commentisfree/2015/oct/14/selfish-proof-ego-humans-inherently-good

with unselfish values than with selfish values. This means that they are more interested in helpfulness, honesty, forgiveness and justice than in money, fame, status and power. The second is that a similar majority – 78% – believes others to be more selfish than they really are. In other words, we have made a terrible mistake about other people's minds.

A Big Lie Requires Big Propaganda

It takes great effort to keep a Big Lie afloat. Let's look at one way the capitalists try to do it.

George Orwell joined the Spanish Revolution and wrote about it in his *Homage to Catalonia*, which describes (and praises) an egalitarian society created by the Spanish people at this time. Of course Orwell also wrote *Animal Farm* to warn the world that Communists in the Soviet Union, for all their talk about equality, were just as bad as the capitalists, and wanted a world in which "some are more equal than others." Orwell was not making a statement about human nature; he was making a statement about Communists. Almost every American school child has read *Animal Farm* or at least has heard the famous line about how the Pigs were more equal than others. But virtually no American learned in our public schools about even the existence of *Homage to Catalonia*, never mind read it. Instead they are given *Animal Farm* and encouraged to view it as a wise book about human nature being selfish. They are also given *Lord of the Flies* by Nobel Prize-winning William Golding, a book whose theme is that human nature is vicious and selfish.

This is no accident. The capitalists need to work very hard to keep people ignorant about the truth of human nature. They need people to hear the Big Lie repeated over and over, so they will accept, as "natural" and "inevitable," the greed-based unequal society that capitalists love so dearly. After reading *Animal Farm* and *Lord of the Flies*, many of our youth go to colleges where the number one major is "Business."

Here they learn to accept and work with the fundamental premises of economics and marketing, all versions of the Big Lie about human nature. Those who become teachers learn that the purpose of education is to enable American children to compete with non-Americans in the world economy when they leave school, again the premise being that competing against others and looking out for #1 is what life is all about--it's human nature.

Marxism Accepts The Big Lie

Marxism (which is discussed in more detail and references in Chapter Twelve) views the working class as the class that will usher in a communist society, a classless society of economic and political equality. One would think that, therefore, Marxism viewed working class people as having egalitarian rather than selfish values. But the fact is that while Marxism views the working class in the abstract as the force that will make the world communist one day, it does not view flesh and blood working class people as having values any different from the selfish values of capitalists.

In Marxism, the working class and the capitalist class have conflicting interests (one wants wages to be higher, the other lower, *etc.*) but the same values: self-interest. Marxists never talk about the conflicting values of working class and capitalist class culture, for example that the former values equality and concern for one another (solidarity) while the latter values inequality, pitting people against one another, and looking out for #1. Marxists only talk about "interests."

Marxism accepts the Big Lie that human nature is the way the capitalists say it is. Marxism also agrees with Adam Smith that there is an "invisible hand" that shapes society in a way that has nothing whatsoever to do with the subjective aims of individual people in that society: the selfish butcher, shoemaker and candlestick maker do not aim, subjectively, to provide people with bread and shoes, *etc.,* but only to make a profit for themselves.

Marxism disagrees with Adam Smith only about how the "invisible hand" will affect society. Whereas Adam Smith said it would lead to everlasting capitalism fulfilling the needs and wants of everybody, Marx said it would lead to an economic crisis for capitalism and its replacement by communism, not because flesh and blood working class people want communism (they don't, he said) but because the working class as an abstraction, as a class whose interests oppose those of the capitalists and whose liberation requires the liberation of all, will cause communism to replace capitalism after the capitalist economic crisis creates the conditions for this to happen.

Good People Accept The Big Lie

Most people who want a more equal and democratic society do not consider themselves Marxists. But whenever somebody who starts to think seriously about how to make society more equal and democratic looks for ideas and books to learn how to proceed, he or she will inevitably come across Marxist ideas that may or may not advertise themselves as Marxist. This is because Marxism is a coherent ideology (even if it is wrong) that tells good people that they should feel hopeful, because an egalitarian communist world is going to emerge in spite of the fact that most ordinary people are just as selfish as capitalists and the last thing on their minds is making the world egalitarian. Good people, who have been raised in a capitalist society that teaches us the Big Lie about human nature, are of course very happy when they discover Marxist ideas. Marxism tells them that, yes, their perception of human nature is accurate, but it's not a problem: communism will arrive despite it.

To see how Marxism affects good people who don't call themselves Marxists, one has only to go to a web site called AxisofLogic.com that is run by good people who oppose oppression and the extremes of inequality and who don't call themselves Marxists. There is an article there called The

Ovarian Lottery[103] by Paul Harris. In this article, Harris calls for making the world less unequal. In the comments that follow the article I said that what we aim for should be a fully egalitarian society, not just one that was less unequal than today. [The comments are no longer online.]

A person named Siv O'Neall objected to my post and wrote:

> *"Socialism is fighting against the innate tendency of man to create a hierarchy. As long as mankind has existed, that is since about 50,000 years ago when we spread out from Africa, there has been inequality. Huge inequality. So what people like Paul and me, both die-hard socialists, are fighting for, goes against the grain of human nature."*

Paul Harris wrote:

> "There is a reason the Spanish spring [I think he is referring to 1936-9--JS] didn't last; and the Vienna spring of the 1920s didn't last. They are not sustainable so long as humans are involved. I'm afraid you think we're a great deal more evolved and civilized than we really are."

O'Neall and Harris, as these comments illustrate, accept the Big Lie about human nature. And this leads them to forsake the idea of revolution to create an egalitarian society.

The Big Lie Leads To Leftist Dictatorships

Some people accept the Big Lie about human nature but, unlike the folks at AxisofLogic.com, still aim to make a revolution to create a classless society in the future. Because, according to the Big Lie, an egalitarian society "goes against the grain of human nature" it follows very logically that if somebody is going to make society egalitarian it must be

---

[103] http://axisoflogic.com/artman/publish/Article_65011.shtml

somebody who is willing to go against the actual conscious desires of ordinary people with their selfish human nature. It will require top-down social engineering. Who will be the social engineers? Whoever they are they will have to be a dictatorship; they dare not let ordinary people have the real say in a genuine democracy because ordinary people would "go against the grain" of where the social engineers want to go. The Marxists say that the Communist Party must be in control. Non-Marxist Socialists might use a different vocabulary, but it amounts to the same thing: a dictatorship of an elite who views ordinary people as going "against the grain" of progress.

Given that an elite needs to have dictatorial power, they will need to do the things dictators must do to stay in power. Fostering solidarity and equality among people is most certainly not something dictators ever do to stay in power. And this is why such elites inevitably become "more equal than others." The egalitarian society they claim to be guiding society towards will remain a far off dream, never today's reality.

Our View Of Human Nature Is Key

As long as we accept the capitalist Big Lie about human nature, we will be resigned to the idea that an egalitarian society is impossible, at least until the far distant future. We will be resigned to accepting inequality and the ideas that legitimate it. There will be winners and losers and the winners will get stronger and stronger because the Big Lie legitimates them and undermines any opposition to them. This is why we need to understand that the Big Lie is a lie, and reject it.

Human Nature And The Reason People Work

What do we actually know about human nature and why people work? Is it true that people wouldn't work reasonably hard in an egalitarian sharing economy because people only work hard to get richer than others?

Some say that society needs to provide some people higher standards of living than others because people will not do excellent work or make the great effort required to learn socially valuable skills (such as medicine or piloting a jet plane) unless the reward for doing so is a higher standard of living than most other people. But many people enjoy learning socially useful skills for reasons having nothing to do with the higher pay they receive. The best doctors love making other people's lives better with their knowledge and skills. Jonas Salk did not patent his polio vaccine or earn any money from it. Good pilots love flying. Carpenters love being very good at what they do. There is a non-monetary reward that people crave: the satisfaction of knowing that they are doing something important that improves the lives of others, that they are doing it skillfully, and that they are admired by others in society for what they do. This is one reason why people would learn skills in the new society.

It is true that people today work hard and learn skills in order to earn more money than they would otherwise. But this is not the same thing as wanting to be richer than other people. To see that this is so, consider what would happen if the typical person who works hard to earn more money in order to have a higher standard of living knew that, as a result of his hard work, everybody else would also enjoy the same higher standard of living. Would he say, "Well, in that case I have no motive for doing the hard work?" Improving one's own life along with the lives of others is a powerful motive for doing work and learning new skills. History demonstrates this is true. Were it not true the facts in Chapter Nine about how the egalitarian economy in Revolutionary Spain 1936-9 out-produced the capitalist economy it replaced would not exist.

CHAPTER TWELVE: EGALITARIANISM IS <u>FUNDAMENTALLY</u> DIFFERENT FROM COMMUNISM

Up to now this book has been trying to give you, the reader, a vision of what an egalitarian society is like. And as good as it all may seem, you may nonetheless be thinking something like this: "Sounds good, but it also sounds like Communism, and I know that Communism turned out to be ugly: totalitarian, not at all democratic, and hypocritical about making things equal—just as George Orwell accused the Communists of being in *Animal Farm*. So what's the story, uh?"

If I were to respond to your concerns by saying something such as, "Oh no. Egalitarianism is much different and better than Communism. Egalitarians would never set up a dictatorship like Stalin's or just pretend to strive for real equality," you would have every right to be skeptical. After all, the Communists say they are for a classless society, and egalitarians say they are for the same thing—abolishing class inequality. So if Communism turned out so bad, what's to say egalitarianism wouldn't also?

That's a fair question. The answer is that what causes Communist practice to be anti-democratic and hypocritical as Orwell described in *Animal Farm*, is Marxism, and the egalitarian ideas presented in this book are (as will be explained next) based on a flat out rejection of Marxism. Furthermore, as will also be discussed below, Marxism, in theory as well as practice, actually rejects the egalitarian goal of a classless society and its associated principle of "From each according to ability, to each according to need"; this is true even though that excellent principle is associated with the name of Karl Marx. These points are not at all well known, which is a major weakness in efforts to make a better world.

Many people love some truly wonderful ideas that existed long before Karl Marx was even born and they think that it was Karl Marx who invented these ideas. There is much confusion about Marxism and Communism that stems from this unfortunate and widespread misconception. The truth is that Marx added to these great ideas something new, what is known as the "science" of Marxism, and it is this wrongheaded "science" that is the source of the ugliness of Communism, not the wonderful ideas that so many people associate with the name Karl Marx.

Let's start with the wonderful ideas.

GREAT IDEAS THAT WERE AROUND LONG BEFORE KARL MARX

Karl Marx was born May 5, 1818. His first major piece of writing was his doctoral thesis in 1841. Here are some great ideas that were around long before Marx began writing.

#1 Class Conflict

Gerard Winstanley, born in 1609 and a leader of the English Diggers, wrote the "Declaration of the Poor Oppressed People of England"[104] in which he said the following:

> *"And we look upon that freedom promised to be the inheritance of all, without respect of persons; And this cannot be, unless the Land of England be freely set at liberty from proprietors, and become a common Treasury to all her children."*

---

[104] Sources for this and the other quotes here of Winstanley can be found by searching for the various text fragments online.

> *"So long as the earth is intagled and appropriated into particular hands and kept there by the power of the sword…so long the creation lies under bondage."*
>
> *"For though you and your Ancestors got your Propriety by murther and theft, and you keep it by the same power from us, that have an equal right to the Land with you, by the righteous Law of Creation, yet we shall have no occasion of quarrelling (as you do) about that disturbing devil, called Particular propriety: For the Earth, with all her Fruits of Corn, Cattle, and such like, was made to be a common Store-house of Livelihood to all Mankinde, friend, and foe, without exception."*

Here is the "property is theft" idea, long before Karl Marx was born.

#2 From Each According To Ability, To Each According To Need

As early as 1775 in his *Code de la Nature ou le Veritable esprit de Ses Lois* a Frenchman named Morelly wrote[105] that his aim was "To distribute work according to capacity; products according to needs." The same idea appears even earlier, in the Bible (Acts, 4:43-35): "Neither was there any among them that lacked: for as many were possessors of lands or houses sold them, and brought the prices of the things that were sold, And laid them down at the apostle's feet: and distribution was made unto every man according as he had need."

Note that while Marx popularized the phrase, "From each according to his ability, to each according to his needs" in his "Critique of the Gotha Program," his point was that society could NOT be based on this principle until far FAR in the future. Here are his exact words:

---

[105] **https://www.marxists.org/archive/hyndman/1921/evrev/chapter23.htm**

"In a higher phase of communist society, after the enslaving subordination of the individual to the division of labor, and therewith also the antithesis between mental and physical labor, has vanished; after labor has become not only a means of life but life's prime want; after the productive forces have also increased with the all-around development of the individual, and all the springs of co-operative wealth flow more abundantly -- only then can the narrow horizon of bourgeois right be crossed in its entirety and society inscribe on its banners: From each according to his ability, to each according to his needs!"

#3 The Need To Abolish Buying And Selling And Commodification Of Things

Gerrard Winstanley (born 1609) wrote:

"Money must not any longer.... be the great god that hedges in some and hedges out others, for money is but part of the Earth; and after our work of the Earthly Community is advanced, we must make use of gold or silver as we do of other metals but not to buy or sell."

"Buying and Selling is an Art, whereby people endeavour to cheat one another of the Land...and true Religion is, To let every one enjoy it."

#4 The Need To Abolish Wage Slavery

Gerrard Winstanley (born 1609) wrote:

"This declares likewise to all Labourers, or such as are called Poor people, that they shall not dare to work for Hire, for any Landlord, or any that is lifted up above others; for by their labours, they have lifted up Tyrants and Tyranny; and by denying to labor for Hire, they shall pull them down again. He that works for another, either for Wages or to pay him Rent, works

unrighteously, and still lifts up the Curse; but they that are resolved to work and eat together, making the Earth a Common Treasury, doth joyn hands with Christ, to lift up the Creation from Bondage, and restores all things from the Curse."

#5 International Working Class Solidarity

In 1676 Bacon's Rebellion broke out in the Virginia Colony. During this rebellion bonded (indentured or slave) laborers--both Africans and British--united against the upper class large property owners and rulers of the Colony. A British naval ship captain, Thomas Grantham, in his report of how he fought the rebels, indicated the solidarity between the African and British laborers this way:

> *"I there met about four hundred English and Negroes in Arms who were much dissatisfied at the Surrender of the Point, saying I had betrayed them, and thereupon some were for shooting me and others were for cutting me in peeces: I told them I would willingly surrender myselfe to them, till they were satisfied from His Majestie, and did engage to the Negroes and Servants, that they were all pardoned and freed from their Slavery: And with faire promises and Rundletts of Brandy, I pacified them, giving them severall Noates under my hand that what I did was by the order of his Majestie and the Governor....Most of them I persuaded to goe to their Homes, which accordingly they did, except about eighty Negroes and twenty English which would not deliver their Armes...."*[106]

Apparently these bonded laborers possessed the idea of international working class solidarity, in 1676.

Before this, in 1524-1525 peasants rose up in armed revolt against the European aristocracy in what is known as the

---

[106] http://clogic.eserver.org/1-2/allen.html paragraph #73

Great Peasants War or Great Peasants Revolt. The uprising united peasants[107] in what are now modern Germany, Switzerland, Austria, Alsace and the Czech Republic. These peasants seemed to grasp the idea of international working class solidarity.

Quite a bit earlier (73 BCE), the slave Spartacus famously led a slave revolt of tens of thousands of slaves against the slave owners of the Roman Empire. This slave revolt united slaves from Thrace and from Gaul (mentioned specifically in the limited historical record) and no doubt from other regions as well. This too reflected the presence of the idea of international working class solidarity, more than two thousand years ago.

#6 The Point Is Not Merely To Understand The World But To Change It

Gerrard Winstanley (born 1609) wrote:

> "..yet my mind was not at rest, because nothing was acted, and thoughts run in me that words and writings were all nothing, and must die, for action is the life of all, and if thou dost not act, thou dost nothing."

#7 Communism, Meaning A Classless Society With Social Wealth Held In Common

John Ball, who led the English Peasant Rebellion in 1381 preached that:

> "things cannot go right in England...until goods are held in common and there are no more villeins and gentlefolk, but we are all one and the same."[108]

---

[107] https://en.wikipedia.org/wiki/German_Peasants%27_War

[108] Life in a Medieval Village, by Frances and Joseph Gies, p. 198

Gerrard Winstanley (born 1609) wrote:

> *A LETTER TO The Lord Fairfax, AND His Councell of War, WITH Divers Questions to the Lawyers, and Ministers: Proving it an undeniable Equity, That the common People ought to dig, plow, plant and dwell upon the Commons, with-out hiring them, or paying Rent to any*
> *A Vindication of Those Whose Endeavors is Only to Make the Earth a Common Treasury, Called Diggers (March 4, 1650)*
>
> *"That we may work in righteousness, and lay the Foundation of making the Earth a Common Treasury for All, both Rich and Poor, That every one that is born in the Land, may be fed by the Earth his Mother that brought him forth, according to the Reason that rules in the Creation. Not Inclosing any part into any particular hand, but all as one man, working together, and feeding together as Sons of one Father, members of one Family; not one Lording over another, but all looking upon each other, as equals in the Creation"* [in The True Levellers Standard A D V A N C E D: or, The State of Community opened, and Presented to the Sons of Men]

The Idea That Karl Marx DID Invent

Marx invented what he viewed as a "science" of social change. This is what makes Communism so ugly, and what is examined closely next.

THE FUNDAMENTAL PROBLEM WITH MARXISM AND COMMUNISM

Are Socialism and Communism good ideas, which unfortunately have been stigmatized because bad people who don't really believe in these ideas do bad things in their name? Or are they truly bad ideas whose implementation by genuine followers leads to very bad things? I think it's the latter, and here is why.

Socialism and Communism, as even their most pure followers would agree, call for the government to own the means of production and to organize economic production for the good of all and not for the profit of a few. There are two key ideas expressed in this formulation: #1) the government owns the means of production and #2) economic production for the good of all and not the profit of a few. Idea #2 is fine. It's idea #1 that is the problem.

What, exactly, is "the government"? Communists and Socialists both mean, by "the government," a strong central[109]

---

[109] Communists call for a centralized state to increase economic production *"as rapidly as possible"* in the Communist Manifesto (by Marx and Engels) as follows:

> *"We have seen above, that the first step in the revolution by the working class is to raise the proletariat to the position of ruling class to win the battle of democracy. The proletariat will use its political supremacy to wrest, by degree, all capital from the bourgeoisie, to centralise all instruments of production in the hands of the State, i.e., of the proletariat organised as the ruling class; and to increase the total productive forces as rapidly as possible."*

Marx advocated a strong central government unambiguously. In the "Address of the Central Committee to the Communist League" [https://www.marxists.org/archive/marx/works/1847/communist-league/1850-ad1.htm] by Marx and Engels, written in 1850, they declare:

> *"In opposition to this plan the workers must not only strive for one and indivisible German republic, but also, within this republic, for the most decisive centralization of power in the hands of the state authority. They should not let themselves be led astray by empty democratic talk about the freedom of the municipalities, self-government, etc."*

After the Paris Commune of 1871, Marx and Engels added to their theory the idea of immediate recall of elected Central Government officials. In 1891 Engels wrote, in his introduction to Marx's *The Civil War in France* [https://www.marxists.org/archive/marx/works/1871/civil-war-france/postscript.htm]:

> *"From the outset the Commune was compelled to recognize that the working class, once come to power, could not manage with the old state machine; that in order not to lose again its only just conquered supremacy, this working class must, on the one hand, do away with all the old repressive machinery previously used against it itself, and, on the other, safeguard itself against its own deputies and officials, by declaring them all, without exception, subject to recall at any moment."*

While immediate recall is a good principle, it is not a substitute for the more important need to reject the authoritarian principle that says, "You must obey the highest level of government (typically the Central government) no matter what." Revolutionary movements aiming for genuine democracy had by this time already rejected this authoritarian principle (see Chapter Eight about this history and why it is vital to reject the authoritarian principle.) Marx and Engels, however, embraced the authoritarian principle. In their view the "deputies and officials" should be empowered--at least until they are recalled--to command (make laws for) everybody else. This is the opposite of how genuine democracy--voluntary federation--works.

government that makes laws and policies that everybody in the nation is obliged to follow or be arrested and face imprisonment. How are the individuals who constitute the central government selected? On this point the Communists and Socialists part ways. The Communists say that their Communist Party must be (or choose) the government in a "one party" state. The Socialists say the government must consist of politicians who won an election by the citizens (or are appointed by a politician or politicians who won such an election) and those they in turn appoint. The United States Constitution or the British parliamentary system are examples of such governments.

In either case, be it the Communist or Socialist method of constituting the central government, the result is the same in that everybody in the nation is obliged to obey laws written by a relatively small number of people, typically meeting in a capital city far away from most citizens. If the citizens disagree with a law, they are obliged to obey it or face imprisonment. Under Communism, there is no way citizens can ever change a law they don't like, except by rebelling against Communism or by persuading the Communist Party to change the law. Under Socialism, citizens can change the law by rebelling against Socialism or by waiting until the next election (which could be many years in the future) and voting for new

---

For Marx, a strong centralized government was needed because it was, in his view, necessary in order to increase economic production to the point where scarcity would be abolished; only then could the state "wither away" in the classless society of communism. Marx was wrong; when economic productivity is a widely shared goal then decentralized power (voluntary federation, *i.e.,* genuine democracy) is far more conducive to economic productivity than anti-democratic domination by a strong central government
[http://newdemocracyworld.org/revolution/which.html].

politicians.

In both cases, ordinary people are not involved in making the laws they are required to obey. This very fact is a recipe for power to be exercised by people whose values and interests are different from those of ordinary people. Lord Acton[110] knew a thing or two!

Why Socialist And Communist Governments Are Always Anti-Democratic

It's not just that the central government might end up becoming an instrument for domination by people whose values and interests are different from those of ordinary people; it's that Communists and Socialists, because of the Marxist theory they both embrace, intend for this to happen, in fact require that it happens. According to Marxism, ordinary people are dehumanized by capitalism; they lack class consciousness; their heads are filled with capitalist ideas and values. Worse, ordinary working class people are, according to Marx, as stupid and ignorant as it is possible for a human creature to become. In his *Capital*, Volume I, Chapter 14, "Division of Labor and Manufacture," Section 5, Marx writes:

[quotation begins here]

> *In manufacture, in order to make the collective labourer, and through him capital, rich in social productive power, each labourer must be made poor in individual productive powers.*

> "*Ignorance is the mother of industry as well as of superstition. Reflection and fancy are subject to err; but

---

[110] Who wrote, "Power tends to corrupt and absolute power corrupts absolutely. Great men are almost always bad men, even when they exercise influence and not authority; still more when you superadd the tendency of the certainty of corruption by authority." [https://acton.org/research/lord-acton-quote-archive]

a habit of moving the hand or the foot is independent of either. Manufactures, accordingly, prosper most where the mind is least consulted, and where the workshop may ... be considered as an engine, the parts of which are men." [45]

As a matter of fact, some few manufacturers in the middle of the 18th century preferred, for certain operations that were trade secrets, to employ half-idiotic persons. [46]

"The understandings of the greater part of men," says Adam Smith, *"are necessarily formed by their ordinary employments. The man whose whole life is spent in performing a few simple operations ... has no occasion to exert his understanding... He generally becomes as stupid and ignorant as it is possible for a human creature to become."*

After describing the stupidity of the detail labourer he goes on:

"The uniformity of his stationary life naturally corrupts the courage of his mind... It corrupts even the activity of his body and renders him incapable of exerting his strength with vigour and perseverance in any other employments than that to which he has been bred. His dexterity at his own particular trade seems in this manner to be acquired at the expense of his intellectual, social, and martial virtues. But in every improved and civilised society, this is the state into which the labouring poor, that is, the great body of the people, must necessarily fall." [47]

45. A. Ferguson, l.c., p. 280.
46. J. D. Tuckett: "A History of the Past and Present State of the Labouring Population." Lond., 1846.
47. A. Smith: "Wealth of Nations," Bk. v., ch. i, art. ii. Being a pupil of A. Ferguson who showed the disadvantageous effects of division of labour, Adam

> Smith was perfectly clear on this point. In the introduction to his work, where he ex professo praises division of labour, he indicates only in a cursory manner that it is the source of social inequalities. It is not till the 5th Book, on the Revenue of the State, that he reproduces Ferguson. In my "Misère de la Philosophie," I have sufficiently explained the historical connexion between Ferguson, A. Smith, Lemontey, and Say, as regards their criticisms of Division of Labour, and have shown, for the first time, that Division of Labour as practised in manufactures, is a specific form of the capitalist mode of production.

[quotation ends here]

The elitist attitude towards working class people and peasants held by Marx and Engels is also explicitly evident in their *Communist Manifesto*, as discussed in "The Communist Manifesto is Wrong."[111]

Marxism purports to be a science of social change. It is based on the axiom that individuals act in their self-interest, and that what is in their self-interest depends on the particular nature of the means of production in a given society and the individual's relation to those means of production.

In the Marxist framework, class conflict is not correctly understood as a conflict between the majority of people who value equality and mutual aid (a.k.a. solidarity) versus the minority who value inequality and greed and domination of the many by the few. No. The Marxist framework understands class conflict to be a conflict between the self-interest of people who do not own the means of production versus the self-interest of those who do. Instead of positive values in conflict with negative values, Marxists see only self-interest in conflict with self-interest.

---

[111] http://newdemocracyworld.org/old/manifesto.htm

Everybody, according to Marx, acts only in his or her self-interest and the changes in society are merely caused by the way changes in the means of production change what is in the self-interest of different parts of the population. As Marx put it[112], "The handmill gives you society with the feudal lord; the steam mill, society with the industrial capitalist." In the Marxist "science" social change (leading eventually to socialism as a transition to the classless society of communism) happens because of impersonal political/economic laws driven by the material nature of the means of production and the self-interests of individuals. The end of capitalism and arrival of communism happen not because this is the subjective conscious explicit aim and desire of flesh and blood working class people, but in spite of the fact that these people are *"as stupid and ignorant as it is possible for a human creature to become."*

To the extent that the process of going from capitalism to a classless society requires conscious human intervention, it must, according to the science of Marxism, be the intervention of people who are not *"as stupid and ignorant as it is possible for a human creature to become."* Who would these people be? Obviously, they are a self-selected elite, who constitute a Socialist or Communist Party, and who believe that they, and not ordinary working class people, must hold the real power in society in order to guide it to the desired goal. This is why Socialist and Communist governments are, and must be, strong central governments that demand obedience by ordinary people.

But what kind of obedience does the Marxist science demand of ordinary people in a Socialist nation? It is obedience to laws that aim to increase economic production. The reason why Marxists believe this is because they believe that before a society can be based on "from each according to ability, to each according to need" economic production must be

---

[112] https://www.marxists.org/archive/marx/works/subject/hist-mat/pov-phil/ch02.htm

ramped up to eliminate scarcity. Marx expressed it this way in his Critique of the Gotha Program[113]:

> *"In a higher phase of communist society, after the enslaving subordination of the individual to the division of labor, and therewith also the antithesis between mental and physical labor, has vanished; after labor has become not only a means of life but life's prime want; after the productive forces have also increased with the all-around development of the individual, and all the springs of co-operative wealth flow more abundantly -- only then can the narrow horizon of bourgeois right be crossed in its entirety and society inscribe on its banners: From each according to his ability, to each according to his needs!"*[114]

---

[113] https://www.marxists.org/archive/marx/works/1875/gotha/ch01.htm

[114] I fully agree with the principle of "From each according to ability, to each according to need." This is the basis of the sharing economy discussed in Chapter Four. But it should be noted that Marx did not invent this idea, he merely popularized it while emphasizing that society could NOT be based on this principle until far FAR in the future, "in a higher phase of communist society."

As early as 1775 in his Code de la Nature ou le Veritable esprit de Ses Lois a Frenchman named Morelly wrote, [https://www.marxists.org/archive/hyndman/1921/evrev/chapter23.htm] long before Karl Marx was even born, that his aim was "To distribute work according to capacity; products according to needs." The same idea appears even earlier, in the Bible (Acts, 4:43-35): "Neither was there any among them that lacked: for as many were possessors of lands or houses sold them, and brought the prices of the things that were sold, And laid them down at the apostle's feet: and distribution was made unto every man according as he had need." According to the authors of this Monthly Review article [https://monthlyreview.org/2010/06/01/capitalism-the-absurd-system-a-view-from-the-united-states]:

Here's the rub. How does an elite governing class make it so that "the productive forces have also increased"? Given the presumption that people act in their self interest, the ruling elite will need to arrange things so that it is in each worker's self interest to work harder and produce more. Well, the capitalists have invented terrific ways of doing just that. The trick is to make society very unequal and lure people to work harder with the promise that if they do they will be rewarded with greater wealth (and privileges wealth can purchase) than others. Another method is Taylorism, which Lenin advocated[115] with great enthusiasm[116]. Taylorism is the "science" of breaking the production process into lots of separate tiny actions and making each worker do just one of those actions over and over and over. Taylorism aims to make each worker as unskilled as possible, thus making workers easily replaceable, which is important for a ruling elite that does not want to be bothered by workers making demands and threatening to bring production to a stop by refusing to work until they are satisfied.

As would have been no surprise to Lord Acton, what actually happens when Socialists or Communists are in power and carrying out their Marxist "science," is that society remains as

---

> *"Back in 1987, a poll of the U.S. population indicated that 45 percent of the population believed that Marx's famous words from the Critique of the Gotha Programme delimiting communism—'from each according to his ability, to each according to his needs'—were enshrined in the U.S. Constitution. This, of course, said more about the absolute ideals of most Americans, and what they thought they should expect, than about the U.S. Constitution itself.19"*

---

[115] http://onlinelibrary.wiley.com/doi/10.1111/1468-232X.00302/abstract

[116] http://www.bus.lsu.edu/bedeian/articles/TaylorLenin-IJE2004.pdf

undemocratic as any capitalist society in terms of ordinary people not having any real say (even if they have the trappings of democracy), and it remains as unequal as any capitalist society. Indeed, from the point of view of ordinary working people, it does not fundamentally differ from capitalism and it gives no indication of ever moving towards a classless egalitarian society at all. And this is true when the Communist or Socialist leaders are genuinely following their Marxist "science."

Actually Existing Socialism

Now let's take a look at what actual self-described socialists do when they have power. [The following information comes from Wikipedia.[117]] Take, for example, the socialist party in Greece, called the Panhellenic Socialist Movement (PASOK) party. It's leader, Georgios Papandreou, became the Prime Minister of Greece in 2009. He was also President of the Socialist International since January 2006. If anybody is a socialist, he is.

Unlike the view in a leaflet[118] distributed by the egalitarian organization, People for Democratic Revolution, the socialist Papandreou thought that the banks must be repaid their debts. Wikipedia reports:

> *"Upon inauguration, Papandreou's government revealed that its finances were far worse than previous announcements, with a year deficit of 12.7% of GDP, four times more than the eurozone's limit, and a public debt of $410 billion.[11] This announcement served only to worsen the severe crisis the Greek economy was undergoing, with an unemployment rate of 10%[12] and the country's debt rating being lowered to*

---

[117] https://en.wikipedia.org/wiki/George_Papandreou

[118] http://newdemocracyworld.org/Debt.pdf

201

BBB+, the lowest in the eurozone.[13] Papandreou responded by promoting austerity measures,[14] reducing spending, increasing taxes,[15] freezing additional taxes and hiring and introducing measures aimed at combatting rampant tax evasion[16] and reducing the country's public sector. The announced austerity program caused a wave of nationwide strikes[17] and has been criticised by both the EU and the eurozone nations' finance ministers as falling short of its goals.[18] ...

"On an opinion poll published on 18 May 2011, 77% of the people asked said they have no faith in Papandreou as Prime Minister in handling the Greek economic crisis.[22]

"On 25 May 2011 the Real Democracy Now! movement started protesting in Athens and other major Greek cities. At the time, the peaceful protests were considered to be a sign of popular rejection of Mr. Papandreou and his government's economic policies,[23][24] with as much as three quarters of the Greek population being against the policies of the Papandreou government.[25] Among the demands of the demonstrations at Athens's central square, who claim to have been over 500,000 at one point,[26] is the resignation of Papandreou and his government."

Whose side are we on? On the side of "three quarters of the Greek population" protesting the same austerity that an egalitarian leaflet also condemns, or on the side of the President of the Socialist International who implemented that austerity? Clearly the former!

What About Sweden?

Sweden, sometimes described as "socialist," is nothing we

should emulate. A *Guardian* article[119] describes rioting in Sweden against "unemployment and poverty." The article reports that:

> "After decades of practising the Swedish model of generous welfare benefits, Stockholm has reduced the role of the state since the 1990s, spurring the fastest growth in inequality of any advanced OECD economy."

Another article reports:

> "With middle class wealth formation being held back by high taxes, Sweden has ironically developed a more unequal wealth distribution than the US. The Gini coefficient for ownership is almost 0.9 in Sweden, compared to slightly above 0.8 in the US."[120]

The Wall Street Journal is very happy about what's happening in Sweden, declaring "It's the free-market reforms, stupid."[121]

Sweden sends troops to Afghanistan in support of the U.S. government's civilian-murdering war.[122]

Yes, The Chinese Communist Party Is Applying Marxism (Unfortunately!)

Some people think that because the Chinese Communist Party is promoting capitalism to the extreme, that therefore it

---

[119] https://www.theguardian.com/world/2013/may/23/swedish-riots-stockholm?guni=Network%20front:network-front%20main-3%20Main%20trailblock:Network%20front%20-%20main%20trailblock:Position5

[120] https://larspsyll.wordpress.com/2012/03/14/inequality-in-sweden-continues-to-increase/

[121] https://www.wsj.com/articles/SB10001424052748704698004576104023432243468

[122] https://www.thelocal.se/20090930/22372

is not really a communist party and that Karl Marx, if he knew what was happening in China in his name, would be turning in his grave. But no, he would likely approve of what the Chinese Communist Party is doing. Here's why.

Marxism defends capitalism--even the most savage and brutal capitalism--as progressive and necessary in regions with economic scarcity. For example, Marx defended British Imperialism in India, which he fully acknowledged was extremely brutal, on the grounds that it was necessary for progress. He makes this point in his article[123] for the *New York Herald Tribune*, June 25, 1853, in which he starts out by noting that,

> *"There cannot, however, remain any doubt but that the misery inflicted by the British on Hindostan is of an essentially different and infinitely more intensive kind than all Hindostan had to suffer before."*

Then he concludes:

> *"England, it is true, in causing a social revolution in Hindostan, was actuated only by the vilest interests, and was stupid in her manner of enforcing them. But that is not the question. The question is, can mankind fulfil its destiny without a fundamental revolution in the social state of Asia? If not, whatever may have been the crimes of England she was the unconscious tool of history in bringing about that revolution."*

What makes the Chinese Communist Party a communist party perfectly in keeping with Marxism is the fact that it is indeed a party of Marxist-Leninists who are (or at least try to be) totally in control of Chinese society, including in control of the capitalists. Using capitalism with all of its "*misery inflicted*" [to use Marx's phrase for the British imperialism he declared to be so necessary] in order to increase economic production to the

---

[123] https://www.marxists.org/archive/marx/works/1853/06/25.htm

maximum before any effort to have *"society inscribe on its banners: From each according to his ability, to each according to his needs!"* is exactly what Marxism is all about. And it stinks!

Cuba, Where Socialism Means Increasing Inequality

Socialism in Cuba, under the rule of the Cuban Communist Party, has resulted in increasing economic inequality[124]. The explanation is that, for Marxists, equality is not the goal; increasing economic production is the goal. Marxists believe that inequality is necessary to motivate people to work hard and produce more. The experience of egalitarianism in Spain in the years 1936-9, however, shows that when there was vastly more equality then economic productivity increased[125], even despite the need for much of the population to be engaged in military service to defend the revolution against the fascist General Franco.

Not Socialism Or Communism, But Egalitarianism

The difference between egalitarians versus Socialists and Communists is that egalitarians, in contrast to the latter, believe that the fundamental conflict in society is between a working class culture of equality and mutual aid versus an elite culture of inequality and pitting people against each other to control and dominate them. Unlike the Marxists, egalitarians know that most ordinary people quite consciously and explicitly favor equality over inequality and favor mutual aid over being pitted against one another. Unlike Socialists and Communists, egalitarians want society to be shaped by the values ordinary people share, and egalitarians see the aim of revolution as the shaping of all of society by the values by

---

[124] See http://www.ipsnews.net/2014/12/cubas-reforms-fail-to-reduce-growing-inequality/ and http://www.wsws.org/en/articles/2008/04/cuba-a17.html and http://www.reuters.com/article/us-cuba-reform-inequality-idUSN1033501920080410

[125] As shown in Chapter Nine

which ordinary people, in their everyday lives, already are trying to shape the little corner of the world over which they may have some real control.

This is why, in contrast to Socialists and Communists who need to control people with a strong central government, egalitarians reject the very idea of a central government. Egalitarians want ordinary people who value equality and mutual aid to have all of the power. The way to do this is voluntary federation, in which local community assemblies of all the people in a community who value equality and mutual aid are invited to participate as equals in the writing of the ONLY laws (and economic policies, *etc.*) that people in that local community must obey; and delegates from local assemblies are given the task of crafting proposals (not laws!) for the local assemblies (in a region whose size could be anywhere from a handful of local communities to as large as the entire planet) to accept and act upon or not as they wish. (In practice, of course, proposals would go through a process of amendments by the delegates and suggestions from local assemblies to the delegates in order to obtain the consent of as many local assemblies as are necessary to implement the proposal.)

Socialists and Communists reject the notion of voluntary federation. The premise for it--that ordinary people are the conscious source of the values that should shape society, values that are the opposite of capitalist values--is one that has no place whatsoever in the Marxist theory that guides Socialists and Communists. The proof of this is that one can search in the Marxist literature as long as one wants and one will never find this premise expressed. Instead one will find only statements about how the material interests (not values) of working class people are different from the interests of capitalists. The Socialists and Communists see their goal not as ensuring that ordinary people have the real power in society, but rather as social engineering society supposedly in the interests of ordinary people. It is a fundamentally elitist outlook: "We know what's best for you; now obey us."[126]

Socialism and Communism have attained the status of derogatory words among billions of people because Socialist

---

[126] Che Guevara expresses this elitist view in his essay, "Socialism and Man in Cuba" [https://www.marxists.org/archive/guevara/1965/03/man-socialism.htm]. In this short essay, Guevara repeats over and over again the theme that ordinary people are defective and must be re-made into a "new man and woman," which is the task of the vanguard Marxist revolutionary party:

> "In our society the youth and the party play a big part. The former is especially important because it is the malleable clay from which the new person can be built with none of the old defects."
>
> "To build communism it is necessary, simultaneous with the new material foundations, to build the new man and woman."
>
> "The resulting theory will, no doubt, put great stress on the two pillars of the construction of socialism: the education of the new man and woman and the development of technology."
>
> "Each and every one of us readily pays his or her quota of sacrifice, conscious of being rewarded with the satisfaction of fulfilling a duty, conscious of advancing with everyone toward the new man and woman glimpsed on the horizon."
>
> "In this period of the building of socialism we can see the new man and woman being born. The image is not yet completely finished — it never will be, since the process goes forward hand in hand with the development of new economic forms."

and Communist governments have demonstrated the utter contempt for ordinary people that underlies the thinking of their Marxist leaders. Billions of people equate Socialism and Communism with the suppression of democracy, and they have good reason for doing this. They also are leery of "democracy" when leaders of the capitalist nations advocate it because they know that this "democracy" is fake democracy, with all the trappings of elections but none of the substance of ordinary people having the real say in society.

As discussed in Chapter Seven, democracy is a way for people with shared fundamental values (and only for people with shared fundamental values) to cooperate for shared fundamental goals that shape society by these values. Voluntary federation of people who share the values of equality and mutual aid is the only way that such people can effectively cooperate to shape society by those values. It is also the way such people can cooperate to prevent (forcibly if necessary, with a militia organized by many local communities with voluntary federation) people with opposite values from shaping society by their contrary (negative) values.

Voluntary federation and a sharing economy—egalitarianism—is the way to make a society that is infinitely more desirable than capitalism or Communism or Socialism. Only in an egalitarian society can one enjoy freedoms discussed in Chapter Five and the trust among people that comes from the abolition of the use of money discussed in Chapter Six. Egalitarianism, as discussed at the end of Chapter Four, is also far more desirable than capitalism or Communism or Socialism especially for small business people, for people who today are relatively well off financially such as professionals or people in management, and for manual workers.

It is time to start thinking about revolution, not for Socialism or Communism, but for egalitarianism. The success of such an egalitarian revolution will depend on understanding why it has nothing whatsoever to do with Socialism or Communism.

CHAPTER THIRTEEN: HOW DOES EGALITARIANISM PREVENT THE ABUSE OF POWER?

There is no way to prevent the abuse of power other than by the vast majority of people having an explicit determination to enforce the key egalitarian principles. What follows is an explanation of how this can indeed prevent the abuse of power.

Let's consider how people could try to abuse their power in a society that is based on the values and principles of egalitarianism: no-rich-and-no-poor equality, mutual aid, from each according to reasonable ability and to each according to need or reasonable desire, and laws made only by local assemblies of egalitarians using voluntary federation to achieve order on a large scale. For an individual or a class of people to abuse power they would have to somehow persuade a lot of people to ignore egalitarian values and principles.

If somebody, for example, abused power to get rich at the expense of other people being poor he or she would have to persuade most people that the no-rich-and-no-poor value for some reason did not apply to him or her. If somebody began commanding others to obey him or her for some selfish purpose (*i.e.,* in violation of the principle of mutual aid) at the expense of others, it would require persuading most people that they were obliged to obey such orders.

Non-egalitarian societies are based on values and principles that make it easy for some people to abuse power and difficult for most people to prevent it. For example, in a capitalist society where the principle is to strive to make a profit and get as rich as possible, a person who gets rich by abusing their power is often not even widely perceived as having done anything wrong because his or her great wealth compared to other people is not in violation of any principle of society. When the abuse of power is not obvious it is much harder for people to prevent it (as discussed below regarding corruption). In an egalitarian society, in contrast, such a person's great wealth would be a huge red flag, alerting people to the fact that some abuse of power was taking place. It would therefore be much easier for people to stop the abuse.

In a **non**-egalitarian society based on the authoritarian principle (*i.e.,* that one must obey the highest body of government no matter what) it is relatively easy for a person or class of people to abuse power by getting control of, or influence over, the highest body of government. The Bolshevik Party got control of the Central Government in the Soviet Union and then easily abused its power. Most people had never heard the authoritarian principle challenged, certainly not by the Bolsheviks. People were used to the idea that the Czar had to be obeyed because he was the highest body of government. When the Bolshevik Party took over the highest body of government most people continued to believe that they were obliged to obey it, just as before. The Bolshevik abuses of power would have been a lot harder to carry off if most people had been clear about the authoritarian principle being wrong!

Big Money abuses power over ordinary Americans today by having taken control of the federal government. It too gets away with this abuse of power largely because people accept the authoritarian principle.

An egalitarian society however is based on a rejection of the authoritarian principle. If a person or class of people seized control of a high level governmental body in an egalitarian society and got it to make abusive proposals (high level bodies in egalitarianism don't make laws, they only craft proposals for local assemblies to accept or reject as they wish) what would happen? If people didn't forget the egalitarian principle that the high level governmental body can only make proposals and not laws, then they would simply refuse to implement the abusive proposal (and they would probably replace their delegates to the higher level governmental body as well, which they can do at any time.)

The moral of the story is that egalitarian values and principles, unlike the values and principles of other kinds of societies, are precisely the ones that enable people to recognize abuse of power when it happens, to understand that such abuse of power has no legitimate excuse, and to stop the abuse of power.

The most effective way to prevent abuse of power is to advocate for, defend, and act upon egalitarian values and principles. If and when abuse of power occurs, it is due to the failure of egalitarian values and principles to be embraced by most people.

Here's How To Eliminate Most Corruption

Everybody--even corrupt people--say they are against corruption. But corruption is rampant nonetheless. How come? It's not because corrupt people, when caught, are not punished. China even uses the death penalty for corruption, as reported in a *Guardian* article[127] titled, "Liu Zhijun, China's ex-railway minister, sentenced to death for corruption."

The reason corruption persists is because it is able to disguise itself as law-abiding respectability. Take Mr. Liu Zhijun, China's ex-railway minister facing the death penalty, for example. His corruption is described this way:

---

[127] https://www.theguardian.com/world/2013/jul/08/liu-zhijun-sentenced-death-corruption

> Chinese media reports suggest the evidence laid out against Liu represented only a fraction of his malfeasance. His charges did not include assets recovered in related cases, including millions of pounds denominated in various currencies, including euros, US dollars and Hong Kong dollars.
>
> The Beijing Times reported that investigations into Liu recovered 16 cars and more than 350 flats[128]. He had 18 mistresses "including actresses, nurses and train stewards", the state-run Global Times reported in 2011.

Liu's corruption apparently went on for many years. The article reports, "Liu stood trial at Beijing No. 2 Intermediate People's Court on 9 June for accepting £6m in bribes between 1986 and 2011 and using his position to help 11 people win promotions or lucrative contracts, according to the state newswire Xinhua."

During the years of Mr. Liu's corruption prior to his recent arrest he was seen as a respectable law-abiding person. Here's the point: He was seen this way in spite of being quite visibly a very rich person enjoying luxuries most Chinese peasants could hardly even dream of. It's not as if Mr. Liu lived a life style apparently indistinguishable from most Chinese peasants in terms of wealth and luxury, and that he was only recently discovered to be secretly enjoying great wealth and luxury. No, his great wealth and luxurious living was known to all who cared to look at it; what was not known to all was that he acquired his wealth and luxury by illegal instead of legal means. Owning (living in, or collecting rents from, it matters not) "350 flats" and owning "16 cars" and having "18 mistresses" is fairly visible to others; but taking a bribe can be virtually invisible.

---

[128] http://www.scmp.com/news/china/article/1258136/seized-assets-much-more-case-against-disgraced-rail-boss-liu-zhijun

In societies that permit some to be rich and others poor, it is not easy to tell whether a rich person is a respectable law-abiding citizen or a corrupt person like Mr. Liu. In such societies corruption can and will persist, using the disguise of respectability quite successfully. Now and then corrupt individuals get caught, like the unfortunate Mr. Liu, but for every one who is caught there are no doubt lots who aren't.

Don't let corruption remain invisible

The obvious way to eliminate most corruption is to make it totally visible, to make it impossible for a corrupt person to disguise him or herself as a respectable law-abiding person. What would this mean, exactly?

It would mean declaring possession of the fruits of corruption--such as 16 cars and more than 350 flats and 18 mistresses (let's be real; they were essentially women forced into prostitution by economic hardship)--to be corruption, no matter how such possession is obtained. In other words, it would mean adopting the morality reflected in the phrase, "From each according to reasonable ability, to each according to need or reasonable desire." It would mean that anybody who saw Mr. Liu enjoying his multiple cars and flats and "mistresses" would be able to see immediately that Mr. Liu was in grotesque violation of "to each according to need or reasonable desire" and would be able to accuse him of corruption, without having to enquire into whether he had been taking bribes or not. It would mean redefining corruption to include taking much more than one needs, no matter how one does it.[129]

---

[129] Thomas Paine put it this way in his essay, "Agrarian Justice" written in 1795-6:

Until we adopt this morality, we are, with respect to financial corruption, in the same position we would be with respect to child molestation if we had a morality that said some people have a right to commit child abuse and others don't. Imagine a society that said it was legal to commit child abuse if one first met certain legal conditions of a private, and hence invisible, nature (the way it is invisible whether one gets rich legally or by accepting bribes.) Imagine a Mr. Smith in this society who quite visibly abuses children. Like Mr. Liu in China, our Mr. Smith, as far as anybody can tell, is a perfectly respectable law-abiding citizen who happens to abuse children, as is his legal right. Maybe one day somebody will discover that Mr. Smith did not obtain the legal right to abuse children and he will be punished. But for every Mr. Smith who is caught, many other illegal child abusers are not.

Obviously, the problem with Mr. Smith's society is that it makes it legal for some people to commit child abuse. And equally obviously, the problem in our current societies is that they make it legal for some to be very rich while others are very poor. The solution is to make "From each according to reasonable ability, to each according to need or reasonable desire" the moral basis of our entire economy.

What About Freeloading Slackers?

"The superstitious awe, the enslaving reverence, that formerly surrounded affluence, is passing away in all countries, and leaving the possessor of property to the convulsion of accidents. When wealth and splendour, instead of fascinating the multitude, excite emotions of disgust; when, instead of drawing forth admiration, it is beheld as an insult upon wretchedness; when the ostentatious appearance it makes serves to call the right of it in question, the case of property becomes critical, and it is only in a system of justice that the possessor can contemplate security."

What would we do in an egalitarian society--with a sharing economy and a voluntary federation system of genuine democracy--about people who want to take from those who work without doing, in return, their own fair share[130] of the work? Today such people[131] (no matter how small or large a

---

[130] What constitutes a reasonable "fair share" of work depends on things like a person's age and health, of course. Children, people who have worked but now are past retirement age and are retired, sick people and truly disabled people would not be expected to work, but people of working age and in good physical and mental health would be expected to make some reasonable contribution to the economy if they are to enjoy the right to take freely from it according to need or reasonable desire, or have access to scarce things when equitably rationed according to need.

[131] Not to be confused with people who merely exercise their right to be lazy and don't claim any right to the fruits of other people's labor. Such people are not really "freeloaders." Maybe a good word for them would be "dropouts." Dropouts would probably not wish to be part of a sharing economy based on "from each according to ability, to each according to need" because they decline to contribute "according to ability" and don't mind not receiving "according to need."

What would happen to dropouts in an egalitarian society based on a sharing economy? What, for example, about a person or family or group of people who want to exercise their right to be lazy or to work (however much or little they wish) on their own land or in their own workshop (or equivalent) and be self-sufficient and not be a member of the sharing economy?

In an egalitarian society dropouts would be perfectly free to drop out this way, if that's what they want to do. They could own, in addition to personal items, as much land or other things related to economic production as they can put to productive use by their own, and only their own, labor; they

percentage they may actually be) can be found collecting welfare (EBT) benefits or disability benefits even though they have no legitimate claim to them, meaning they are not really trying to find gainful employment or they are lying when they claim to be disabled or unable to work for some other reason. What would we do with such freeloaders?

In an egalitarian society freeloaders would have no right to enjoy the fruits of the sharing economy. Unlike those who are members of the sharing economy because they contribute reasonably to it, as they are able, by working or learning a skill, freeloaders would not be able to take products and services for free from the sharing economy. They could barter something for something else, if somebody was willing to make such a trade, but that's all. People in the sharing economy could also decide, if they want to, to provide (from what they have a right to individually own) whatever they feel like providing to freeloaders, but they would be under no moral or legal **obligation** to provide anything. Note that this principle conflicts with the (understandably!) very popular slogan, "Health care is the right of all people." Is this a paradox? No. But to untangle this confusing question see the section below titled "Is Health Care a RIGHT for Freeloaders?"

The principle of the sharing economy is "From each according to reasonable ability, to each according to need or reasonable desire."[132] Reasonableness is assumed, of course. People are expected to contribute according to ability reasonably, meaning a reasonable amount of work, not the maximum work

---

cannot, however, hire other workers. What they do with the fruits of their labor is up to them; but since society is no longer based on money and they have chosen not to be in the sharing economy, they might decide to barter some of the fruits of their labor with individual members or economic enterprises in the sharing economy, which is fine.

[132] It is NOT unconditional "Free access."

physically possible! Children and the elderly and the truly disabled and sick are not expected to work. People are free to take according to reasonable need and also reasonable desire (people deserve not just bread but roses too.) Things in short supply are rationed equitably in some reasonable manner according to need. Reasonableness is defined by the democratic local community and workplace assemblies, which, being open equally to all the people in the community or workplace who support the values of equality and mutual aid and democracy, will almost certainly be guided by reasonableness in their decisions.

At first glance, denying freeloaders a right to enjoy the fruits of the economy sounds the same as what right wing Republicans advocate. These right wingers devote lots of talk radio time to complaining about the freeloaders defrauding the welfare system and buying caviar with their EBT cards and enjoying the "Life of Riley" at the expense of hard working honest people.

An egalitarian society, however, is not what right-wingers--at least not the top leaders of the right-wingers--have in mind. Here are the key differences between what egalitarians want and what the right-wingers want:

> 1. Egalitarians deny ALL freeloaders a right to enjoy the fruits of the work of others. Right-wingers only deny this right to poor freeloaders, not rich freeloaders.

> 2. Egalitarians say that there should be no obstacle preventing a person from contributing his or her fair share of work to the economy. They say that if you want to work reasonably, all you need to do is go to where people are working and volunteer to help them, or go to a school to learn a skill so as to be able to help do skilled work in the future, or propose to your local assembly a plan to do something the assembly will agree is useful and then do it (with the necessary human and material resources being available for free) or help work on a new project that somebody else has just had approved. In an

egalitarian society there is no such thing as involuntary unemployment. Every effort is made to make sure that those who want to contribute their fair share of work are actually able to do so. This, after all, makes life better for all because it shares the required work of society among more people, making it possible for everybody to do less work. Thus all that is needed to work and be a member of the sharing economy is a willingness to work reasonably.

But right-wingers disagree. They say that if you cannot find an employer who is willing to hire you or you cannot find somebody who will pay your tuition to attend a school, then tough luck; you're unemployed no matter how eager you are to work or study. In the right-wingers' view, people only deserve to be hired or paid to study if it will increase some capitalist's profits. If more profits can be made by not hiring some people, then it's just too bad for them: their lot in life is to be unemployed regardless of their willingness to work.

In conclusion, the choice for how to deal with freeloaders comes to this. Egalitarians say: Deny[133] all freeloaders the right to take from those who work, and ensure that anybody who truly wishes to do their fair share of the work is able to do so. Right wingers say: Deny only poor freeloaders the right to live as a parasite off of others but give this right to rich freeloaders, and furthermore deny many people an opportunity to do their fair share of the work.

But what do the liberals say? The liberals who lead the Democratic Party pretend not to notice that there are any freeloaders living unfairly at the expense of regular working people at all. The liberals portray, as "racism" or "selfishness," the justifiable anger of working people against freeloaders. The liberals claim to be the champions of the poor, including the unemployed and disabled, and they ignore the fact that

---

[133] The nuts and bolts of how to do this are discussed in Appendix VII

some (no matter how small a percentage) of the people they claim to champion are indeed freeloaders. Why do the liberals do this?

The liberal leaders don't do it out of any real concern for the poor, freeloaders or not. These liberal leaders are as unconcerned about regular people as the most right wing Republican Party leaders. What's going on is this. The liberal and conservative leaders are playing a kind of "Good Cop/Bad Cop" (or rather "Friend of freeloaders/Foe of freeloaders") routine to divide and rule the American people with the "freeloader" issue. Their purpose is to protect the enormous inequality of our capitalist society. The Democratic Party deliberately acts in a way that makes it seem to working people as if the government is coddling freeloaders at the expense of honest workers. This is a set-up for the Republican Party to direct anger at poor freeloaders into support for policies that give the very rich (the rich freeloaders) exactly what benefits them (the rich) the most while making life harder for all working people.

If the Democratic Party liberals really cared about poor people, they would be egalitarians. They would do whatever it takes to enable people who want to work to find employment. They wouldn't accept the capitalist principle that nobody gets hired unless it maximizes some capitalist's profits to hire them. The Democrats are no friends of the poor; it was Democrat Bill Clinton who "abolished welfare as we know it" and orchestrated the shipping of higher paying factory jobs to Mexico with his anti-worker North American Free Trade Agreement. The Democratic Party leaders are pro-capitalists who cry crocodile tears for the poor in order to divide and rule Americans.

Is Health Care A <u>Right</u> For Freeloaders?

Almost all of the people who presently do not have adequate health care insurance deserve to have it. Why? Because the relevant moral principle is "From each according to reasonable ability, to each according to need or reasonable desire" and these people contribute (or at least are willing to contribute even if wrongfully denied employment) to society according to ability. (The ability of children and of people physically or mentally incapable of doing useful work, or of people past a reasonable retirement age is of course considered to be zero, which means they are considered to be contributing reasonably according to ability no matter what; also attending school or an apprentice program, *etc.*, is considered doing useful work.)

Today, the only choices for health care policy that the politicians ever talk about are these two:

a) A policy (such as Obama Care) that leaves many people without adequate (or even any) health insurance. This kind of policy denies the principle of "From each according to reasonable ability, to each according to need or reasonable desire" (in particular the second part of that principle).

b) A policy (such single payer universal health care for all) that is based on the idea that health care is the right of all (whether they contribute reasonably according to ability or not, *i.e.*, whether they are freeloaders or not). This kind of policy also denies the "From each according to reasonable ability, to each according to need or reasonable desire" moral principle (in particular the first part of that principle).

Given these two morally flawed choices, good people very understandably go with the second choice because they don't want people who truly deserve health care as much as anybody else not to have it when they need it.

But do freeloaders--people who can but who simply refuse to contribute according to reasonable ability--have a <u>right</u> to health care? Here's a thought experiment to shed light on the question.

221

Do you remember that rich woman, Leona Helmsley, who famously declared[134], *"We don't pay taxes. Only the little people pay taxes"?*

Imagine a freeloader (a person who similarly says, "I don't work. Only the little people work") in need of medical care arriving at a hospital and demanding that the doctors and nurses and orderlies care for him/her because it is his/her "right."

Are those health care workers obliged to agree that they MUST provide the freeloader health care because it is that person's right to receive it? Note that this question is not the same as the question, "Should the health care workers provide the freeloader health care?"

Health care workers might decide--for any of a number of reasons[135]--that it would be a good idea to provide health care to the freeloader. At the same time, if I were one of those health care workers I would make it clear to all concerned that "Even freeloaders have a right to health care" is NOT one of those reasons.

If, for some reason such as the scarcity of health care resources (perhaps an organ needed for a transplant or a team of surgeons faced in an emergency with more cases than they can handle), health care workers had to prioritize who would receive scarce health care and who would not, what is the applicable moral principle? I think the priority

---

[134] https://en.wikipedia.org/wiki/Leona_Helmsley

[135] For example, a national health care system might offer health care free to everybody no matter what, instead of only to people who are not freeloaders, simply because it would cost more to check if a person is a freeloader every time somebody requests health care. Fine. Or the health care workers may not want to live where sick people are dying on the street; or they may just feel sorry for the freeloader, or hope to improve their chances of going to heaven if they give the freeloader care. But note that these reasons have nothing to do with the notion that freeloaders have a *right* to have health care provided to them by those who do contribute reasonably according to ability.

should be to care for people who have contributed according to ability, and the freeloader--contrary to the idea that health care is the <u>right</u> of all--has no right to complain about this.

How "health care is a right for all" harms good people

Some good people (*i.e.*, people who are not freeloaders but who for some reason are unable to work) today who have Medicaid health insurance feel guilty for having this insurance, when they have no valid reason for feeling guilty; this is harmful to them emotionally.

These good people feel guilty because they know that other people-- taxpayers--are paying for their health care and that they are not paying for it themselves. They feel like a freeloader and they know freeloading is morally wrong.

But these people are not freeloaders and have no reason to feel guilty. These people contribute to the wealth of society according to reasonable ability; what their reasonable ability is varies according to their individual circumstances: some work normally until they become disabled or otherwise incapable of working; some may try but fail to find reasonable employment; some may never be able to work because of a physical or mental illness.

In receiving health care according to need or reasonable desire these people are acting perfectly morally, consistent with the moral principle of "From each according to reasonable ability, to each according to need or reasonable desire." These people have a moral right to take health care and other things according to need or reasonable desire. They wouldn't have this right if they had refused to contribute according to reasonable ability (*i.e.*, if they really were freeloaders), but they did not refuse and so they have no reason to feel guilty for getting health care paid for by taxpayers.

Unfortunately these good people seldom hear the appropriate moral principle articulated at all, never mind applied to their situation as a person on Medicare. What they hear instead is the wrong moral principle, that "Health care is the right of all." These good people know that if *this* is the principle by which they receive health care courtesy of the "hard working taxpayers" then they are receiving it for the same reason freeloaders also receive it. This makes them feel as if they were a freeloader because they focus on what they have in common with a freeloader--not working--and lose sight of how they are very different from a freeloader--working according to reasonable ability.

We would do a lot to promote the emotional health of good people by embracing the principle that "Health care is a right for those who contribute reasonably according to ability" so that these good people would know that the health care they receive is deserved by them for the *same* reason that "hard working taxpayers" deserve their health care, and *not* because health care is a right even for freeloaders.

The freeloader issue discussed here with respect to health care applies equally to the newest "big idea," Universal Basic Income, which I discuss online[136].

---

[136] https://www.opednews.com/articles/Beware-of-the-Universal-Ba-by-John-Spritzler-Basic-Income-Guarantee_Class_Equal_Income-Inequality-170314-184.html

CHAPTER FOURTEEN:
REFORM OR REVOLUTION?

People quite naturally and quite rightly wage all sorts of reform struggles all the time. Sometimes people try to stop the rulers from making things worse in some particular way. And sometimes people try to improve conditions of life for ordinary people in some way. When the explicitly stated aim of the struggle is something short of all-out egalitarian revolution then this is called a reform struggle.

An egalitarian revolutionary movement supports reform struggles. The WAY it supports them is this. It strives to increase widespread public support for the struggle by not only communicating to the public the particular facts about the reform demand, but also the **fundamental** values and aspirations that motivate the people who are waging the struggle.

Invariably, when people wage a reform struggle, they do it because they want to make society closer in some particular way to being an egalitarian society; they want to make it more equal (in the egalitarian sense of no rich and no poor), and they want to make it based more on people helping each other (mutual aid, solidarity) instead of being pitted against each other, and they want to make it more genuinely democratic instead of just a fake democracy as it is today. People waging reform struggles, in other words, have egalitarian values and aspirations. Their motive for waging their struggle is to bring the day closer when the goal of egalitarian revolution is accomplished: to remove the rich from power, have real--not fake democracy--with no rich and no poor.

Egalitarian revolution means <u>removing the rich from power</u> so that people--the vast majority of whom want an egalitarian society--are able to shape ALL of society by their egalitarian values.

An egalitarian revolutionary movement wants people waging reform struggles to know something extremely important that is generally not known and even disputed. The fact is that their struggle would **GAIN,** not lose, support from the public if they told the public what truly motivated their struggle--that they want an egalitarian society with the rich removed from power and with real not fake democracy and with no rich and no poor.

Videos of "person on the street" interviews[137] in Boston show that practically everybody (no cherry-picking in the videos!) says they would support a progressive organization **MORE** if it sincerely said it wanted to remove the rich from power to have real not fake democracy with no rich and no poor.

An egalitarian revolutionary movement encourages people waging a reform struggle to tell the public explicitly about their egalitarian revolutionary values and aspirations. This will not only strengthen public support for the reform struggle, but will also strengthen the egalitarian revolutionary movement by giving people greater confidence that they are part of the majority (not a hopelessly weak minority) in wanting an egalitarian revolution.

The rich, however, will remain in power, and class inequality will continue, and ordinary people will be treated like dirt forever (for the reason discussed in Chapter Two**), until we make an egalitarian revolution; and this can only happen when millions of people EXPLICITLY**

---

[137] https://www.youtube.com/watch?v=acmNtxyzEf4 (a compilation) and
https://www.youtube.com/watch?v=UDasqHqijX8 and
https://www.youtube.com/watch?v=EkGThwhSipU and
https://www.youtube.com/watch?v=Ku8wzaMMLEo and
https://www.youtube.com/watch?v=py0kqr2q9mc

make egalitarian revolution their goal. Movements against the ruling elite can win what they explicitly aim to win; but they never win more than that.

Reform struggles are not the opposite of egalitarian revolution or a substitute for it; they are a way that the egalitarian revolutionary movement gains strength and confidence from people learning that they are part of a large majority in wanting to shape all of society by egalitarian values, and in wanting to remove the rich from power in order to be able to succeed in this great effort.

Most Marxists disagree with the above view

Karl Marx, and the modern Marxists whose thinking is based on his writings, have, in contrast to the viewpoint expressed here, a very negative view of ordinary (working class) people (see Chapter Twelve about this.) These Marxists do not agree that most people waging reform struggles have, themselves, egalitarian revolutionary values and aspirations. Marxists believe that people in reform struggles are motivated merely by self-interest and have no desire to create a classless society. Nor do these Marxists agree that people waging a reform struggle would gain, not lose, public support if they explicitly declared their egalitarian revolutionary values and aspirations (since the public likewise supposedly only cares about its self-interest.)

Marxists, therefore, view the motives of people in a reform struggle as being very different from their (the Marxists') motives as revolutionaries. Some Marxists see their role as persuading people in a reform struggle to **change** their goal (and their values) from a self-interest reform goal to the nobler revolutionary goal. These Marxists look down on reform struggles as "not revolutionary" and they take some pride in not getting involved in such struggles.

Other Marxists join and even try to lead reform struggles. They do this while down playing their revolutionary aspirations.

Their aim is to persuade the people in the reform struggle that they (the Marxists) are good leaders, so that the people in the reform struggle will follow the Marxists' revolutionary party in spite of the fact that they (supposedly) don't share its revolutionary goals. This way the revolutionary party will be able to seize power one day and then use that power (very un-democratically, of course) to re-mold ordinary people so they will stop just "thinking with their belly" and become (as Che Guevara put it) "Socialist Man."

The point is that neither of these ways of relating to reform struggles is useful. Marxists act as if people in reform struggles did not want an egalitarian revolution. The Marxists get all tangled up in debating amongst themselves how to relate to these "un-revolutionary" struggles. They miss the point entirely. Reform struggles are only "un-revolutionary" because the people waging them do not know that the majority of the public shares their egalitarian revolutionary aspirations. The role of a revolutionary is to help people (including those in reform struggles) learn that in having egalitarian revolutionary aspirations they are in the great majority. When this is well known, people waging reform struggles will declare their revolutionary aims and strengthen both the reform struggle AND the egalitarian revolutionary movement. This is how people can get off of the "treadmill of defeat."

Let's get off the treadmill of defeat

The aim of the Bernie Sanders movement, as spelled out by Bernie Sanders himself, was essentially a new New Deal, like the original one implemented by FDR. The Green Party has its new New Deal, and Donald Trump also (sort of) has one. What happened as a result of FDR's New Deal is a warning to us about all such New Deals.

FDR's New Deal made things better for some people, but only for a while. Then what happened?

What happened is what we see today all around us--obscene economic inequality, obscene racial discrimination, obscene warmongering (Orwellian wars of social control, based on lies), obscene U.S. government support for Israel's racist ethnic cleansing, and a U.S. "hear no evil, see no evil, but sell weapons to" policy towards the obscene Saudi Arabian head-choppers. This is where the last New Deal landed us, and it's what Bernie Sanders's new New Deal or the Green Party's new New Deal, or Donald Trump's new "Make America First" New Deal would (will) get us more of too. How come?

The problem with these "New Deals" is that they leave class inequality firmly intact; they leave our society one in which money is power and a few have lots while most have none; **they thus leave a ruling plutocracy in power** that, in order to *keep* its power and wealth and privilege, must treat regular people like dirt (for the reason discussed in Chapter Two), must take back tomorrow whatever it grants us today to pacify us[138], and must do disgusting things to control us by

---

[138] Here's just one example of how the rulers take back with one hand what they give with the other. The ruling class has, in response to the large $15/hr minimum wage struggle, allowed the minimum wage to be raised in some cities and states. Some low-wage (a.k.a. "low- skill") workers did indeed see their hourly earnings increase. But, as discussed in some detail at

http://www.bostonglobe.com/opinion/editorials/2016/10/29/for-low-skilled-workers-life-hard-minimum-wage-hikes-make-harder/a5kOAZlfl8Pzncfki2Pu9J/story.html?p1=Article_Recommended_ReadMore_Pos2_, employers responded by using fewer hours of low-skill labor. This increased the number of low-skill workers who had either no job at all or a reduction in their hours of work, resulting in the gains enjoyed by some workers coming from losses suffered by others.

Conservatives (such as Jeff Jacoby, whose article is linked to above) who advocate abolishing minimum wage laws argue (gleefully!) that raising the minimum wage doesn't actually

pitting us against one another with lies and manipulation to make the lies credible (the racist War on Drugs' purpose is to make the lie that blacks are a criminal race seem convincing, as discussed in Chapter Fifteen.)

These New Deals leave us on the treadmill of defeat.

If we want to get off the treadmill of defeat then we need to aim to solve the Big Problem at its root with a Big Solution. We need to aim at abolishing class inequality, the way the abolitionist movement aimed at abolishing--not reforming!--slavery. This is what egalitarianism is all about. Chapter Eighteen is about how we can actually do this.

---

raise the income of low-skill workers overall, it only helps the decreasing number of them who remain fully employed. This conservative argument is actually true and airtight, but only if one accepts its unstated premise, which is that our society (at least the dominant private sector) remains based on the free market in which everything--commodities and labor--is bought and sold for prices determined by the law of supply and demand.

But who says our society must remain this way? We can have an egalitarian society that is not based on money, not based on buying and selling, but rather based on the common-sense principle of "From each according to reasonable ability, to each according to need or reasonable desire, with scarce things equitably rationed according to need."

CHAPTER FIFTEEN: HOW THE RULING CLASS DIVIDES-AND-RULES US WITH "SOCIAL ISSUES" AND HOW TO OVERCOME THIS

Why is it that Americans are split, conservative versus progressive, right down the middle: one half the population versus the other half and not, say, 20% versus 80%? The 2017 election, like the last several, was exceedingly close to a 50-50 split (48.2% Clinton vs. 46.1% Trump). The split on social issues such as same-sex marriage and abortion and bathroom gender laws is also right down the middle, with each camp having utter contempt for the other. And yet at least 80% of Americans want to remove the rich from power to have real--not fake--democracy with no rich and no poor (as Chapter One demonstrates.) Why are we, the American public, so divided despite our profound agreement with each other?

I believe that the explanation is that the ruling class goes to great lengths to deliberately split the American public into bitterly opposing camps, right down the middle, which is where a split is most effective for divide-and-rule. The ruling class needs to divide us against each other to prevent us from realizing that we—the vast majority—are in agreement about the most important thing, that we want an egalitarian revolution. If the American public knew this fact about itself, then it would be curtains for the ruling class. The ruling class knows this full well.

This is why the ruling class orchestrates public debates on "social issues" in a manner that ensures that there will be two approximately equal sized camps, each regarding the other as beyond-the-pale horrible. The ruling class uses as many private opinion polling results and focus groups as it takes to determine the most divisive way to frame these debates. These frameworks deliberately exclude from consideration any viewpoint that the vast majority of the population would agree with. The ruling class uses the media it controls, some with progressive audiences and others with conservative audiences, to specifically censor views and factual information (especially about what "the other side" really believes and is concerned about) that would unite most people on social-issue questions or at least result in each side having respect for, if not agreement with, with other side's concerns.

What I'm saying here is that the ruling class pits half of the American population against the other half with the same disgusting methods that it uses to get the American population as a whole to approve of violent unjust warfare against a foreign people: big lies, censorship, and manipulation (such as false flag attacks.) It does this because it fears what would happen if it didn't—egalitarian revolution.

Before looking at how the ruling class uses specific social issues to divide us, I want you to be fully aware of just how deliberately and knowingly ruling class leaders lie to us to make us think another category of people are our enemy, even though the truth is otherwise. I want you to have not just my word for it, but proof. But how can I prove this? These ruling class people are good at covering up their crimes.

Well, it turns out, as you no doubt know, that the older the crime, the more likely it is that documents about it will be declassified. Because of this, it recently became possible for us to learn how President Lyndon Johnson and his buddies deliberately and knowingly lied us—big time!--into the Vietnam

War. The proof of this crime is finally available to us. I'm going to start this chapter, therefore, by giving you proof. I'm hoping that after you read it, you'll be more willing to believe the truth about how the ruling class lies us into forming extremely hostile camps over social issues.

Here's The Proof

Go to the U.S. Naval Institute's Naval History Magazine issue online[139] that has an article by Lieutenant Commander Pat Paterson, U.S. Navy, titled "The Truth About Tonkin." The author is (or was when the article was posted) "the African desk officer at Special Operations Command, Europe in Stuttgart, Germany. A 1989 graduate of the U.S. Naval Academy, he is also a surface warfare and foreign area officer." This article is based on formerly secret documents only recently declassified for public inspection: it takes many decades for us to learn the truth about these things.

If you spend the half-hour or so it takes to read this article, you will learn what really happened in the famous so-called Gulf of Tonkin Incident that was used by President Lyndon Johnson to get Congress to pass the Gulf of Tonkin Resolution, which dramatically escalated the War in Vietnam.

Specifically, you will read how Defense Secretary Robert McNamara *"distorted the evidence and mislead Congress"* and *"intentionally mislead Congress and the public"* and *"lied"* and how *"McNamara's intentional distortion of events prevented Congress from providing the civilian oversight of military matters so fundamental to the congressional charter"* and how *"McNamara deceived the American people and Congress."*

Referring to the American sailors who supposedly shot at attacking North Vietnamese ships in self-defense in the Gulf of Tonkin, this article quotes President Johnson remarking, *"Hell,*

---

[139] https://www.usni.org/magazines/navalhistory/2008-02/truth-about-tonkin

those damn, stupid sailors were just shooting at flying fish."

Defense Secretary Robert McNamara LIED, deliberately, for the purpose of getting Congress to approve the escalation of the Vietnam War (the first overt attack by the United States on North Vietnam). The Vietnam War resulted in killing 1.3 to 3.9 million (estimates vary) Vietnamese peasants and 58,000 American GIs, and it split the American population (not to mention the world's population!) into mutually hostile camps. It was based on the most explicitly deliberate lie there ever was!

Not only did Robert McNamara lie to jump start the atrocious Vietnam War, there is strong evidence that the reason people such as McNamara wanted that war had nothing whatsoever to do with the official purpose of stopping Communist aggression. Had this been the actual motive then the United States government would not have been providing enormous quantities of military equipment to the Soviet Union, which delivered them, in turn, to the North Vietnamese against whom American GIs were sent to fight. And yet this is precisely what the United States government did, and had been doing for decades, as discussed in great detail in my online article, titled "The U.S. Armed the Soviet Union During the Cold War."[140] The purpose of the war was to implement a strategy to keep the American plutocracy rich (from selling high-priced weapons to the government) and in power (by keeping Americans fearful of the Communist bogeyman enemy in an Orwellian war of social control.

McNamara was president of the Ford Motor Company before President Kennedy appointed him Defense Secretary, after which he went on to become the President of the World Bank. He thus travelled in circles where you and I don't ever go, among the kind of people--the ruling class--that you and I never get to know personally and seldom even see. These are indeed the kind of people who would deliberately tell a lie to start a war.

---

[140] http://newdemocracyworld.org/war/sutton1.html

These people live in a very different culture from the one we know. For them, it is praiseworthy to tell a lie that enables the very rich to gain at the expense of ordinary people, and especially praiseworthy to tell a lie that divides ordinary people right down the middle for divide-and-rule. This is known as "serving one's class." They imbibe this culture with their mother's milk and learn it as children at the dinner table and at their private schools and clubs. A few can enter this circle from the ranks of the "commoners" but only if they demonstrate total loyalty to the upper class culture.

These are the kind of people who control the United States, who have (or are beholden to those who have) billion dollar fortunes. These people know that ordinary people want society to be equal and democratic, not ruled by and for the exclusive benefit of a billionaire class and its highly paid servants. They know that to prevent ordinary Americans from making ours a genuinely equal and democratic society they must be divided against each other to be controlled. These people employ experts in social control to figure out what lies to tell and what phony divisive public debates to orchestrate.

Most of us have never personally encountered people who are THAT awful, that devious on such a huge scale. Who has ever seen a person orchestrate a NATIONAL debate designed to deliberately pit hundreds of millions of people against each other? Is it possible that such persons even exist?

If such persons do not exist, then the only explanation for why all of the above divide-and-rule "social issue" frameworks do exist, with the censorship they require, would have to be random luck--bad luck for us and good luck for the ruling class. We would have to assume that the ruling class is just extraordinarily lucky!

One can be forgiven for doubting that such incredibly evil persons exist. But as we've seen now, they do exist!

The lies (remember WMD[141], and the phony testimony[142] about Saddam killing babies in incubators?) are concocted at the very top. Everybody lower in the hierarchy learns very quickly what to say or not say in order to please those above them and hold onto their careers. The underlings don't need to know WHY they must say and do what they must say and do, *i.e.,* why it is important for divide-and-rule; it is sufficient merely that they know what to say and do. Those that don't intuit what pleases and displeases those above them don't remain in, or ever get into, important corporate or government positions. Newspaper editors, for example, know not to print refutations of the key ruling class lies, because if they did so they would regret it: they'd lose big advertising accounts, or worse.

If you would like to learn how to defeat the ruling class's use of social issues to divide and rule us, here's what I suggest. For each of the social issues listed below, read the following online articles I have written about them. They expose how the ruling class has lied and used censorship and manipulation to create hostile camps, and they offer an approach to each social issue that would unite most people and defuse the bitter anger between those who may still disagree. Very likely you have never heard of these approaches to these issues; the ruling class censors mention of them in the mass (and alternative!) media. Unfortunately, the American Left, rather than exposing how the ruling class uses social issues to divide and rule, accepts the divisive ruling class frameworks. This is discussed in my article, "The Dangerous Naiveté of the American Left."[143]

Race

---

[141] http://www.newsweek.com/2015/05/29/dick-cheneys-biggest-lie-333097.html

[142] https://en.wikipedia.org/wiki/Nayirah_(testimony)

[143] http://newdemocracyworld.org/culture/naivete.html

Is it a 'Privilege' Not to be Discriminated Against?[144]

Why and How Big Money Promotes "White Privilege" Rhetoric[145] (also read the articles this one links to at the top)

We need THIS, not Affirmative Action[146]

Appendix X: Race, Crime and Egalitarianism

What Do "White Supremacists" Believe?[147]

Same-sex Marriage

Video: Same-Sex Marriage & Anonymous Sperm/Egg Donation: What's the Connection and Why Does it Matter?[148]

Links to Online Sources of Information about Same-Sex Marriage and Gamete Donation (a supplement to the above video)[149]

Conception Of Children: View #1[150]

Feminism

---

[144] http://newdemocracyworld.org/culture/privilege.html

[145] http://newdemocracyworld.org/culture/white.html

[146] http://newdemocracyworld.org/culture/affirmative.html

[147] http://newdemocracyworld.org/culture/supremacists.html

[148] https://www.youtube.com/watch?v=u6CSCXnK3P4

[149] http://newdemocracyworld.org/culture/links.html

[150] https://www.pdrboston.org/conception-of-children-1

Misandry: An Obstacle to Solidarity Between Men and Women[151]

Transgender bathrooms

Bathroom Policy Regarding Transgender People: The Ruling Class Is Using This Issue To Divide-And-Rule[152]

Abortion

How the Ruling Class Uses the Abortion Issue to Divide-and-Rule[153]

Immigration

Illegal Immigration[154]

Muslim refugees

What About the Mass Muslim Immigration of Refugees?[155]

Links to Some Facts about Muslims & Islam[156]

---

[151] http://newdemocracyworld.org/culture/misandry.html

[152] https://www.pdrboston.org/bathroom-policy-re-transgender

[153] http://newdemocracyworld.org/culture/abortion.html

[154] https://www.pdrboston.org/illegal-immigration

[155] http://newdemocracyworld.org/culture/muslim-refugees.html

[156] http://newdemocracyworld.org/culture/muslims2.html

Palestine and the part of it called Israel (This issue is extremely divisive globally, and becoming more so domestically.)

What the "Existence of the State of Israel" Really Means and Why It Should NOT Exist[157] (Be sure to read the key articles this in turn links to.)

Israel/Palestine: "It's Complicated!"...Or Is It?[158]

Why Our Government Supports Israel's Government, and Why We Shouldn't[159]

The Israel Lobby's Power Comes from The American Ruling Class[160]

Newt Gingrich's Brilliant Insight about Palestinians[161]

Should There Be a Jewish State?[162]

Albert Einstein Quotations Opposing a Jewish State in 1938, 1946 & 1952 and Labeling Future Israeli Prime Minister Menachem Begin a Fascist in 1948[163]

---

[157] http://newdemocracyworld.org/palestine/existence.html

[158] http://www.newdemocracyworld.org/old/War/Complicated.leaflet.pdf

[159] http://www.newdemocracyworld.org/old/War/Why_Our_Government-Aug-9-07.pdf

[160] http://newdemocracyworld.org/old/War/Lobby2.htm

[161] http://spritzler.blogspot.com/2011/12/newt-gingrichs-brilliant-insight-about.html

[162] http://newdemocracyworld.org/old/state.htm

[163] http://www.newdemocracyworld.org/old/einstein.htm

Universal Basic Income

Beware of the Universal Basic Income[164]

Trump versus Clinton (worth reading about even though the election is over)

The Clinton/Trump Team[165]

How The Ruling Class Deliberately Fomented A Race War In Boston In 1974

The school busing crisis in Boston in the early 1970s developed into a virtual race war with racial violence carried out with fists, knives and rocks, and a surge of support for an overtly racist leader--the Boston School Committee chairwoman Louise Day Hicks--who formed an overtly racist organization (ROAR) against blacks and those who supported integrating the schools.

The only reason that Hicks was able to build her racist movement was because the ultra-liberal federal Judge W. Arthur Garrity, who ordered the school busing, demanded that integration be implemented with a plan that (quite unnecessarily!) maximized the distances that little children would be bused; the plan was designed, in other words, to anger people for reasons having nothing to do with integration *per se*. The proof of this deliberateness is that Judge Garrity refused to even consider an integration plan that

---

[164] https://www.opednews.com/articles/Beware-of-the-Universal-Ba-by-John-Spritzler-Basic-Income-Guarantee_Class_Equal_Income-Inequality-170314-184.html

[165] http://newdemocracyworld.org/culture/team.html

black and white parents proposed that would minimize the distance children would be bused and would have even eliminated some busing (it took advantage of the fact that black and white neighborhoods were like a checkerboard pattern in Boston, and called for building schools near the borders between black and white neighborhoods so children could go to schools that were both integrated AND near their homes.)

Furthermore, the liberal leaders provided the racist Louise Day Hicks everything she needed ideologically. How? By never refuting the racist argument against integration. This racist argument asserted that the presence of black students in a classroom caused white students in that classroom to receive an inferior education. For example, when white parents in Boston had complained to the principle of the newly integrated Patrick O'Hearn elementary school about the slow and boring pace of the schoolwork, they were repeatedly told, "We have to go slow because the black children can't keep up." Yet black parents were upset that their children were bored because they weren't being challenged; they knew the work was harder at the all-black school their children had been at before.

Similarly, when the same school became overcrowded because of the busing in of black students, the principle told white parents, "These new students are ruining the school." These attempts to turn white parents against blacks and against the idea of integration failed at the Patrick O'Hearn school, but such racist arguments, made throughout the school system in Boston, helped the racist Louise Day Hicks build her racist anti-busing movement. The oh-so-liberal *Boston Globe* editorialized about the importance of integrating the schools and ending racial discrimination, but it never refuted the racist lies that undermined its preaching. In this way the *Boston Globe* actually helped the racist Hicks, while appearing to oppose her. This kind of ruling class device is common (as the articles above about Affirmative Action and "white privilege" demonstrate.)

Additionally, the *Boston Globe* not only accused any white person who objected to Judge Garrity's logistically nightmarish busing plan of being a "racist" but also accused any black person who objected to it (and there were many) of being an "Uncle Tom." No well-known black leader dared stand up against the busing plan. This ensured that black opposition to the busing plan would be virtually invisible and thus create the false impression that only whites opposed it, and only for racist reasons. The racist Louise Day Hicks absolutely needed these actions by liberal politicians and the *Boston Globe* in order to succeed in mobilizing white parents around a racist "blame the blacks" ideology.[166]

Race is still no doubt the most divisive issue in the United States. The progressive half of the population thinks the conservative half are horrible racists. The conservative half thinks that "anti-racism" is code for anti-white. The Boston busing example illustrates how the ruling class manipulates us to pit us against each other this way. The articles listed above about numerous different "social issues" show how the rulers do this with virtually all them, not only race. To achieve the solidarity we need to remove the rich from power requires, chiefly, gaining an understanding of how the ruling class is manipulating us, and then spreading that understanding far and wide.

---

[166] The facts about the Patrick O'Hearn school are from Dave Stratman's *We CAN Change the World*, pages 16-17 at http://www.newdemocracyworld.org/old/Revolution/We%20Can%20Change%20the%20World%20book.pdf . Other facts are from my personal experience living in Boston at this time.

CHAPTER SIXTEEN: WHAT CAN INDIVIDUALS REALISTICALLY DO TODAY TO START BUILDING AN EGALITARIAN REVOLUTIONARY MOVEMENT?

I've written this chapter to be read by a person who has a very busy and demanding life, just personally trying to make the best of things in our society. It's for a reader who may be working at a job (or more than one job) most of his or her waking hours; or for a reader taking care of children all day (and some of the night); or for a student with a heavy course load and maybe even a part time job too; or for a retired person who has taken on a full and busy post-work lifestyle. This chapter is for people who may not belong to any kind of formal or informal group that considers itself to be political in any way. If you are such a person, this chapter is for you. (It's also for people who are politically active, of course.)

The phrase, "building an egalitarian revolutionary movement," might conjure up in your mind an image of picking up a gun and, like Che Guevara, heading into the hills (or wherever) to organize a guerrilla band of revolutionary soldiers. But this is not what I mean by the phrase at all—not even close. What I mean by the phrase is to do something (described below) that you can do in the normal course of your present-day routine; it will require virtually no extra time from your busy schedule; it will cost you nothing; it is legal and safe; and—surprise!—it is FUN! Not only that, it is truly the most appropriate thing today for people to do to start building an egalitarian revolutionary movement that really CAN remove the rich from power so that we can have real—not fake—democracy with no rich and no poor.

What is this amazing activity I am proposing you do? It is "buttoning," as described in Chapter One. The way others and I have "buttoned" is by using PDR buttons (the image of which is shown in Chapter One), which are available to you absolutely free[167], courtesy of donations people have made to a "buttonship fund." But one could just as usefully pay a commercial online button-making company to make a button with the same words and your own design; or even simpler and cheaper, you could just write the words on 3x5 cards to show to people. In the following paragraphs I assume for simplicity of writing that you're using the PDR button when I describe what "buttoning" means and why it is so important at this point in time. But the choice is yours.

As stated in Chapter One, "buttoning" means going to a public place and asking passers-by, while handing them the PDR button, "Do you think the message on this button is a good idea or a bad idea?" and, when they say it's a good idea (as most do), giving them the button and a flyer (Appendix IV) that explains why we "button." "Buttoning" also means doing the same thing, but with individuals one may know personally or individuals one encounters during the normal routine course of one's day at work or school or while doing errands.

Granted, going to public places and "buttoning" passers-by takes extra time out of your busy day, and maybe it even seems

---

[167] https://www.pdrboston.org/button

almost as daunting to you as mimicking Che Guevara's suicidal bravado. So let's just focus on buttoning "with individuals one may know personally or individuals one encounters during the normal routine course of one's day at work or school or while doing errands." I personally have buttoned sales people while shopping, the cash register operators when buying groceries, bank tellers when doing banking business, the persons who hand me my prescription drugs at the pharmacy, fellow passengers in elevators in professional buildings, the women (it's always been women) who drew my blood for blood tests I needed, the mail-carrier and the UPS person for the building where I live, my neighbors and (before I retired) my co-workers, and people sitting next to me on the bench while waiting for the trolley bus to arrive.

None of this took any extra time out of my life, and it invariably was FUN because the response to the button was so positive. People would read the button I handed them and then, after seeing that it wasn't supporting some politician or some stupid idea, their face would light up with a smile because the button said something they agreed with so very much. This is when I would tell them that the button was not a joke, but part of a very serious effort. This is important because many people have never heard anybody who seriously thought it was possible to, as the button says, remove the rich from power to have real—not fake—democracy with no rich and no poor. Most people think this is impossible to do, and so figure that anybody advocating it must just be joking.

OK, I hope I've persuaded you that "buttoning" is something you could do if you wanted to. But now the question is, why would you want to? I've mentioned that it is fun, but there are lots of fun things you don't do. Why is "buttoning" a fun thing that you would especially want to do? Here's why.

If you "button," then you will discover that you are surrounded by people who, like you, want an egalitarian revolution. Before you "button" you may wish that this were true. You may hope that it is true. You may suspect it is true. You may even believe (from reading Chapter One?) that it is true. But you won't KNOW it is true. You won't know it the same way you know that if you drop a stone it will fall down instead of up. That's the kind of confidence people need to have, in the egalitarian revolutionary aspirations of their fellow Americans, in order to seriously even begin thinking about how to build an egalitarian revolutionary movement that can grow large and strong enough to actually win (as discussed in Chapter Eighteen.) The main reason you should "button" is to gain this confidence. A secondary reason is to let the "buttonee" also learn that he or she is not alone in having egalitarian revolutionary aspirations, and to provide him or her with the PDRBoston.org URL so they can learn more about egalitarianism.

"Buttoning" may seem pointless when the goal is to remove the rich from power, given that the rich have so much power (money, government, police, military) at their disposal, but it's not. "Buttoning" is an effective tactic implementing a larger revolutionary strategy that CAN remove the rich from power.

The Strategy For Which "Buttoning" Is A Key Tactic

Millions of Americans know that we are living in a fake democracy that is really a dictatorship of the rich. Millions of Americans would love it if there were an egalitarian revolution to, as the PDR button says, "Remove the rich from power. Have real not fake democracy, with No Rich and No Poor."

AND YET, HARDLY ANY AMERICANS KNOW THAT IN FEELING THIS WAY THEY ARE PART OF A LARGE MAJORITY, NOT A HOPELESSLY SMALL AND HENCE IMPOTENT MINORITY.

The ruling class's #1 method of social control is to prevent this majority from KNOWING it is the majority and thereby to keep people paralyzed by hopelessness. This is why one never sees egalitarian revolutionary aspirations expressed in the mass (or alternative!) media even though most people share these aspirations. The plutocracy that owns these media censor such views to ensure that we will think that hardly anybody else shares them. (See Appendix XIV to read how, in 1969, I learned about the explosive result--a political sea change!--that happens when people who know their anti-establishment goal is morally right ALSO learn that they are the majority in having that goal.)

To build the kind of mass egalitarian revolutionary movement that can eventually win over a critical mass of rank-and-file soldiers (see Appendix XV about why this will be possible) to its side (they didn't enlist to keep the rich in power, you know!); and to persuade these soldiers that the revolutionary movement is large enough and determined enough so that if they support it and refuse to obey orders to attack it they will likely be on the winning side and not executed as a traitor for going over to the losing side; and thereby actually to remove the rich from power, the first step is to help the majority of Americans who would love for this to happen to see that they are in fact a majority. This is what is required for millions of Americans to gain the hopefulness and confidence to build such a revolutionary movement, to create explicitly egalitarian revolutionary organizations that enable people to act together on a very large scale.

"Buttoning" is not, by itself, going to remove the rich from power, obviously. But it is the most practical way to take the first step towards increasing the number of people (starting with oneself!) who have the confidence to organize on a larger scale as discussed in Chapter Eighteen, which CAN remove the rich from power.

Furthermore, the strategy for which "buttoning" is a first tactic, is a strategy that is realistic. It is not based on wishful thinking that we can vote the rich out of power (see Appendix Five for why not.) It is not a (please excuse this metaphor) "get rich quick" strategy. Nor is it a strategy that aims merely for some band-aid solution on the grounds that it is impossible to remove the rich from power. There are all sorts of such unrealistic or defeatist strategies being promoted by this or that person or organization. If wishful thinking or defeatism is your cup of tea, then don't "button." Otherwise, please "button."

Speaking Of "Band-Aid" Solutions…

In the previous paragraph I mentioned "band aid" solutions in a way that might be misleading. The problem with "band aid" solutions (otherwise known as reforms) is not that they are bad things to try to win. Indeed, they are great things to win if they make life better for some people (without making life worse for others, and not at the expense of undermining the solidarity of all ordinary people.) The problem with "band aid" solutions is if people view them as a <u>substitute</u> for solving the problem of class inequality at the root by abolishing class inequality (*i.e.,* by making an egalitarian revolution.) When this happens, people end up on a treadmill of defeat, forever and forever, as discussed in Chapter Fourteen.

The Short-Term Goal Of The Egalitarian Revolutionary Movement Is To Win Good 'Band Aid' Reforms

The short-term goal of the egalitarian revolutionary movement is to win improvements in our lives quickly, and--as explained below--the WAY to achieve this short-term goal is to increase the size of the egalitarian revolutionary movement itself.

The egalitarian revolutionary movement's short-term goal is the same as the goal of countless people today who are fighting for all sorts of improvements: a $15/hr. minimum wage, stopping evictions caused by gentrification, better pay and working conditions and benefits at work, affordable health care and college education that doesn't drive working class people into debt slavery, an end to unjust wars and an unjust foreign policy that attacks innocent people and supports their oppressors, and many similar reform demands large and small.

One way that the egalitarian revolutionary movement strengthens these reform struggles is by increasing public support for them, as discussed in Chapter Fourteen.

Furthermore, the stronger the egalitarian revolutionary movement grows, the more fearful the ruling class becomes that the only way to prevent a revolution is either to grant people their reform demands or else rely on increasingly overt repression. Sometimes the rulers do choose repression but this poses a danger to them because it risks polarizing society even further and drawing yet more people to oppose the ruling class and favor the idea of revolution.

The most important reforms that have been won in U.S. history were won when the ruling class feared that a serious, *explicitly* revolutionary movement was developing and that in order to prevent an actual revolution it was necessary to give people what they were demanding.

This is why President Franklin D. Roosevelt gave us the New Deal's government-sponsored employment of the unemployed, unemployment compensation and Social Security. This is why the U.S. Congress with all its racist members voted for the Civil Rights Act of 1964 and abolished the racist Jim Crow Laws. This is why the warmonger President Nixon pulled troops out of Vietnam in 1975 in an ignominious (for the ruling class!) defeat. The huge strike wave in the 1930s[168] and the increasingly radical Civil Rights Movement and its linking up (thanks to Martin Luther King, Jr.) with the likewise increasingly radical and revolutionary Anti-Vietnam War Movement, scared the hell out of the ruling class.

Had the ruling class not seen increasingly revolutionary movements "on the streets" at these times, there would have been no granting of these reforms.

This is why those who believe that the best way to win reforms is by *avoiding* any mention of egalitarian revolutionary aspirations are mistaken. The exact opposite is true. When the ruling class is comfortable in knowing it has no reason to fear revolution, then it is comfortable in refusing to grant any reform demands.

The larger the *explicitly* egalitarian revolutionary movement is, the more afraid the ruling class will be of NOT granting reform demands. What frightens the rulers most is when large

---

[168] Here's just one of many instances. When a longshoremen's strike in 1934 led to a general strike in San Francisco of 130,000 workers, which spread to Oakland and then up the Pacific Coast, the *Los Angeles Times* wrote: "The situation in San Francisco is not correctly described by the phrase 'general strike.' What is actually in progress there is an insurrection, a Communist-inspired and led revolt against organized government. There is but one thing to be done--put down the revolt with any force necessary." FDR's National Recovery Administration chief, General Hugh S. Johnson, went to San Francisco and declared the general strike a "menace to the government" and a "civil war." See Jeremy Brecher, *Strike*, South End Press, Boston, Massachusetts, 1997, pp. 169-74. More about this huge strike wave is in my *The People As Enemy: The Leaders' Hidden Agenda in World War II*.

numbers of people declare that they aim for no less than to remove the rich from power to have real, not fake democracy, with no rich and no poor.

There is both a short-term and a long-term goal in building the egalitarian revolutionary movement. The short-term goal (winning reform demands) may make life better, but the problem is that as long as the ruling class remains in power it will take back tomorrow what we win today. In this sense we remain on a treadmill of defeat until we achieve our long-term goal of egalitarian revolution.

Even if one feels that the long-term goal's attainment is too far in the future to justify devoting time and energy towards building the egalitarian revolutionary movement today, please keep in mind that the *short*-term goals are *also* an important reason for working to build the egalitarian revolutionary movement.

What Else Besides "Buttoning"?

"Buttoning" is just a first step. For discussion of subsequent steps, please read Chapter Eighteen, titled "How We CAN Remove the Rich from Power."

CHAPTER SEVENTEEN: WHAT ABOUT FEAR AND REPRESSION?

Fear, Yes. Paralysis, No

It's unfortunate to need a chapter about a negative subject--fear—in a positive book about how we can make a truly equal and democratic society called egalitarianism. But many people, for quite understandable reasons, worry about getting in trouble--maybe ending up on an NSA "troublemakers" list or something--if they even demonstrate interest in a book like this one or the ideas in it. So I want to address that concern honestly and forthrightly here.

It's perfectly reasonable to fear the very rich and powerful people who actually rule the country--the ruling class. The ruling class, with the private and governmental power that its billions of dollars can buy, has the means to attack those who challenge its power. It would be naive to believe that this is not so.

Fear of such retaliation or repression is certainly one of the main things that sometimes prevents some people from expressing their true feelings about our dictatorship of the rich, never mind taking concrete steps to remove the rich from power.

Of course it makes sense to be fearful of the ruling class and to try to avoid being harmed by it. But must we be paralyzed by this fear? Must we simply accept that the ruling class will always remain in power? Or can we take useful steps towards removing the rich from power in a way that people with a sensible appreciation of the risks would nonetheless find reasonable?

Minimize The Danger; Maximize Our Strength In Numbers

The "buttoning" tactic (described and discussed in Chapter Sixteen) is designed to be minimally dangerous for the people doing it, while at the same time being extremely useful (given our current situation) for increasing the number of people who have confidence that it is possible (and hence sensible) to build a majority-based egalitarian revolutionary movement.

Why is "buttoning" only minimally dangerous? To see why, compare it to the kinds of acts that are indeed very dangerous.

It's extremely dangerous to corner a rat

It would be extremely dangerous for an individual to confront a powerful member of the ruling elite with the threat of publicly documenting that he or she, *personally*, had engaged in a criminal (or legal, but reprehensible) act. This amounts to "cornering a rat." People who do that are sometimes assassinated.

When people in positions of power even at a relatively low level in society (such as corrupt local labor union "leaders") fear that a relatively small number of people are doing things that will quickly lead to their being removed from power, then they may very well respond like a "cornered rat" and strike back violently to protect their power, essentially forcing their foes to decide if it is worth losing their lives just to remove some low level bad guys from power. This writer knows of one instance of corrupt local union leaders carrying out a drive-by shooting of live bullets into the homes of the leaders of an anti-corruption caucus in the union for this very reason.

It's extremely dangerous to lead <u>millions</u> of people in a more revolutionary direction

Another example of a maximally dangerous thing to do would be for an individual who is the respected leader of millions of people in a reform struggle to begin to give unprecedented good leadership that makes that struggle more revolutionary and more *immediately* threatening to the ruling class than before. Martin Luther King, Jr. did this when he joined the Civil Rights Movement to the Anti-Vietnam War Movement and began framing the conflict in class rather than racial terms. Malcolm X did this when he too began towards the end of his life framing the conflict in class rather than racial terms. Both of these leaders were assassinated.

It's extremely dangerous for small numbers of people without widespread public support to use violence against the ruling class

The Black Panthers in the late 60s armed themselves with rifles and made it clear they would shoot police if necessary to protect black people from police brutality. The Panthers had substantial support for this in the black community, but very little in the general white population, which did not know the truth about police brutality against blacks. As a result of the lack of support for the Panthers in the general public, the ruling class calculated that it could literally murder the Panthers without risking it leading to a revolution, and so murder[169] them it did, with the FBI. From the ruling class's point of view, this murder made sense: the risk (triggering a revolution) was very small while the benefit (ending a very real and *immediate* threat to the power of the police) was very large.

"Buttoning," in contrast, is not very dangerous at all.

"Buttoning" doesn't "corner a rat," it doesn't involve giving revolutionary leadership to millions of people, and it's totally non-violent. From the point of view of anybody with the means

---

[169] https://www.democracynow.org/2014/12/4/watch_the_assassination_of_fred_hampton

of striking back at a "buttoner" there is very little motive to do so. Those of us who have been buttoning have experienced no retaliation whatsoever.

Is there absolutely zero risk if one "buttons"?

Of course not. There is at least a small risk involved in doing *anything* not 100% approved of by the ruling class. Whispering in private to one's son or daughter a slightly anti-establishment opinion carries some risk, since the child could innocently mention it to somebody else who might report one to the authorities resulting in one "getting on a list" of troublemakers to be dealt with punitively at some point.

The ruling class relies on this kind of fear to cause people to self-censor their egalitarian revolutionary (or even just slightly anti-establishment) views, so that the Big Lie--that hardly anybody has such views--will remain credible. The ruling class wants people to feel so alone that they will abandon all hope of building an egalitarian revolutionary movement and not even try taking the first step of talking to others about it. To frighten people into silence, the ruling class thus makes a point of telling us that the NSA monitors our communications.

There are two ways of responding to this fear of "getting on a list."

One way is to refrain from absolutely all expressions of anti-establishment views by both word and deed, and thereby resign oneself (and one's children and grandchildren) to living in the kind of world the ruling class wants, with its unjust Orwellian wars of social control[170] and divide-and-rule along race and religious lines and its treatment of ordinary people like dirt (as discussed in Chapter Two)--all for the purpose of maintaining its domination over us.

---

[170] https://www.youtube.com/watch?v=oOVICOudMVI

Another way is to do things that that are only minimally dangerous but may nonetheless result in "getting on a list," while encouraging lots and lots of other people to do likewise, so that the list ends up having so many people on it that it becomes as useless to the ruling class as the telephone directory and the risk from being in the "troublemaker list" is hardly more than from being in the telephone directory.

In deciding which way to respond, it may be helpful to read about how Americans obtained the right of free speech (in the online article, "How the Wobblies Won Free Speech"[171].) As late as 1912 the most recent Supreme Court's ruling had interpreted the First Amendment as allowing local government authorities to make it illegal to pass out a leaflet or speak to a crowd on public property. The reason we have this right of free speech today is because huge numbers of workers broke these laws against free speech and filled the jails. Had these workers not accepted the risk of being thrown in jail back then, we and our children and grandchildren would not be able legally to even hand out a flyer on the street if the government objected to its content.

Rights that we cherish and take for granted exist on a "use it or lose it" basis. If we retreat and stop using our rights to challenge the ruling class then we and our children and grandchildren will lose these rights and go back to the days when we couldn't even pass out a flyer on the sidewalk. Something to think about, no?

One might object that there is nothing to prevent the ruling class from cracking down hard on the first wave of people who "get on the list" in order to "make an example" of them and stop the growth of a revolutionary movement by "nipping it in the bud." While there is some truth to this objection, it is not the whole story. Ruling elites only remain in power if they

---

[171] https://connecticuthistory.org/how-the-wobblies-won-free-speech/

grasp some key facts about how small elites can remain in power.

Why Does the Ruling Class Let Us "Button"?

One of the facts that ruling elites know about how to remain in power is that for an elite--no matter how ruthless--to remain in power it needs at least the grudging tolerance of a substantial part of the population. Ruling elites always worry that if they use overt repression it may reduce the amount of grudging tolerance below the point where the ruling elite can remain in power. There are many cases in which the ruling class allows people to engage in anti-establishment, even revolutionary, acts without forcibly stopping them with overt repression. This happens when the ruling class has good reason to fear that the amount of repression required to stop the acts would be counter-productive to the ruling class because it would reduce the level of grudging acceptance to a dangerously low level.

This is why the ruling class lets us "button," and why it lets countless other people do things it does not want them to do. It is thus possible to leverage the ruling class's fear (of losing the amount of public tolerance it requires to remain in power) to gain a relatively safe space for overtly revolutionary activity.

The Antidote to Fear is Strength in Numbers

The point here is not that buttoning alone will remove the rich from power; it won't. But buttoning is a way to develop our strength in numbers, which is the antidote to fear. Buttoning gives people confidence that they are not alone in wanting to remove the rich from power and in fact are literally surrounded by people who want what the button says: "Let's remove the rich from power, have real--not fake--democracy with no rich and no poor" (in other words an egalitarian revolution.)

This confidence paves the way for people to start acting like the **majority** they really are instead of like the hopelessly small and hence impotent minority they think they are today. This in turn can lead to people acting collectively in large numbers--meaning **a majority of the U.S. population!**--to demonstrate to themselves and to the members of the military forces that they are determined to make an egalitarian revolution. Only when this happens will a critical mass of members of the military think it makes sense to refuse orders to attack the revolutionary movement and instead to go over to its side. This is how the rich can be removed from power.

When a majority of the people are rising up for egalitarian revolution, what people will think is sensible versus just crazy and dangerous because of the risk of ruling class repression and violence, will be different from what seems sensible to those same people today. This is because people naturally weigh the risk versus the potential benefit. When the potential *immediate* benefit is enormous--egalitarian revolution or at least a major step in that direction--the acceptable risk is greater than when, as today, the potential *immediate* benefit from whatever we might do is definitely not going to be huge compared to an actual egalitarian revolution.

The "buttoning" tactic is a very low-risk act with an extremely large *but non-immediate* potential benefit, and with a smaller but less distant potential benefit as well, namely the short-term goal of the egalitarian revolution that is discussed in Chapter Sixteen. It is sensible to "button" despite the fact that the ruling class is truly scary.

We Cannot Prevent Repression, But We Can Succeed Despite It

In "Thinking about Revolution"[172], *Dave Stratman and I wrote the following.*

How Do We Overcome Repression?

The political power of the ruling elite depends mainly on the assent of the governed. People may be deeply unhappy with

---

[172] http://newdemocracyworld.org/revolution/Thinking.pdf

the government and the direction of society, but as long as they see no alternative, they go along with things as they are. As the revolutionary movement grows, people will see an inspiring alternative and withdraw their assent to the status quo. The government will then be forced to use police and the military power to keep people in line.

But the government can use force against the people only at great political cost to itself. The more it attacks a revolutionary movement that is deeply embedded in our communities, the more it exposes itself as a tool of the rich and angers a wider circle of people.

Once revolutionary movements include the bulk of society, ruling elites become powerless to act effectively against them. French President Charles DeGaulle and his wife fled France in the dead of night in the face of the French workers' and students' movement in 1968. He was convinced that the army would not support him against the workers. It was only the treachery of the powerful Communist unions in France, which persuaded workers to abandon their strikes that allowed the elite to stay in power. The U.S.-backed Shah of Iran used all the means at his disposal to keep his grip on society, including a huge army and SAVAK, secret police known for their brutal methods. Yet so many Iranians opposed the Shah that his regime collapsed.

The strength of the revolutionary movement lies in speaking with the voice of the people and spreading its views as widely as possible. The ultimate success of the revolution depends on the movement having a deeply democratic character, based on a democratic and positive view of human beings. We cannot prevent repression, but we can succeed despite it.

But Won't A Revolution Just Produce A Lot More Horrible Violence?

I know that some people will say, after reading all of the above, that revolution, though possible, is still a bad idea. There are two arguments such people may make. The first argument is that revolutions just provoke the ruling class to commit horrible violence. The second argument is that revolutionaries, themselves, commit horrible violence, as happened in, say, the French Revolution.

The first argument is made by people who do not grasp how violent the ruling class already is—today; they don't appreciate the magnitude of mass murder the ruling class commits routinely. (See my online article, "The U.S. Government is Run by Mass Murderers"[173] for more on this.)

The second argument is, frankly, based on a wrong and elitist view of ordinary people. Ordinary people who want to shape society by the values of equality and mutual aid, and who think that local communities should be sovereign and thus have the right to shape society this way in the manner they, and only they, choose, are not the kind of people who lust to kill innocent people.

There were indeed revolutions in the past in which some people did lust to kill innocent people. The French Revolution is often cited as such an example. What happened then? The French Revolution was not led by ordinary people; it was led by upper middle class people such as lawyers. These revolutionary leaders were fanatics in the sense that they believed that there was a single "will of the French people" that only they knew, and anybody who disagreed with them was the enemy of the people who had to be executed. When these leaders disagreed with each other then leaders in the majority sent leaders in the minority to the guillotine, in a repeating and macabre process that eventually left few alive. There was also some wrongful violence by ordinary people against innocent people perceived as enemies of the revolution. Much of this wrongful violence stemmed from the fanaticism of the revolution's leaders.

In contrast to the French Revolution's leaders, the leaders of

---

[173] http://newdemocracyworld.org/war/murder.html

the American Revolution, though also not ordinary people (many of them were slave owners), did not share the fanaticism of the French revolutionaries. This is why the American Revolution, unlike the French Revolution, is not known for being particularly violent against innocent people.

The Bolsheviks were also fanatics in the sense of believing that only the Bolshevik party should rule because ordinary people only "think with their belly" and don't aspire to create a classless society (as discussed in Chapter Twelve and in the "Communism" section of Appendix III). To enforce the dictatorship of the Bolshevik Party its leaders did indeed commit terrible violence against innocent people.

The point is that what revolutionaries do in a revolution depends on who are the revolutionaries and what are their guiding beliefs. It is just elitist to believe that ordinary people who are egalitarians trying to shape society by the wonderful and decent values of egalitarianism will necessarily turn out to be vicious killers of innocent people. The ruling class wants us to think this way so we'll just give up and let it rule the world forever. This book is for people who don't want to do that.

CHAPTER EIGHTEEN: HOW WE CAN REMOVE THE RICH FROM POWER

Most Americans want an egalitarian revolution, as Chapter One shows. What prevents Americans from making such a revolution? What prevents us from thoroughly shaping our society by our values of equality (no rich and no poor) and mutual aid?

Most people know that the billionaires with the real power were never elected and thus cannot be un-elected. Even if we get a wonderful person elected president, so what? As anybody who seriously studies power in the United States knows, the real power is not in the Oval Office, and the real power always has the option of killing the person in the Oval Office if and when that is necessary to carry out the policies desired by the billionaires, as discussed in Appendix V.

Everybody knows that the obstacle to making an egalitarian revolution is the fact that the rich in power have military forces that are overwhelmingly more powerful than we are in terms of raw violence

But what is not as well known is that under the right circumstances military forces go over to the other side and refuse to obey orders to attack the people they are ordered to attack. American GIs did this in Vietnam, as discussed in

Appendix XV. Soldiers in Iran did this in 1979[174], forcing the Shah of Iran to flee the country even though he thought--up to the last moment--that his military force, which he knew was the strongest in the Middle East, would keep him in power. Similarly, the Czar of Russia was forced to abdicate in February of 1917 when his Cossack soldiers decided to defend, instead of follow orders to attack, the workers demonstrating against the Czar in the streets of St. Petersburg. In the French Revolution, the King's power was defeated when people in the streets successfully took over the famous Bastille prison on July 14, 1789. This decisive battle "could not have been won without the support of the troops in the capital, or at least their benign neutrality. Within the French Guards, the mutinies at the company level in early June were soon followed by the outright participation of entire regiments in the popular uprising." (*The Third Revolution*, vol. 1, pg. 278, by Murray Bookchin)

Far more important than the size and power of an army's weapons is the direction that soldiers decide to aim those weapons--at the people opposed to the ruling regime, or at those using violence against foes of the ruling regime!

Professor of history at Harvard University, Crane Brinton, who from 1942 to 1945 was Special Assistant to the Office of Strategic Services in the European Theater of Operations, wrote in his 1965 book, *The Anatomy of Revolution (pg. 88)*,

> *"[T]he nowadays common view that modern weapons have for the future made street-risings impossible is probably wrong. Modern weapons have to be used by police or soldiers, who may still be subverted, even in the atomic age."*

---

[174] In this case, however, the Iranian soldiers stood down because President Jimmy Carter told them to [see https://www.theguardian.com/world/2016/jun/10/ayatollah-khomeini-jimmy-carter-administration-iran-revolution?CMP=share_btn_fb]

The way we can remove the rich from power is to create the circumstances that will cause a critical mass of soldiers to a) refuse any orders they may get to attack people who want to remove the rich from power and b) use their weapons to help the egalitarian revolutionary movement defend itself against anybody who may attack it violently[175]. This is how the rich lose power! (A video[176] shows how it might start.)

But in order to persuade substantial numbers of soldiers to do this we will need to persuade them that the egalitarian revolutionary movement is so large and determined that, if soldiers support it, it can actually win. If soldiers are not convinced of this then they will not refuse orders to attack the movement, even though most of them support the goal of the movement for the same reasons their civilian friends and neighbors and relatives support it. Why not? Because when a soldier refuses an order to attack "the enemy" he or she risks being severely punished--perhaps even executed--for mutiny or even treason. For substantial numbers of soldiers to take this risk they must be persuaded that the risk is relatively low because, with their support, the revolutionary movement has a good chance of winning, in which case soldiers who refuse to attack it won't be punished.

The key to removing the rich from power is, thus, to build a movement of a large majority of Americans (and of people in

---

[175] Soldiers are more likely than police to refuse orders to attack the revolutionary movement. This is because soldiers see themselves as defenders of Americans against foreign enemies, and it violates their sense of legitimate purpose to attack their fellow Americans, especially if they are ordered to attack a very large movement clearly representative of the majority of Americans. In contrast police are trained to use violent force against their fellow Americans for the purpose of protecting "law and order" (*i.e.*, the wealth, property and privilege of the rich) and routinely do so. It is not unlikely that soldiers will use their weapons to stop the police from attacking us. This is what happened in Russia in February 1917.

[176] https://www.youtube.com/watch?v=HwW5i-ukKOs&sns=fb

other countries as well[177]) that can persuade lots of soldiers to support it because it can actually WIN. This is very possible, because it is already the case that most people would LOVE an egalitarian revolution, even if they presently think it can never happen.

The movement needs to be one that *explicitly* declares its goal to be egalitarian revolution (for the reasons I discuss in this important footnote[178]). It needs to involve people in every walk

---

[177] Rich people in different nations help each other to stay in power and defeat egalitarian revolutionary movements. This is why we need a world-wide egalitarian revolutionary movement. Otherwise the American rich, when they see American soldiers refusing to obey their orders, could rely for help on an invasion of soldiers from another nation. But if there is an egalitarian revolutionary movement in that other country as well, then there is a good chance those soldiers would refuse to attack egalitarians in the United States, much as American GIs by 1975 were refusing to obey orders to attack Vietnamese peasants fighting foreign occupation, as discussed in Appendix XV.

[178] The need for **explicitly** aiming for an egalitarian revolution is twofold:

#1) Movements against a ruling class often win what they explicitly aim for, but they never win more than that. For example, the Civil Rights Movement explicitly aimed to abolish the Jim Crow laws, but it did not explicitly aim to abolish class inequality (even though practically all who joined the Civil Rights Movement wanted to end class inequality.) As a result, the Jim Crow laws were indeed abolished, but class inequality remained and this enabled the ruling plutocracy to institute the New Jim Crow [see http://newdemocracyworld.org/culture/newjimcrow.html] of racist prison incarceration. Likewise, the South African anti-apartheid movement explicitly aimed to abolish apartheid, but it did not explicitly aim to abolish class inequality. As a result, apartheid was indeed abolished, but class inequality remained and the ruling corporate elite have made life for ordinary black South Africans worse in many ways than even under apartheid [see http://www.newdemocracyworld.org/revolution/decision.html].

of life in challenging the unequal and undemocratic *status quo* on the grounds that it violates the values of egalitarianism. And it needs to promote people standing in solidarity with each other for these values and in defense[179] against those who attack them. Only this kind of movement--very large and very determined--will be able to gain the support of soldiers that is required to remove the rich from power. My online article, "Why Progressive Organizations Don't Advocate Egalitarian Revolution"[180] discusses the reason progressive organizations today are not even trying to build this kind of movement.

The first step towards building this egalitarian revolutionary movement is for people to discover that the vast majority of people want an egalitarian revolution. Chapter Sixteen **is about how you, personally and by yourself, can do this.**

Form Local Assemblies Of Egalitarians NOW

One important way to build such a movement, once you have gathered a few others in your community similarly inclined, is by forming a local assembly of egalitarians in your community. Here's the idea.

#2) People don't get on a bus if they don't know where it's going; likewise people don't join and passionately support a movement unless they know explicitly what it is aiming for and are inspired by that goal. Egalitarianism--abolishing class inequality to have real, not fake, democracy with no rich and no poor--is the goal that IN FACT inspires the vast majority of Americans when they believe it is possible.

---

[179] I believe that the egalitarian revolutionary movement should use violence in self-defense when the circumstances make that appropriate. This is discussed in Appendix VI titled "Nonviolence or Non-Cruelty?"

[180] http://newdemocracyworld.org/culture/fund.html

In your local community (a population of around 30 to 40 thousand, typically), announce meetings of the Local Assembly of Egalitarians of [Your Community]. At the Assembly meetings, discuss what laws you, as the Assembly, would enact and decisions you would make if your community were an egalitarian one, meaning one in which the sovereign power in the community is the Local Assembly of Egalitarians, to which all egalitarians in the community have a right to belong and participate as equals. Some laws could be very general, and others very specific about particular community resources--land, buildings, *etc.*; and decisions could be general or specifically about particular organizations or individuals.

Then post a single "Notice" from the Assembly after each of its meetings announcing its latest law or decision. Post the "Notices" throughout your community so people can start to get a sense of what it could be like if they lived in an egalitarian society, see how wonderful it could be, and converse with each other about this to find out that their neighbors feel the same way.

To give you an example of what such "Notices" might look like, see the "Notices" for the imaginary town of Somewhereville in Appendix I. These "Notices" try to convey several things: a) how fundamentally different an egalitarian society is from what we have today, b) how practical egalitarianism can be, c) how all of the novel laws and policies fit together coherently and consistently reflect the positive values of egalitarianism, and d) how WONDERFUL it would be if society were like this. To the extent that the "Notices" do this, and do it in both general and locally specific terms, they will help everyone in the community see that there really is a MUCH better alternative to the unequal society that we have today--one worth fighting for (this is what Chapter Two is all about).

I hope these "Notices" for Somewhereville inspire you to want to write and post your own "Notices" by your own Local

Assembly of Egalitarians, expressing your vision of what egalitarianism could mean. You may choose to express your vision very differently, but I trust you will add to the growth of an egalitarian revolutionary movement however your notices are worded.

These local assemblies at first, when they have only a small number of participants, can inform others in the community about egalitarianism, what it is and why it is both very practical and much better than our *status quo*. These early assemblies can also explain that local assemblies of egalitarians open to all egalitarians in the community are the **only** bodies that ought to make laws people in the community must obey. These assemblies can provide a place where people meet to figure out how to involve more and more people in advocating for egalitarianism, challenging the power of the rich, and creating relations of solidarity with other egalitarians near and far.

In my online article, "Lessons for Today from the Spanish Revolution 1936-9,"[181] I note that the ability of workers and peasants to make about half of Spain essentially egalitarian (in the revolution known generally as the Spanish Civil War) was due to the fact that for decades prior to doing it Spanish workers and peasants had been engaged in a deep, sophisticated and extremely widespread conversation about what they called "The Idea": the idea of how society **ought** to be. Today, local assemblies of egalitarians can promote this same kind of public conversation.

When lots of people are participating in their local assembly of egalitarians, and the assemblies are coordinating with each other by sending delegates to non-local assemblies to craft proposals for the local assemblies to implement if they agree, and when this voluntary federation of local assemblies

---

[181] http://newdemocracyworld.org/revolution/spain.html

involves tens or hundreds of millions[182] of Americans, and when similar local and non-local assemblies of egalitarians are formed in workplaces, then something extremely important happens. Then, for the first time, there is an egalitarian government in place, with which egalitarians have ALMOST everything they need to shape *all* of society by egalitarian values. This egalitarian government can begin doing some things to start making society egalitarian.

The crucial thing this egalitarian government lacks is the power to prevail against the violence of soldiers and police obeying anti-egalitarian orders. This is when a critical mass of soldiers, however, can realistically be expected to side with the revolutionary movement. **This is how the rich lose power.** Like the Czar. Like the Shah. But unlike in those previous revolutions, when the leaders of the revolution advocated anti-democratic and anti-egalitarian goals, this time it will be egalitarianism that replaces the dictatorship of the rich.

The main obstacle today in the United States that prevents people from acting together on a large scale to build an egalitarian revolutionary movement is that people feel it is hopeless to even try. Hopelessness comes, for most people, from believing that there is no better alternative to our current society based on class inequality. Even when people discover that there IS a much better alternative--egalitarianism--hopelessness continues to come from feeling virtually alone in having revolutionary aspirations for an egalitarian society.

The obstacle to egalitarian revolution is not that most people don't want it (they'd <u>love</u> it!); the obstacle is that most people don't <u>know</u> that most people want it.

---

[182] See "Historical Evidence that Voluntary Federation Can Quickly Replace the Status Quo in a Revolution" at http://newdemocracyworld.org/revolution/arendt.html .

But when most Americans **know** that most Americans want to remove the rich from power to have real—not fake—democracy with no rich and no poor, and **know** that they are in the **majority** in wanting an egalitarian revolution they will no longer feel alone. They will have the confidence to start **acting** like the majority they actually are (as illustrated by the event described in Appendix XIV), by taking concrete steps to build an egalitarian revolutionary movement with explicitly egalitarian revolutionary organizations. Such a movement can indeed remove the rich from power.

APPENDIX I: EXAMPLES OF POSSIBLE EGALITARIAN LAWS

Some say that despite all of the faults of our capitalist society, there is no alternative to it that is both better and realistic. The egalitarian laws ("Notices") indicated at the bottom of this page show this is not true. These laws are imaginary laws written by the imaginary Local Assembly of Egalitarians of Somewhereville, USA. Their purpose is simply to make a bit more concrete what the possibilities are when egalitarians are finally in power. Egalitarianism means that egalitarians are free to pass and enforce great laws such as these.

These Notices are in the approximate chronological order that they might have been written, stating general principles first and then applying them more specifically.

The footnoted links below are to online PDF files with one Notice per page. Below I have printed the same Notices. You are welcome to make copies and use them as you wish.

Notice #1[183] (announcing the first Assembly meeting, who's invited)
Notice #1.5 [184](The Golden Rule is the Basic Law)
Notice #2[185] (Gentrification is Illegal)
Notice #3[186] (Squatting is Legal)

---

[183] http://media.wix.com/ugd/20615e_9e6e5749f5144202962820b6f6ae4231.pdf

[184] http://media.wix.com/ugd/20615e_cfe38969f98c41b5ae37bcb0ad101cf1.pdf

[185] https://media.wix.com/ugd/20615e_0c127435f67f4fcabee04c1b1491f08e.pdf

[186] http://media.wix.com/ugd/20615e_9fa634e605d84d96bca9e3a53c8ccd56.pdf

Notice #4[187] (Public Transportation is Free)
Notice #5[188] (All Health Care is Free)
Notice #6[189] (School Policies Are Set Only by those who Reside or Work in Somewhereville)
Notice #7[190] (All Education, pre-K through PhD, is Free)
Notice #8[191] (Entrepreneurs Get What they Need for Free)
Notice #9[192] (There Are No Taxes)
Notice #10[193] (There Are No Politicians Any Longer--this explains 'voluntary federation')
Notice #11[194] (Somewhereville Decides With What Other Egalitarian Communities to Share Goods and Services According to Reasonable Need and Desire--explaining the 'sharing economy')
Notice #12[195] (Somewhereville Decides Its Own Foreign Policy)
Notice #13[196] (Workplaces are Democracies where All Have an Equal Say)
Notice #14[197] (Mr. John D. Hog is Not in Good Standing)

---

[187] http://media.wix.com/ugd/20615e_8606eb6ec5644fab84c0a90533f00df2.pdf

[188] http://media.wix.com/ugd/20615e_638f63d0ba564f268a8c1bdc7634d513.pdf

[189] http://media.wix.com/ugd/20615e_c316664fa2444c528d3f7c315a64199d.pdf

[190] http://media.wix.com/ugd/20615e_88608426e65c430192e6a1376301f35b.pdf

[191] http://media.wix.com/ugd/20615e_531d8c6b723a43f5b27019d42f6e45b8.pdf

[192] http://media.wix.com/ugd/20615e_2fe8e4de307f429b936a4e365466e228.pdf

[193] http://media.wix.com/ugd/20615e_fd521de8c3db421289e355076f683a1a.pdf

[194] http://media.wix.com/ugd/20615e_2e28ad4d872e4e629002d63e7794be2a.pdf

[195] http://media.wix.com/ugd/20615e_0f115640dffb4175bf311a71b61b1e79.pdf

[196] http://media.wix.com/ugd/20615e_4f99ff638da34493abc890ea1caee4de.pdf

[197] http://media.wix.com/ugd/20615e_bd398ef557df4815a787616b1ff26bc3.pdf

Notice #15[198] (Somewhereville Will Not Share with Greedyville--explaining more about the 'sharing economy.')
Notice #16[199] (It's Officially "Reasonable" to Work a Bit Less)
Notice #17[200] (A Good Reputation, Not High Profits, Is the Basis for Being in Good Standing)
Notice #18[201] (Involuntary Unemployment is Abolished)
Notice #19[202] (The Local Assembly Alone Decides How Land and
Buildings in Somewhereville Shall be Used)
Notice #20[203] (Retirement)
Notice #21[204] (Parental Leave and Child Day Care)
Notice #22[205] (Membership in the sharing economy is voluntary)

---

[198] http://media.wix.com/ugd/20615e_980fa6ef967543a9a5389f26f3a9057d.pdf

[199] http://media.wix.com/ugd/20615e_af734033c035413a9eefd8a5825047a3.pdf

[200] http://media.wix.com/ugd/20615e_a64432559a494bcebbfb3ad68e073c63.pdf

[201] http://media.wix.com/ugd/20615e_17cc3fc03d66433cb9b42540a77bcaa6.pdf

[202] http://media.wix.com/ugd/20615e_fbe7ba0376ba4edfacdab6c0f5ca8fa7.pdf

[203] http://media.wix.com/ugd/20615e_1b6ae04dd05e49bbba1a6eb6e28f26c6.pdf

[204] http://media.wix.com/ugd/20615e_5d82d1184d264a50bfba525269254e08.pdf

[205] http://media.wix.com/ugd/20615e_0e01d3684c3245b38c718fe35aeb3a1f.pdf

LOCAL ASSEMBLY
of
SOMEWHEREVILLE EGALITARIANS

NOTICE

The 1st meeting of the Assembly will be July ??, 2014 at the ????

All egalitarians* (and only egalitarians) of Somewhereville are invited and encouraged to attend and participate as equals in writing the ONLY laws that residents of Somewhereville must obey in an egalitarian society.

Agenda: gentrification

*An egalitarian is any person who supports:

- **Equality** (in the sense of "no rich and no poor," not "equal opportunity" to get richer than others) and
- **Mutual Aid** (or **Solidarity**, meaning helping each other, not being pitted against others in competition by an oppressor to control us)

More information: PeopleforDemocraticRevolution@gmail.com   PDRBoston.org/#!jp/c1txi   Jul xx xxxx

LOCAL ASSEMBLY
of
SOMEWHEREVILLE EGALITARIANS

NOTICE

THAT IN AN EGALITARIAN SOMEWHEREVILLE IT WOULD BE THE LAW THAT

The Golden Rule is the Basic Law

It is illegal to infringe upon a person's reasonable right to enjoy, equally with all others, personal safety, well-being, happiness and freedom, except when and to the extent it is necessary to prevent a person from, him or herself, infringing upon this same right of another.

All egalitarians (and only egalitarians) of Somewhereville are encouraged to attend the Local Assembly and participate as equals in writing the ONLY laws that residents of Somewhereville must obey in an egalitarian society. An egalitarian is any person who supports:

- **Equality** (in the sense of "no rich and no poor," not "equal opportunity" to get richer than others) and
- **Mutual Aid** (or **Solidarity**, meaning helping each other, not being pitted against others in competition by an oppressor to control us)

The next meeting of the Assembly will be ?? ??, 201? at the ????

More information: PeopleforDemocraticRevolution@gmail.com   PDRBoston.org

LOCAL ASSEMBLY
of
SOMEWHEREVILLE EGALITARIANS

NOTICE
THAT IN AN EGALITARIAN SOMEWHEREVILLE IT WOULD BE THE LAW THAT

Gentrification is Illegal

Doctors, scientists & professionals are welcome to live in Somewhereville, but:

- No resident in good standing of Somewhereville shall be coerced by economic hardship or any other means into leaving their home in Somewhereville unwillingly.
- Every resident in good standing has an equal right to freely take products from the economy (housing, food, clothing, services, etc.) according to need and reasonable desire, or to receive scarce products equitably rationed according to need.
- A resident is in good standing unless, in the judgment of the Assembly, he/she is unreasonably violating the principle of "from each according to ability, to each according to need." If not in good standing a person may only beg or barter for things.

All egalitarians (and only egalitarians) of Somewhereville are invited and encouraged to attend the Local Assembly and participate as equals in writing the ONLY laws that residents of Somewhereville must obey in an egalitarian society. An egalitarian is any person who supports:
- **Equality** (in the sense of "no rich and no poor," not "equal opportunity" to get richer than others) and
- **Mutual Aid** (or **Solidarity**, meaning helping each other, not being pitted against others in competition by an oppressor to control us)

More information: PeopleforDemocraticRevolution@gmail.com   PDRBoston.org

LOCAL ASSEMBLY
of
SOMEWHEREVILLE EGALITARIANS

NOTICE
THAT IN AN EGALITARIAN SOMEWHEREVILLE IT WOULD BE THE LAW THAT

Squatting is Legal

Any reasonable* number of persons in good standing** who do not otherwise have a safe place to live may live together **for free** in any house or apartment that is safe and not already reasonably used by others as their primary place of residence.

Residential buildings shall be used for shelter, not rental income.

Houses and apartments belong to those who reasonably use them as their primary place of residence, for as long as they do so.

All people in good standing** have no need for rental income or any other money because they have an equal right to freely take products from the economy (housing, food, clothing, services, etc.) according to need and reasonable desire, or to receive scarce products equitably rationed according to need.

* What is reasonable is determined by the local Assembly of Egalitarians***
** All persons are in good standing unless the Assembly determines that, after taking into account the particular circumstances and reasonableness, they are violating the principle of "from each according to ability, to each according to need."
*** Egalitarians are those who support equality (no rich and no poor) and mutual aid.

The next meeting of the Assembly will be ??? ??, 201? at the ????

More information: PeopleforDemocraticRevolution@gmail.com   PDRBoston.org/#ljp/c1txi   Jul xx xxxx

LOCAL ASSEMBLY
of
SOMEWHEREVILLE EGALITARIANS

NOTICE
THAT IN AN EGALITARIAN SOMEWHEREVILLE IT WOULD BE THE LAW THAT

Public Transportation is Free

All persons in good standing* may ride public transportation for free.

People in good standing deserve to ride public transportation for free because the people in good standing, by their work for the economy, collectively produce all public transportation, from building the trains and buses and trolleys, laying the tracks and electric lines, driving and maintaining the vehicles, administering the entire MBTA and providing all goods and services required by those who do the above.

* All persons are in good standing unless the local Assembly of Egalitarians** determines that, after taking into account the particular circumstances and reasonableness, they are violating the principle of "from each according to ability, to each according to need."
** Egalitarians are those who support equality (no rich and no poor) and mutual aid. Only Somewhereville egalitarians may be members of the Local Assembly.

LOCAL ASSEMBLY
of
SOMEWHEREVILLE EGALITARIANS

NOTICE
THAT IN AN EGALITARIAN SOMEWHEREVILLE IT WOULD BE THE LAW THAT

All Health Care is Free

All persons in good standing* may receive all of their health care **for free.**

People in good standing deserve to receive all of their health care—of the highest quality—for free because the people in good standing, by their work for the economy, collectively produce all health care, from building the clinics and hospitals and medical schools and maintaining and cleaning them, growing the food and building the homes and providing the water and electrical service and teaching the K-12 subjects and providing the child care and so on and so forth *ad infinitum* without which there could be no doctors or nurses of clinics or hospitals.

* All persons are in good standing unless the local Assembly of Egalitarians** determines that, after taking into account the particular circumstances and reasonableness, they are violating the principle of "from each according to ability, to each according to need."

** Egalitarians are those who support equality (no rich and no poor) and mutual aid. The next meeting of the Assembly will be ??? ??, 2014 at the ????

More information: PeopleforDemocraticRevolution@gmail.com PDRBoston.org/#ljp/c1txi   Jul xx xxxx

LOCAL ASSEMBLY
of
SOMEWHEREVILLE
EGALITARIANS

NOTICE

THAT IN AN EGALITARIAN SOMEWHEREVILLE IT WOULD BE THE LAW THAT

All Education, pre-K through PhD, is Free

- Any person in good standing may attend school for free, from pre-K through PhD.
- All persons are in good standing unless the Local Assembly of Egalitarians determines that, after taking into account the particular circumstances and reasonableness, they are violating the principle of "from each according to ability, to each according to need."
- Getting an education counts as reasonable work, *i.e.*, contributing according to ability.
- Egalitarians are those who support equality (no rich and no poor) and mutual aid.

The next meeting of the Assembly will be ??? ??, 201? at the ????

More information: PeopleforDemocraticRevolution@gmail.com
PDRBoston.org/#!jp/c1txi   Jul xx xxxx

LOCAL ASSEMBLY
of
SOMEWHEREVILLE EGALITARIANS

NOTICE
THAT IN AN EGALITARIAN SOMEWHEREVILLE IT WOULD BE THE LAW THAT

School Policies Are Set <u>Only</u> by those who Reside or Work in Somewhereville

- As long as schools abide by Local Assembly* laws, the policies of a particular school shall be determined by, and only by, a school assembly open to all the school's teachers, staff, parents of students in the school and adult students in the school (if any).
- The assembly shall operate democratically in a manner of its own choosing with every participant having equal formal status.
- Schools shall promote the egalitarian values of equality and mutual aid, and provide an education that prepares students to help one another and the rest of society to the best of their ability—and to compete against others only for fun in sports, games and contests, <u>not</u> dog-eat-dog competition in the global economy.

*All egalitarians (and only egalitarians) of Somewhereville are encouraged to attend the Local Assembly and participate as equals in writing the ONLY laws that residents of Jamaica Plain must obey in an egalitarian society. An egalitarian is any person who supports:
- **Equality** (in the sense of "no rich and no poor," not "equal opportunity" to get richer than others) and
- **Mutual Aid** (or **Solidarity**, meaning helping each other, not being pitted against others in competition by an oppressor to control us)

The next meeting of the Assembly will be ??? ??, 201? at the ????

More information: PeopleforDemocraticRevolution@gmail.com   PDRBoston.org/#ljp/c1txi   Jul xx xxxx

LOCAL ASSEMBLY
of
SOMEWHEREVILLE EGALITARIANS

NOTICE

THAT IN AN EGALITARIAN SOMEWHEREVILLE IT WOULD BE THE LAW THAT

Entrepreneurs Get What they Need for Free

- An "entrepreneur" is a person with a great idea for producing a new and wonderful product, or for providing a new and wonderful service, or for a new and wonderful way of producing an old product or providing an old service.
- Entrepreneurs will, upon the approval of the Local Assembly, be able to set up shop and carry out their idea, taking **for free** the material things they require from the economy such as a work place, raw materials, etc. This product or service, like all others, shall be free to those in good standing.
- Every person who works reasonably on this project (and takes reasonably from the economy) is in good standing.
- Successful entrepreneurs will be greatly honored!

The next meeting of the Assembly will be ??? ??, 201? at the ????

More information: PeopleforDemocraticRevolution@gmail.com   PDRBoston.org/#ljp/c1txi   Jul xx xxxx

LOCAL ASSEMBLY
of
SOMEWHEREVILLE EGALITARIANS

NOTICE
THAT IN AN EGALITARIAN SOMEWHEREVILLE IT WOULD BE THE LAW THAT

There Are No Taxes

- The government, i.e., the Local Assembly of Somewhereville Egalitarians*, has no need to tax anybody because it has no need for money.
- The Local Assembly needs no money to determine the purposes for which the community's resources shall be used, or to call for volunteers to work on this or that project, or to decide if a person is not in good standing**, or to decide how to equitably ration scarce things, or to send delegates to meet with delegates from other localities to craft large-scale proposals.
- The Local Assembly needs no money to pay wages or salaries because people in good standing may take from the economy whatever they reasonably need or desire for free or receive scarce products equitably rationed according to need.
- An egalitarian society is not based on money, has no rich and no poor, and thus has no need to collect taxes.

* All who support equality (no rich and no poor) and mutual aid are egalitarians; they and only they are equal members of the Assembly.
** A resident is NOT in good standing if, in the judgment of the Assembly, he/she refuses to work or attend school or apprentice training reasonably, or possesses more property or takes more products or services from the economy than is reasonable.

The next meeting of the Assembly will be ??? ??, 201? at the ????

More information: PeopleforDemocraticRevolution@gmail.com   PDRBoston.org/#!jp/c1txi   Jul xx xxxx

LOCAL ASSEMBLY
of
SOMEWHEREVILLE EGALITARIANS

NOTICE
THAT IN AN EGALITARIAN SOMEWHEREVILLE IT WOULD BE THE LAW THAT

There Are No Politicians Any Longer

- Politicians, *i.e.*, people who write, and then command egalitarians* to obey, laws that they (the egalitarians) are not allowed to participate as equals in writing, are no longer needed.
- Laws are written by the Local Assembly of Egalitarians, in which **all** local egalitarians, and only they, are encouraged to participate with equal status democratically.
- The Assembly decides how to enforce the law, and delegates people to do it. The Assembly selects delegates to meet with delegates from other local assemblies (in non-local assemblies) to craft proposals (**not laws!**) for the Assembly to implement or not as it sees fit. Non-local assemblies likewise send delegates to larger-region non-local assemblies to craft larger-region proposals. This is "voluntary federation."

* Egalitarians are those who support equality (no rich and no poor) and mutual aid.

The next meeting of the Assembly will be ??? ??, 201? at the ????

LOCAL ASSEMBLY
of
SOMEWHEREVILLE EGALITARIANS

NOTICE
THAT IN AN EGALITARIAN SOMEWHEREVILLE IT WOULD BE THE LAW THAT

Somewhereville Decides With What Other Egalitarian Communities to Share Goods and Services According to Reasonable Need and Desire

A "sharing economy" is one in which all its members mutually agree to contribute reasonably according to ability, to share non-scarce goods and services for free, and equitably ration scarce things, all according to reasonable need and desire.

The Somewhereville Local Assembly of Egalitarians* may, if, when and on whatever terms it wishes, mutually agree with local assemblies of other communities to participate in a larger-than-local sharing economy, and may unilaterally stop participating whenever it sees fit.

Voluntary federation can facilitate such mutual agreements among **millions** or even **billions** of people.

* Egalitarians are those who support equality (no rich and no poor) and mutual aid.

The next meeting of the Assembly will be ??? ??, 201? at the ????

LOCAL ASSEMBLY
of
SOMEWHEREVILLE EGALITARIANS

NOTICE

THAT IN AN EGALITARIAN SOMEWHEREVILLE IT WOULD BE THE LAW THAT

Somewhereville Decides Its Own Foreign Policy

- The Somewhereville Local Assembly of Egalitarians*, and nobody else, determines whether Somewhereville is at peace with other people or at war with them. Somewhereville egalitarians will decide what course of action best promotes and defends egalitarian values, based on having access to all relevant information and opinions of others.
- If Somewhereville is at war with other people, it will rely on volunteers to join a Military Organization (MO) based on these principles:
    - Rank and file democratic selection (and recall) of all ranks of officers
    - Soldiers either obey the orders of higher-ranking officers or else leave the MO
    - No privileges (other than command) or special insignias for officers
    - The Assembly decides the MO's good standing status**

*Egalitarians are those who support equality (no rich and no poor) and mutual aid. The next meeting of the Assembly will be ??? ??, 201? at the ????

** See PDRBoston.org/#ljp/c1txi for details. Email PeopleforDemocraticRevolution@gmail.com Jul xx xxxx

LOCAL ASSEMBLY
of
SOMEWHEREVILLE EGALITARIANS

NOTICE
THAT IN AN EGALITARIAN SOMEWHEREVILLE IT WOULD BE THE LAW THAT

Workplaces are Democracies where All Have an Equal Say

- All organizations in which people cooperate to produce goods or perform services by working reasonably are democracies. The workers all have an equal say in determining the policies of the organization consistent with laws enacted by the Local Assembly of Egalitarians.*
- If the Assembly says an organization is in good standing then so are all of its workers except any individuals judged by the Assembly to be taking more goods or services from the economy than reasonable. People or organizations in good standing, and only they, can take for free (or receive equitably rationed, in the case of scarcity) goods and services they reasonably need or desire, from the sharing economy**.
- There are no wages or salaries. Being in good standing is all anybody needs to live well.

* Egalitarians are those who support equality (no rich and no poor) and mutual aid.
** "sharing economy" is discussed at PDRBoston.org/#ljp/c1txi
The next meeting of the Assembly will be ??? ??, 201? at the ????

More information: PeopleforDemocraticRevolution@gmail.com   PDRBoston.org/#ljp/c1txi   Jul xx xxxx

LOCAL ASSEMBLY
of
SOMEWHEREVILLE EGALITARIANS

NOTICE
THAT IN AN EGALITARIAN SOMEWHEREVILLE IT WOULD BE THE LAW THAT

Mr. John D. Hog is Not in Good Standing

- The Assembly rules that Mr. John D. Hog is not in good standing. The reason is that he claims to own the entire apartment building at 123 Main Street, in which reside 20 families in separate apartments.
- Not being in good standing, Mr. Hog is not entitled to take for free any product from, or use any service provided by, the sharing economy* that Somewhereville is part of. He is essentially a beggar.
- Each family in an apartment at 123 Main Street owns that apartment for as long as it uses it as its primary place of residence.
- If and when Mr. Hog renounces his claim to own the entire building at 123 Main Street, and works reasonably, the Assembly will consider reinstating him in good standing.

* "sharing economy" is discussed at PDRBoston.org/#ljp/c1txi
The next meeting of the Assembly will be ??? ??, 201? at the ????

More information: PeopleforDemocraticRevolution@gmail.com   PDRBoston.org/#ljp/c1txi   Jul xx xxxx

LOCAL ASSEMBLY
of
SOMEWHEREVILLE EGALITARIANS

NOTICE
THAT IN AN EGALITARIAN SOMEWHEREVILLE IT WOULD BE THE LAW THAT

Somewhereville Will Not Share with Greedyville

- Currently Somewhereville is, by mutual agreement, in a sharing economy with many other communities encompassing approximately two billion people. It has come to the attention of the Somewhereville Assembly, however, that Greedyville, also in this sharing economy, is being unreasonable and not at all acting according to "from each according to ability, to each according to need."
- Therefore, we have notified the non-local assembly of delegates representing the entire sharing economy that if Greedyville is not excluded from our sharing economy then we will leave it.
- The non-local assembly must now facilitate the re-negotiation of a new mutual agreement among all the local assemblies. We will notify you what is eventually agreed upon, and by whom. We hope Greedyville is excluded and not us.

* "sharing economy" is discussed at PDRBoston.org/#ljp/c1txi
The next meeting of the Assembly will be ??? ??, 201? at the ????

More information: PeopleforDemocraticRevolution@gmail.com   PDRBoston.org/#ljp/c1txi   Jul xx xxxx

LOCAL ASSEMBLY
of
SOMEWHEREVILLE EGALITARIANS

NOTICE
THAT IN AN EGALITARIAN SOMEWHEREVILLE IT WOULD BE THE LAW THAT

It's Officially "Reasonable" to Work a Bit Less

- The local assemblies of communities encompassing all of the approximately two billion people in our sharing economy* have mutually agreed (facilitated by proposals crafted by our delegates in many small- to large-region non-local assemblies) that it is reasonable for us all to work a bit—10%--less, because economic productivity is presently more than necessary to satisfy our needs and desires.
- This relaxation of the criteria for "reasonableness" will be reflected in the Somewhereville Local Assembly's determination of the "in good standing" status of economic enterprises and other organizations (such as schools, etc.).
- Enjoy your greater leisure!

* "sharing economy" is discussed at PDRBoston.org/#ljp/c1txi
The next meeting of the Assembly will be ??? ??, 201? at the ????

More information: PeopleforDemocraticRevolution@gmail.com   PDRBoston.org/#ljp/c1txi   Jul xx xxxx

LOCAL ASSEMBLY
of
SOMEWHEREVILLE
EGALITARIANS

NOTICE
THAT IN AN EGALITARIAN SOMEWHEREVILLE IT WOULD BE THE LAW THAT

A Good Reputation, Not High Profits, Is the Basis for Being in Good Standing

- The basis for the Assembly determining that an economic enterprise or organization (such as a school) is in good standing* is primarily its reputation for providing its product or service reasonably, based in turn on the quality of the product or service, how useful or desirable it is, how well it is made available to the appropriate people, etc.
- To judge an organization's reputation, the Assembly currently consults all relevant sources, including the various certification organizations, newspaper reports, and communications from concerned individuals. **Please submit suggestions** how to improve on this.

* People or organizations in good standing, and only they, can take for free (or receive equitably rationed, in the case of scarcity) goods and services they reasonably need or desire, from the sharing economy (discussed at PDRBoston.org/#ljp/c1txi.)

The next meeting of the Assembly will be ??? ??, 201? at the ????

LOCAL ASSEMBLY
of
SOMEWHEREVILLE EGALITARIANS

NOTICE
THAT IN AN EGALITARIAN SOMEWHEREVILLE IT WOULD BE THE LAW THAT

Involuntary Unemployment is Abolished

- Any resident of Somewhereville who sincerely wishes to be in good standing* by acting reasonably according to the principle of "from each according to ability, to each according to need" shall be provided with a mutually agreeable way for him/her to do so.
- If such a person cannot find an economic enterprise or organization (such as a school) of his/her own choosing that agrees to accept him/her as a worker (or student), then the Assembly will either order one to accept him/her, or set him/her up as a new entrepreneur, or grant him/her "good standing" status pending a search for a better solution.

* People or organizations in good standing, and only they, can take for free (or receive equitably rationed, in the case of scarcity) goods and services they reasonably need or desire, from the sharing economy (discussed at PDRBoston.org/#ljp/c1txi.)

The next meeting of the Assembly will be ??? ??, 201? at the ????

More information: PeopleforDemocraticRevolution@gmail.com PDRBoston.org/#ljp/c1txi Jul xx xxxx

LOCAL ASSEMBLY
of
SOMEWHEREVILLE EGALITARIANS

NOTICE
THAT IN AN EGALITARIAN SOMEWHEREVILLE IT WOULD BE THE LAW THAT

The Local Assembly Alone Decides How Land and Buildings in Somewhereville Shall be Used

- The assembled egalitarians of Somewhereville, acting democratically and as equals (nobody is rich or poor), determine how land, buildings and other resources of Somewhereville shall be used.
- People who volunteer to work reasonably to use these resources for the purpose determined by the Assembly thereby satisfy the "from each according to ability" requirement to be in good standing*.
- The organization that uses these resources reasonably for the purpose determined by the Assembly may take for free whatever goods and services it reasonably requires to do so.

* People or organizations in good standing, and only they, can take for free (or receive equitably rationed, in the case of scarcity) goods and services they reasonably need or desire, from the sharing economy (discussed at PDRBoston.org)

The next meeting of the Assembly will be ??? ??, 201? at the ????

More information: PeopleforDemocraticRevolution@gmail.com PDRBoston.org

LOCAL ASSEMBLY
of
SOMEWHEREVILLE
EGALITARIANS

NOTICE
THAT IN AN EGALITARIAN SOMEWHEREVILLE IT WOULD BE THE LAW THAT

RETIREMENT: All People in Good Standing and Meeting the Criteria for Retirement May Retire and Continue to Take Freely (or Receive Equitably Rationed in the Case of Scarcity) All Reasonably Needed or Desired Products and Services From the Economy

- Retirement is voluntary.
- The criteria for retirement (being at least a certain age, and having been in good standing for a certain length of time) are determined by the Local Assembly of Egalitarians*.
- A person is in good standing unless the Local Assembly judges that he/she is either not contributing reasonably according to ability or is taking more products or services from the economy than is reasonably needed or desired.
- A person meeting the criteria for retirement need no longer contribute to the economy to be in good standing.

*An egalitarian is any person who supports:
- **Equality** (in the sense of "no rich and no poor," not "equal opportunity" to get richer than others) and
- **Mutual Aid** (or **Solidarity**, meaning helping each other, not being pitted against others in competition by an oppressor to control us)

All egalitarians (and only egalitarians) of Somewhereville are invited and encouraged to attend the Local Assembly and participate as equals in writing the ONLY laws that residents of Somewhereville must obey in an egalitarian society.

LOCAL ASSEMBLY
of
SOMEWHEREVILLE
EGALITARIANS

NOTICE
THAT IN AN EGALITARIAN SOMEWHEREVILLE IT WOULD BE THE LAW THAT

PARENTAL LEAVE & CHILD DAY CARE: Any Person Who Is the Primary Person Caring for a Child During the Day and is in Good Standing, Or Who is a Member of a Child Day-Care Enterprise that is in Good Standing, May Take Freely (or Receive Equitably Rationed in the Case of Scarcity) All Reasonably Needed or Desired Products and Services From the Economy

- A parent, or a worker in a child day-care enterprise, who provides reasonable child-care during the day satisfies the "contribute reasonably according to ability" requirement to be in good standing.
- A person or enterprise is in good standing unless the Local Assembly of Egalitarians* judges that he/she/it is either not contributing reasonably according to ability or is taking more products or services from the economy than is reasonably needed or desired.

*An egalitarian is any person who supports:
  - **Equality** (in the sense of "no rich and no poor," not "equal opportunity" to get richer than others) and
  - **Mutual Aid** (or **Solidarity**, meaning helping each other, not being pitted against others in competition by an oppressor to control us)

All egalitarians (and only egalitarians) of Somewhereville are invited and encouraged to attend the Local Assembly and participate as equals in writing the ONLY laws that residents of Somewhereville must obey in an egalitarian society.

LOCAL ASSEMBLY
of
SOMEWHEREVILLE EGALITARIANS

NOTICE

THAT IN AN EGALITARIAN SOMEWHEREVILLE IT WOULD BE THE LAW THAT

Individual Membership in the Sharing Economy is Voluntary

- The sharing economy is a mutual agreement among people to work reasonably in the economy according to ability and to take freely (or receive as equitably rationed in the case of scarcity) from the economy according to reasonable need or desire.
- Any person or group of people may choose not to be members of the sharing economy.
- Non-members of the sharing economy may own personal property and as much land and other things as they can, by themselves alone, reasonably use to produce goods and/or services for themselves or to barter with individuals or enterprises in the sharing economy.
- In any economic enterprise, in or outside the sharing economy, all workers have an equal say in decision-making and an equal standard of living: inherently unequal employer-employee relations are not allowed.

*An egalitarian is any person who supports:
  - **Equality** (in the sense of "no rich and no poor," not "equal opportunity" to get richer than others) and
  - **Mutual Aid** (or **Solidarity**, meaning helping each other, not being pitted against others in competition by an oppressor to control us)

All egalitarians (and only egalitarians) of Somewhereville are invited and encouraged to attend the Local Assembly and participate as equals in writing the ONLY laws that residents of Somewhereville must obey in an egalitarian society.

APPENDIX II: EYEWITNESS REPORT OF A LOCAL ASSEMBLY OF EGALITARIANS IN REVOLUTIONARY SPAIN, AROUND 1937

A fascinating eyewitness account, by Gaston Leval, of a local assembly meeting in the rural village of Tamarite de Litera, in the province of Huesca, in the Aragon region of Spain during the Spanish Revolution (1936-9), is available online in the online version of his 365-page book, *Collectives in the Spanish Revolution*, published by Freedom Press, London, 1975[206].

Egalitarian ideas (known as anarchist ideas in Spain at this time) were implemented as people saw fit throughout about half of Spain. In this local assembly meeting two frequently used words are (in Spanish) "Collective" and "individualist." "Collective" is the word that the Spanish people used for what I call (see Chapter Four) the "sharing economy." "Individualist" is the word that the Spanish people used to refer to people who did not wish to belong to the collective. Of note, "individualists" were not hostile to the egalitarian revolution; they were not fascists who hoped General Franco would succeed in crushing the revolution and restoring the

---

[206] https://libcom.org/library/collectives-leval-2 , in which a search for the word "pregonero" will bring you to the beginning of the account

large land owners and big capitalists back to power, and they were not large land owners or big capitalists, all of whom had fled from the village of Tamarite de Litera and would, no doubt, not have been welcomed at the local assembly meeting.

Among the numerous issues addressed and resolved by this assembly meeting were the following:

Whether to let the "individualists" who came to the meeting remain

Whether to replace four comrades in a standing Commission

Who should retain control of the bakehouses being used by some members of the collective who recently left the collective

Whether to ration bread

How many hours per day the potters should be expected to work

Should young girls be taught dressmaking (instead of just being allowed to "waste time gossiping in the street.")

Who should be the new hospital director

How often should the assembly meet

APPENDIX III:

EGALITARIANISM VERSUS THE OTHER "ISMS": SOCIALISM, COMMUNISM, ANARCHISM, LIBERTARIANISM, CAPITALISM

SOCIALISM

Socialism is not a very well defined idea. To the extent that it is defined by the large political parties that call themselves "socialist" and that occasionally win elections and control national governments[207] (in places like France and Greece, for example), it is the idea that the government, as opposed to private individuals, should own the means of production in at least certain industries of the nation, and the workers in these industries should be employees of the state.

Some individuals and small organizations that call themselves "socialist" might define the word differently (although I am not aware of any organization calling itself socialist and supporting egalitarianism as defined here.) In either event, since the word "socialism" is known to most people in the world to mean what

---

[207] https://en.wikipedia.org/wiki/List_of_socialist_states

the large socialist parties that sometimes control national governments mean by the word, and because what they do in the name of "socialism" stinks, I have decided to let these large socialist parties own and define the word "socialism." This is the socialism that I oppose, for reasons discussed below.

Because socialism is not a well-defined idea, it can only be judged by looking at what governments that claim to be socialist actually do. France and Greece, for example, have had governments controlled by Socialist parties on and off during the 20th and 21st centuries. When Socialists come to power, class inequality continues just as before. Capitalists remain a wealthy and powerful class just as before. Workers' strikes are repressed just as before. Society remains as unequal as before.

Socialism appears to be a word that some politicians use merely to get working class votes with a vague promise to "make things better for workers."

Some Communists call themselves Socialists in order to avoid the stigma of Communism's ugly anti-democratic nature that so many people are aware of.

The reason that governments (Socialist or Communist) based on Marxism are so anti-democratic is discussed in Chapter Twelve.

An Open Letter To Socialists [from PDRBoston[208], the revolutionary egalitarian organization I co-founded]

Dear Socialist,

If, as is very likely, you agree with PDR--Boston's egalitarian revolutionary aims, you may wonder how come PDR--Boston says "NO to Socialism." There are two main reasons. You may

---

[208] https://www.pdrboston.org/

think it is for a third reason that is discussed below, but it is not.

Reason #1

The main reason we say No to Socialism is because, for most people in the world, the meaning of the word "socialism" is the meaning that the large socialist parties give to the word by the policies they enact when (as happens now and then) they gain control of a national government. These socialist parties do terrible things. We are about telling people who don't like the things that socialist parties do when in power that we **agree** with them that these things are terrible. We are NOT about telling people that they don't know what socialism "really" means (as if anybody does.)

Socialist parties give socialism the bad reputation that it now **deservedly** has.

The socialist president of France banned demonstrations[209] in solidarity with Palestinians. And the French socialists in parliament voted for a bill that would let the government tap phones and emails[210] without even having to get any judicial permission. People in France are outraged, and opponents of the bill "launched a last ditch campaign against it under the banner: '24 hours before 1984.'" In July of 2016 the working class rose up[211] against anti-worker[212] reforms to French labor law demanded by the socialist government.

---

[209] http://www.dailymail.co.uk/news/article-2697194/Outrage-France-country-world-ban-pro-Palestine-demos.html

[210] https://www.theguardian.com/world/2015/may/05/france-passes-new-surveillance-law-in-wake-of-charlie-hebdo-attack

[211] http://yournewswire.com/media-blackout-as-france-witnesses-biggest-revolution-in-200-years/

[212] http://www.cnn.com/2016/06/02/europe/france-strikes-labor-reform-bill/index.html

The socialist prime minister of Greece in 2009 (Georgios Papandreou, who was the president of the Socialist International since January 2006) insisted banks must be repaid their debts and he therefore promoted austerity[213] measures to do this, thus (understandably!) infuriating the Greek population and causing three quarters of it to demand his resignation.

The gaggle of political parties associated with the word "socialist" include, for example the Greek party, named Syriza, which was[214] "originally founded in 2004 as a coalition of left-wing and radical left parties." Syriza gained enormous support by 2015 because it promised to oppose the draconian austerity that the European banks were insisting the Greek people had to endure. Syriza became the largest party in the Greek parliament and its leader became--and remains as of May 22, 2016--the prime minister.

Then what? The May 22, 2016 *Guardian* newspaper reports[215] under the headline "Greece pushes fresh austerity drive through parliament," that:

> *The Greek parliament has approved a fresh round of austerity incorporating €1.8bn in tax increases – and widely regarded as the most punitive yet – amid hopes the move will lead to much-needed debt relief when eurozone finance ministers meet next week[216].*
>
> *Alexis Tsipras, the prime minister, mustered the support of 152 of his 153 deputies on Sunday to vote through policies that many have previously rejected.*

---

[213] https://en.wikipedia.org/wiki/George_Papandreou

[214] https://en.wikipedia.org/wiki/Syriza

[215] https://www.theguardian.com/world/2016/may/22/greece-to-unveil-fresh-round-of-austerity-to-unlock-bailout-funds

[216] https://www.theguardian.com/world/2016/may/09/eurozone-ministers-to-examine-how-to-ease-greeces-debt-burden

> *Addressing the 300-seat house during the heated three-day debate that preceded the ballot, Giorgos Dimaras, an MP in Tsipras' leftwing party, said he was appalled at being forced to support measures he had spent a lifetime opposing.*
>
> *"I am in mourning," he said. "This is what can only be called wretchedness."*

Socialist parties don't call for removing the rich from power and having no rich and no poor. This is what most people really want. And this is the only way to prevent the rich from continuing to have the real power in society. It is the only way to get off the treadmill of defeat in which people are forever forced to fight the rich for every single crumb we are able to get.

Socialist parties, when they control the government, boss people around in the name of the working class, and people don't like it.

Whatever benefits people have in nations ruled by socialist parties is obtained IN SPITE of the fact that a socialist party is in power, not because of it; these benefits are obtained by people fighting for them and often they have to fight the socialist parties to do so.

Where is the socialist party today that calls for ending wage slavery--the system in which people have to work for an employer (often the government itself when socialists have their way) and obey that employer on the job every bit as much as people have to obey a dictator?

Where is the socialist party today that says there should be real democracy, meaning that the only laws people who support equality and mutual aid have to obey are the ones they themselves (not so-called "representatives") have an equal say in writing in local assemblies (with voluntary federation of local assemblies used to achieve order on a large scale)?

To hear some people defend socialism by pointing to government benefits in socialist nations you'd think these people would call it socialism if the slave-owners in the American slavery era gave the slaves benefits such as good food and housing and "job security" and health care (the way a farmer takes good care of his/her farm animals)! We say, "Forget socialism. We need egalitarianism."

Reason #2

PDR--Boston also disagrees with some important things that practically every person who calls him or herself a socialist agrees with. For example, practically everybody who calls him or herself a socialist believes that the huge numbers of people who oppose same-sex marriage do so because of bigoted ("homophobic") and anti-equality ("reactionary" as some socialists would say) thinking. We believe, on the contrary, that for many people their opposition to same-sex marriage stems from a very reasonable concern for children. Specifically they believe that social laws should promote the opportunity for a child to know and be known by its biological mother and its biological father. They believe that, since a marriage certificate confers formal social approval for a couple to make a child of their own, that therefore making same-sex marriage legal gives formal social approval to same-sex couples to make a child of their own, but the only way such a couple can do that is by third party gamete donation, which means the child will be denied the opportunity to know and be known by its biological father (or mother as the case may be) in a genuine parent/child relationship if-- as is legal today and as is typically the case--the gamete donor remains anonymous.

We call for a mutually respectful discussion of this question among egalitarians, and promote that discussion online[217],

---

[217] https://www.pdrboston.org/conception-of-children-1

where we propose making same-sex marriage legal only when anonymous gamete donation is illegal and anybody who deliberately conceives a child with their gamete must, by law, at the time of conception genuinely intend to be fully in the life of the child as its co-primary (with the other biological parent) parent, regardless of any marriage or non-marriage status.

PDR--Boston believes that very good and well-intentioned people who are genuine egalitarians can disagree about whether the psychological harm to a child caused by being deprived of knowing and being known by its biological father (or mother) is sufficiently harmful to be a reason to ban same-sex marriage. Before penicillin was available to cure syphilis, most people, because of a concern for the child such a marriage might produce, agreed that being infected with syphilis was a reason to make it illegal for a person to marry, which is why most states used to require a blood test to get a marriage certificate. Virtually everybody agrees that siblings should not be allowed to marry because of the potential harm to the children such a couple might produce. Nobody says this former ban on syphilis-infected marriage or the ban on sibling marriage stems from bigotry against people infected with syphilis, or bigotry ("sibling-phobia"?) against siblings, or opposition to equality. Likewise, it does not follow that concern for a child's right not to be deliberately denied the opportunity to know and be known by its biological mother and father stems from bigotry or opposition to equality.

The fact that a very large proportion of people who call themselves socialists view huge numbers of good and decent people as awful people simply because these good and decent people have a genuine concern for the welfare of children and believe that the welfare of children trumps the desires of adults--well, this makes us want to distance ourselves from the word "socialism."

Another topic on which PDR--Boston disagrees with an opinion held by very many people in the "socialist camp" is this. We think that racial discrimination against blacks and Hispanics is a) rampant (socialists would agree here) and b)

NOT a benefit to those ("white") working class people who are not discriminated against. The "socialist camp" disagrees. It refers to racial discrimination against blacks and Hispanics as "white privilege," which means something that benefits whites (the word "privilege" means a benefit.) We on the contrary say that "An Injury to One is an Injury to All" as discussed here[218].

Reason #3 is NOT why we don't call ourselves socialists.

The reason we do not call ourselves socialists is NOT that we believe some things that socialists stand for but we are reluctant or afraid to say so openly. The most radical things that some socialists (you, perhaps?) stand for are the very things that we say most prominently and clearly to the public. We are for revolution. We are for having no rich and no poor. We are for abolishing the system of wage slavery and class inequality altogether. We are for a society based not on money with its buying and selling but rather based on sharing according to need among those who contribute reasonably according to ability (Note that we **disagree** with Karl Marx on this point. Marx argued[219] that society could NOT be based on "from each according to his ability, to each according to his need" until "a higher phase of communism" is reached when "all the springs of co-operative wealth flow more abundantly," in other words far FAR in the future. We say it can be done now, and in fact was done in 1936-9 in about half of Spain to a very large degree (when peasants and workers acted on the basis of revolutionary non-Marxist ideas and the economy's level of productivity was quite primitive compared to today.)

We strongly encourage you to think about the very serious problems that come from calling oneself a socialist.

---

[218] http://newdemocracyworld.org/culture/race2.html

[219] https://www.marxists.org/archive/marx/works/1875/gotha/ch01.htm

Unless you go around telling everybody, "No, socialism doesn't mean what you and millions of others think it means" and people **believe** you (not always the case!), then you are pretty much guaranteeing that most people will believe that you support terrible, in fact oppressive, governments as long as they have a socialist president or prime minister. Calling yourself a socialist amounts to telling huge numbers of good and decent people that you think they are nothing but a bunch of homophobic anti-equality bigots. It amounts to telling white working class people that racism benefits them and (as they naturally infer) that "anti-racism" is code for "anti-white." (The ruling class is delighted that socialists do this, as discussed here[220] and here[221].)

If you are for egalitarianism, you belong in PDR--Boston!

COMMUNISM

Chapter Twelve is about why Communists create such ugly anti-democratic regimes in which, as George Orwell so famously put it in his Animal Farm, *"Some animals are more equal than others."*

The fundamentally elitist thinking behind Communism is discussed in the online article "The Communist Manifesto is Wrong."[222]

---

[220] http://newdemocracyworld.org/culture/white.html

[221] http://media.wix.com/ugd/20615e_f48e4aa2d79c49e1bcc8da9013af189d.pdf

[222] http://newdemocracyworld.org/old/manifesto.htm

Of note in regard to Communism is the online article "The U.S. Armed the Soviet Union During the 'Cold War'"[223]

Communism (with a capital C) is a theory developed by Karl Marx about how society will inevitably eventually become what Marx called a communist (with a small "c") society. There is a huge difference between **C**ommunism and **c**ommunism. Small c communism is a classless society in which, by definition, class inequality is abolished. Small c communism is based on the principle, "From eac__h__ according to ability, to each according to need." This phrase was first published[224] by the French utopian Étienne-Gabriel Morelly in 1775, 43 years before Karl Marx was even born, and it is a principle that had been cherished by many people going as far back in time at least to the early Christians [Acts 4: 32-36]; Karl Marx, however, insisted--wrongly!--that society could ***not*** be based on this principle until the "higher phase of communist society" was attained.

An egalitarian society and the small c communist society that Big C Communists hope one day to achieve in the far distant future (by means of social engineering to make people very different from how they are today) are essentially the same thing. But the way that egalitarians aim to make an egalitarian society is vastly different from the way the Communists aim to do it--so different that egalitarianism and Communism are, in theory and in practice, hostile to each other today.

The conflict between egalitarianism and Communism stems from their having diametrically opposite views of ordinary people as they are today. Egalitarians understand that most ordinary people value equality (in the sense of no rich and no poor, not in the sense of "equal opportunity" to get richer than others), mutual aid (people helping each other) and

---

[223] http://newdemocracyworld.org/war/sutton1.html

[224] https://en.wikipedia.org/wiki/From_each_according_to_his_ability,_to_each_according_to_his_needs

democracy (people having an equal say in decisions) and try to shape the small corner of the world over which they have any real control with these values. Egalitarians believe that an egalitarian society will come into being because it is what most people want. Egalitarianism means shaping society on a large scale by the same values with which most people today are already trying to shape the little corner of the world over which they have any real control.

Communists (based on the writings of Karl Marx[225]), in stark contrast, believe that most ordinary people care only about their self-interest, that they "think with their belly" and have no desire for a classless society based on equality and mutual aid and democracy. Communists have a thoroughly negative view of most ordinary people as they are today, that they are "dehumanized by capitalism," that they are as selfish as capitalists, that they are "racist" and "homophobic," and "complicit" in the crimes of the ruling class.

But Communists still believe that a classless society is inevitable one day and that it will happen because of the working class's leading role in history. This "working class," however, is not flesh and blood real individuals that exist today but rather a purely abstract conception. How does this abstract "working class" usher in a small c communist society if it is made up of people for whom that goal is the last thing on their minds? Here's how it works in Marxist "science."

Communists believe in something like Adam Smith's "invisible hand."[226] Adam Smith said that people acting in their self-interest resulted in a better world for everybody even though they did not care about or even think about making a better world for everybody. Thus the baker who only thinks of making a profit provides bread for all, and the candlestick maker who only cares about making a profit provides candlesticks for

---

[225] http://newdemocracyworld.org/revolution/socialism.html

[226] https://en.wikipedia.org/wiki/Invisible_hand

all, *etc.* The Communists similarly argue that people acting only in their self-interest leads to something good happening to society despite it not being the subjective aim of anybody.

But whereas Adam Smith thought that capitalism itself was what made something good for society happen, Marx said that the thing that was good for society, that would happen as a result of people acting in their self interest, was the ending of capitalism and its replacement by small c communism. How this happens is what Marx's supposed "science" of social development is all about. It is all based on impersonal economic laws that assume everybody acts only in their self-interest: the capitalist's self interest being to maximize profits and the worker's conflicting self-interest being to get a higher wage.

The Communists say that people acting in their self-interest will lead inevitably to a crisis in capitalism that will prevent capitalism from increasing economic productivity as it had initially done; and this will lead to Socialism (*i.e.*, the working class, which Marx views as an abstract force of history, taking over society) and this in turn will enable economic production to continue to increase so that one day in the far off future there will no longer be any scarcity; and when scarcity is eliminated then, and only then, will it be possible for Communists to socially engineer people to be fundamentally different and better than they are today so they will accept small c communism. As the Marxist Che Guevara says in his "Socialism and Man in Cuba"[227]:

> *"To build communism it is necessary, simultaneous with the new material foundations, to build the new man and woman."*

Communists believe that small c communism will come not because it is what most people **today** want, but rather in spite of the fact that it is NOT what most people today want. This is

---

[227] https://www.marxists.org/archive/guevara/1965/03/man-socialism.htm

why Communists are so anti-democratic. Communists fear democracy because they think most people do not want what the Communists want. Communists think that the way to achieve small c communism is to have power exclusively in the hands of the Communist Party (whose members are trained in the science of Marxism and who will, in the name of an abstract "working class," work to hasten the impersonal laws of economic development[228] by increasing economic productivity to end scarcity so that one day people will accept small c communism.[229])

Communists think that increasing economic productivity is the crucial task today. And because they think that people act only in their self-interest, Communists think that the way to increase economic productivity is with a combination of the stick, *i.e.,* authoritative control over workers by a strong central government (controlled by the Communist Party) and the carrot, *i.e.,* letting some get much richer than others if they produce (or make workers produce) more. This explains why the Chinese Communist Party is promoting capitalist billionaires and factories with brutal sweatshop conditions for workers. Lenin did similar things in the Soviet Union, and likewise Stalin.

Egalitarians, in stark contrast, think that the way to achieve a classless society (*i.e.,* egalitarianism) is to help the vast majority of people today **who already want an egalitarian society** to act together (using voluntary federation of

---

[228] An example of how Marxism is about hastening impersonal laws of economic development even when this means supporting extremely oppressive capitalist rulers is Karl Marx's 1853 letter [https://www.marxists.org/archive/marx/works/1853/06/25.htm] declaring that British imperialism in India, despite its cruelty, was necessary in order to bring about the "social revolution" that India needed.

[229] The notion that scarcity has to be abolished before most people will share--on the basis of "From each according to ability, to each according to need" with scarce things equitably rationed--is just flat out wrong. This wrong notion comes from the elitist view of ordinary people held by Marxism--that ordinary people only think with their belly and are motivated only by self-interest. It is a disgusting view of working class people, and it is why Marxist regimes are always so anti-democratic.

egalitarians and only of egalitarians) to make society egalitarian, and to prevent anti-egalitarians from stopping them.

Chapter Eight[230] in Dave Stratman's *We CAN Change the World,* titled "From Marx to Lenin," is about the relationship between Marxism and Leninism; it shows how the anti-democratic practice of Lenin was in fact the practical application of Marxist theory, not a deviation from it.

ANARCHISM

The nineteenth century writers, Mikhail Bakunin[231] and Peter Kropotkin[232], advocated a vision of society with no government and no class inequality; they called their vision anarchism. While numerous other writers have also called themselves anarchists and have advocated having no government, they did not all envision an end to class inequality and some envisioned capitalism minus government.

The Spanish Revolution of 1936-39 (often called the "Spanish Civil War") was inspired by the writings of Bakunin and Kropotkin. In the decades leading up to the revolution, workers and peasants in huge numbers were reading (or, since many were illiterate, having people read to them) books by these authors. The vision these authors wrote about was essentially the same as what we now call egalitarianism. In a part of Spain with approximately four million people, large numbers of workers and peasants described themselves as anarchists, and they made this part of Spain very close to egalitarian.

---

[230] http://www.newdemocracyworld.org/old/Revolution/WCCTW-Ch8.htm

[231] https://en.wikipedia.org/wiki/Mikhail_Bakunin

[232] https://en.wikipedia.org/wiki/Peter_Kropotkin

What, then, is the difference between egalitarianism and anarchism? To answer this question, let us first speak only of the anarchism that inspired the Spanish Revolution, and not the numerous other ideas that are advocated by people who have in the past, or do today, call themselves anarchists.

The difference between egalitarianism and Spanish-Revolution-Anarchism is not about the vision but rather about the way to achieve it. The Spanish Revolution was defeated by the fascist General Franco (with overt help from Hitler, indirect help from other so-called "democratic" governments such as the United States, and sabotage of the anarchists by Stalin.) There was an important weakness in Spanish-Revolution-Anarchism theory that enabled its enemies to defeat it. This weakness concerns the Spanish-Revolution-Anarchist misunderstanding of governmental power.

To understand this anarchist misunderstanding of power it helps to be familiar with the Spanish Revolution, so here's a brief account of it. In early 1936 Spain was the Republic of Spain with an elected government of liberal pro-capitalist politicians. Capitalists and large landowners oppressed workers and peasants severely. Very large numbers of workers and peasants were anarchists and the largest labor union was anarchist. In 1936 the fascist General Franco launched a military attack on the government to overthrow it and ruthlessly repress the workers and peasants whose movement was growing increasingly revolutionary. The Republican government, fearing its own workers and peasants as much as it feared Franco, refused to give arms to the anarchists who wanted to defeat Franco. But in Barcelona the anarchists seized arms and defeated the Franco forces in that city. The anarchists then led a social revolution in a large part of Spain (with a population of about four million people) that, with variations in different regions and villages, essentially removed the capitalist and landlord class from power and allowed peasants and workers to begin creating an egalitarian society. This part of Spain was known as Republican Spain, as opposed to the part where Franco was in power.

Initially, right after the anarchists defeated the fascist forces in Barcelona, their power in that city and its entire province of Catalonia was unchallenged. The anarchists could easily have established a government that would have explicitly defended egalitarianism from the anti-egalitarian forces, and they could have done this in the larger region of Republican Spain. But they did not. The reason they didn't was because the anarchists had a theory that said that all governmental power was bad. This was a huge error in anarchist theory that resulted in the defeat of egalitarianism in Spain.

In the absence of an egalitarian government defending egalitarianism in the part of Spain where the anarchist-led social revolution was happening, the anti-egalitarian forces there were able to, and did indeed, set up an anti-egalitarian government (it was the "Spanish Republic") that attacked egalitarianism; in particular it tried to define the goal of the people in Republican Spain as merely to defend the old liberal rule of capitalists and big landowners against fascism. The anti-egalitarians were the capitalists and landlords and their politician allies, as well as Communists sent by Stalin to Spain, and some (but not all) Communist followers of Leon Trotsky.

The anarchists were confused about what to do and in this confusion they ended up collaborating with the anti-egalitarian government (known now as The Republic). The defeat of egalitarianism in Spain was due largely to this huge mistake.

If the anarchists had created a government to defend egalitarianism, they would have had a much better chance of defeating the anti-egalitarian forces of General Franco and others. The reason is this. The anti-egalitarian government did everything it could to suppress and hide the egalitarian aims of the people fighting General Franco's fascist attack on egalitarians. The more the anti-egalitarian government succeeded in this effort, the harder it was for people in the parts of Spain controlled by Franco to see why they should support the anarchist revolutionaries, and the easier it was for

General Franco to enlist them in his army to attack the anarchists. General Franco relied heavily on recruits for his army from the Spanish Protectorate of Morocco. The Moroccans wanted independence from Spain. If Republican Spain had been Egalitarian Spain instead, then it would have told the Moroccans, "The fascists want to keep Morocco a protectorate of Spain, but we--the egalitarians--want no such thing because we are for voluntary federation. Join us in defeating the fascists." But the opposite happened. Republican Spain told the Moroccans, "We intend to keep Morocco a protectorate of Spain," which amounted to telling them, "So you have no particular reason for supporting us against General Franco." This is a major reason why General Franco was able to recruit soldiers and defeat the egalitarians.

A group of Spanish anarchists came to understand this error of Spanish- Revolutionary-Anarchism and tried to correct it, but it was too late to succeed. This group of Spanish anarchists called themselves the "Friends of Durruti Group"[233] after Buenaventura Durruti who was a much beloved, inspiring and courageous anarchist leader who had been killed in November of 1936, shortly after the revolution broke out.

Egalitarianism today, learning from this mistake of Spanish-Revolution-Anarchism, advocates a government (based on voluntary federation (described in Chapter Four) of local assemblies of egalitarians) to defend egalitarianism from anti-egalitarianism. This key point is what Chapter Seven ("Why Should Only Egalitarians Make the Laws?") is all about.

What about anarchism today? Today in the United States there are people who call themselves anarchists and who may even agree with the vision of egalitarianism, but who disagree with egalitarians about how to achieve it. Some of these people have a very wrong, negative view of ordinary people; they simply fail to appreciate that most ordinary people would love to live in an egalitarian society. Due to this failure, these

---

[233] http://www.spunk.org/texts/places/spain/sp001780/

anarchists think of themselves as being very different from (better than!) most people--different in the sense of having different values from most people and in having aspirations for an egalitarian society that are not shared by people who don't call themselves anarchists. Some of these anarchists even glorify this supposed difference between them and non-anarchists by calling themselves "a minority within a minority within a minority" or "Satanists" or other such things that are intended to shout out to the public, "We're not like you!" For an example of self-described "anarchists" referring to themselves as "Satanist" and as "a minority within a minority within a minority" read the article on page 4 of the Prison Action News Zine[234] by "Dark Desyre Zine Network, which begins:

> *"We are a radical anarchist collective of GLBTQ individuals who also self-identify as Satanist, Lucifarian, Setian, Gothic Witch, Dark Pagan. We are heterodox and thus eclectic with various antimonion and left hand path strains. We are anti-racist, anti-fascist and severely opposed to these and all other forms of cultural intolerance. As a minority within a minority within a minority we know the human-primate craves social intercourse and seek, via a zine network, to buffer the pain of isolation, provide a forum for expression and free exchange of ideas, through aiding in both individual and collective augmentation and evaluation."*

Anarchists who think this way have contempt for ordinary people and therefore, **despite** their wanting an egalitarian society, are as likely to help bring about an egalitarian society as Bill Gates or Dick Cheney. The contrast between anarchists who declare themselves to be "a minority within a minority within a minority" and the Spanish Revolutionary anarchists is revealed by the fact that when the Spanish Revolutionary anarchist leader, Buenaventura Durruti, died, "over a half million people[235] filled the streets to accompany

---

[234]   https://bostonanarchistblackcross.files.wordpress.com/2014/02/pan_7-1_screen.pdf

[235] https://en.wikipedia.org/wiki/Buenaventura_Durruti

the cortege during its route to the Montjuïc cemetery" in Barcelona when the total population of Barcelona at this time was only 1.1 million![236]

Some of these modern-day "minority within a minority within a minority" anarchists believe that the way to get non-anarchists to become anarchists is by supporting people (non-anarchists) in their struggles (*e.g.*, organizing strike support for workers where one is not personally employed, or helping to lead a strike or union drive or related action where one is employed) and, while doing so, telling the workers, "I am an anarchist" so they will see that anarchists are good people. Such anarchists fail to do what is most important, however, which is talking to people in struggles about how egalitarian revolution is the shaping of society on a large scale by the very same values of equality and mutual aid that motivate these people to engage in their struggles in the first place. This failure, again, stems from a failure to understand that most people already share and try to act upon the values that define egalitarianism.

This weakness of modern anarchism seems to reflect the influence of Marxism's negative view of ordinary people (discussed above in the section on Communism) on anarchists, which is ironic because anarchists vehemently reject the anti-democratic **practice** of Marxists.

In conclusion, egalitarianism is very similar to Spanish Revolutionary Anarchism as modified by the Spanish anarchists in the Friends of Durruti Group. But the word "anarchism" refers to so many other ideas about how society should be and how to make it that way that there is little to be gained by using that word, which is why I use the word "egalitarianism."

---

[236] http://libcom.org/library/population-spain-its-distribution

LIBERTARIANISM

Libertarianism is capitalism with minimal government. The focus of libertarianism is on why there should be only minimal government and what it should be limited to doing (protecting the nation from foreign attack and enforcing contractual agreements.)

There is nothing in the philosophy of libertarianism that challenges capitalism or that challenges the class inequality that is inherent in capitalism.

Libertarians emphasize individual freedom, meaning freedom from government coercion and freedom from aggressive violence from any other person. They emphasize the importance of people having no obligations except those agreements made with others freely and by mutual agreement, voluntarily. So how does class inequality arise from this?

Class inequality arises from this libertarian kind of society because a) there is no limit on how much property (including the means of production) an individual (or group of individuals) may own, and b) this libertarian society is based on buying and selling things (with money) in a free market. If one imagines such a libertarian society in which, initially, all individuals are equal with respect to the amount of wealth they own, it is not hard to see how a capitalist class and a working class will inevitably emerge. Here is why.

Some people are lucky and others unlucky. One person's house burns down and another person's doesn't. One person has good crops and another one has crop failures. What happens? The unlucky person, quite voluntarily, must make a deal with a lucky person to get out of a hard spot. The lucky person is in the driver's seat, able to take advantage of the hardship of the unlucky person. The result is that the lucky person comes out the winner, the unlucky person the loser;

the lucky person gets wealthier and the unlucky person poorer. Wealth inequality inevitably emerges because there is nothing in the libertarian morality that prevents it from emerging.

Likewise, some people have many siblings and others none. The "only child" inherits more than the child with many siblings. More wealth inequality develops.

By countless means, some become wealthier than others. The wealthier ones thereby have more power and can take advantage of more opportunities. Eventually they buy more means of production, while the unlucky ones are forced to sell their means of production (land, tools, etc.) to make do in hard times. Wealth begets more wealth. The rich get richer, the poor get poorer. Nothing in libertarianism prevents this. Full-blown class inequality inevitably emerges. Libertarians do not consider this a problem. As long as the government is minimal and nobody uses violence to coerce anybody and all contractual agreements (enforced by the government with violence when necessary) are entered into voluntarily, then all is well according to libertarians. But class inequality is not ok according to egalitarians.

For a little fictional story that illustrates how class inequality develops inevitably in a pure libertarian society, see "Libertaria: a Libertarian Paradise" in Chapter Two (Why Have No Rich And No Poor?).

CAPITALISM

I tried to find a real live capitalist to debate me in public on the resolution, "We should remove the rich from power and have no rich and no poor." Having failed to find a willing capitalist, I wrote how I imagined the debate might have gone, in "We

Debate Mr. Billionaire," online[237] *for your amusement and edification.*

Capitalism can exist in many forms, from those with minimal government intervention (which is libertarianism) to those in which the government plays a very large role (*e.g.*, what exists in countries like Sweden, sometimes called "welfare state" capitalism) and those somewhere in between. **In all cases, however, capitalism is a system of class inequality.**

This inequality arises from the five defining features of capitalism:

1) that virtually all of the means of economic production (farm land, mines, factories, commercial-use buildings such as warehouses and office buildings and retail stores, intellectual property such as computer software, *etc.*) are owned as the personal property of individuals or of groups of individuals (*e.g.*, as a corporation) but **not owned by society as a whole**;

2) that whoever owns the means of production, and only they, own the products or services that are produced with those means of production (typically by many people--the hired workers--who do not own the means of production[238]);

3) that economic products and services are commodities that are bought and sold by individuals (or groups of individuals) in the "free market" as an exchange of equal value (of the commodity) for an equal value (of money);

4) that society is based on the belief that it is both innate human nature and also morally right for people to try to

---

[237] https://www.pdrboston.org/mr-billionaire

[238] The problem of class inequality remains even if the workers in a capitalist economic enterprise are the only owners of it, as discussed in my online article, "Why Cooperative Businesses Are Not the Answer" at http://newdemocracyworld.org/revolution/coops.html .

increase their personal wealth as much as possible (by making a profit by buying low and selling or renting high) and to become richer than other people; the argument for this "morality" asserts that when everybody acts in their self-interest this way the result is (via Adam Smith's famous "invisible hand"[239]) that everybody in society benefits; and

5) that money is, and ought to be, power because virtually everything can be bought, not only material things but also the obedience of people (hiring an employee means buying their obedience for certain hours of the day.)

Here is how class inequality inevitably arises and increases in any capitalist society. Even if one imagines a capitalist society starting out with everybody equal in terms of their personal wealth, inequality in wealth will inevitably emerge merely because of facts such as that some people are lucky and others unlucky (one person's house burns down and another's doesn't, one person has a crop failure and another doesn't) and some people have many siblings and inherit very little while others are an only-child and inherit more, *etc. etc.*, as discussed in the section on libertarianism above. This wealth inequality means that the society will eventually have three kinds of people:

#1) Capitalists: those who own means of production on a scale so large that the productive use of them requires the labor of those who do not own them.

#2) Workers: those who do not own sufficient means of production (or, typically, any means of production) with which to provide for themselves (directly or by trade) enough to live satisfactorily and who therefore either sell their labor to capitalists for wages in order to obtain money to buy what they need to live, or rely on public welfare or private charity. (Government employees are workers whose employer is the

---

[239] https://en.wikipedia.org/wiki/Invisible_hand

capitalist class as a whole, which uses the government for its collective needs.)

#3) Small business owners: those who own sufficient means of production with which to provide for themselves (directly or by trade) enough to live by using only their own labor, but who do not own enough means of production that would require the labor of others to be productive. (Self-employed professionals such as doctors and lawyers are a kind of small business owner. Their "means of production" is their education and office and books, *etc.*, and their "product" is the service for which their clients pay them.)

(Defenders of capitalism don't like to talk about how capitalists **actually** came to own so many of the means of production in the first place, preferring to say, "They bought them fair and square." But if one asks, "How did the person they bought them from come to own them?" and work backwards in history this way, it usually turns out that the first private owner of the means of production seized them violently from people who used them but did not consider them to be anybody's private property. Early feudal lords seized land violently from the tillers of the land. European upper class people seized land from the natives in the New World and in other colonies in Africa and Asia, and forced "not-so-lucky" people (indentured servants, slaves, prisoners, *etc.*) to work the land. Capitalism is based on ruthless violence; it is not "natural.")

Capitalists grow richer than workers because in any capitalist business only the capitalists own the commodity produced by the workers; hence only the capitalists possess the money obtained from selling the commodity, and only the capitalists have a say in determining how much, if any, of the profit (the sale price of the commodities minus their cost of production) goes to the workers and how much to the capitalists. The "admirable" (in the morality of capitalism) reason the capitalists go into business in the first place is to get richer, so it is not likely that they would take for themselves less of the profits than possible by, say, sharing their profits with their workers or, say, freely sharing their commodities with others according to need rather than selling them for their full value to obtain the maximum profit.

Small business owners cannot grow rich the way capitalists can because they can only produce a very limited amount of commodities (in a retail store the commodity is the service of making a product conveniently available to the customer) with only their own labor, and hence can obtain only a very limited amount of profit from their sale, compared with a capitalist who can profit from the sale of an enormous amount of commodities produced by the labor of many other workers.

Not only do capitalists grow richer than workers, they also are, in a very real sense, masters in a master versus "wage-slave" relationship with workers. When a worker accepts a job from a capitalist he or she must agree to obey the "on-the-job" commands of the capitalist or else be fired. Within the capitalist business there is not even a pretense of democracy--it is an overt dictatorship of the owners over the workers.

The result of the above is that capitalists gain greater power in society than workers because they grow richer and because money in a capitalist society is power, and capitalists also have direct power over workers "on the job." Based on these sources of unequal power and privilege, capitalists form a dominating upper class over the working class. Capitalists use their greater amount of money than workers have to achieve yet more power and then use that power to obtain yet more money (for example, by controlling the government and using it to enrich themselves in countless ways, and by pitting working class people against each other to prevent them from being united in solidarity against the capitalist class.) A capitalist society is thus a society in which there is always a class war between the capitalists trying to maintain or even increase their unequal (compared to workers) wealth and power and privilege versus workers trying to make society more equal and democratic and based on people helping each other.

To prevent workers from making society more equal and democratic, the capitalist class needs to use a combination of a) cowing workers into submission, b) pitting workers against each other so as to divide-and-rule them, and c) making workers believe that they are, in some way, inferior human beings who do not deserve to live as well and have as much say in society as capitalists (one way of doing this is by treating working class people like dirt, as discussed in Chapter Two).

Many of the worst aspects of our present society stem from capitalists doing these kinds of things, such as 1) using standardized "high stakes" tests in public schools that have--by design--a built-in failure rate so that no matter how well children learn their lessons the failure rate will be what the test-makers want it to be, the purpose of which is to make working class children believe they are not smart enough, or didn't study hard enough, to deserve a decent-paying job; 2) waging Orwellian wars of social control based on lies (*e.g.,* Saddam's "Weapons of Mass Destruction") in order to make ordinary people believe that it is unpatriotic not to obey their capitalist rulers (*i.e.*, the politicians who are beholden to the capitalist class), 3) making workers of different races mistrust and fear one another and 4) forcing workers to work for lower wages by telling them that if they don't the company will hire other workers (often foreigners) who will work for those lower wages.

Appendix IV: THE FLYER WE GIVE TO PEOPLE WHO SAY THE PDR BUTTON'S MESSAGE IS A GOOD IDEA

The flyer is shown below. A pdf version is online[240] and you are welcome to download and print it, handwrite local contact information on it, and make copies to hand out.

---

[240] https://media.wix.com/ugd/20615e_33a870daa4784f8da8b999a8060fdf68.pdf

THANK YOU FOR WEARING THE PDR BUTTON

OR PINNING IT TO YOUR BACKPACK OR PURSE, IF NOT AT WORK THEN ELSEWHERE

We invite you now to do a simple experiment. Ask random ordinary people you encounter during the course of your day—at work or school or while doing errands—"What do you think of what my button says? Good idea or bad idea?" (You have to ask people because most people just ignore buttons otherwise.)

It may surprise you, but most people will say it's a good idea, or even a great idea. See for yourself!

But most people will also say "It's impossible; it can never happen because hardly anybody else wants it to."

This is exactly what the billionaire class wants people to think. This is why the rich who own and control the mass AND alternative media censor all expressions of support for the button's message; it's to make people feel hopeless and think that resistance is futile. This is how the rich remain in power.

We produced these buttons to make it easy for people to discover that they are NOT alone in wanting to remove the rich from power to have real not fake democracy with no rich and no poor. We hope you'll carry extra buttons with you and give them to people who want to wear them so they too can discover the truth about what most people REALLY want.

Please visit www.PDRBoston.org to see how to obtain buttons (and similar stickers) and to read about why it really is possible to remove the rich from power and have a genuinely democratic society with no rich and no poor—an egalitarian revolution.

It won't be easy, and it will take more than voting since the billionaires with the real power were not elected and thus cannot be un-elected. But when millions of people KNOW that millions want to do it, then the resulting confidence will turn hopelessness into hopefulness, and it will indeed be possible—for the vast majority that honors the Golden Rule to prevail over the small minority that attacks it with inequality and domination.

Let's Win Our Short Term Goals Too, Fast!

Nothing makes the rulers more willing to grant our short term demands--for things such as a $15/hr minimum wage, or better pay and conditions and benefits at work, or affordable health care and college—than a growing egalitarian revolutionary movement that makes them fear there will be revolution unless they grant such demands.

PDR-Boston (888) 506-8881 or (617) 213-5095
PeopleForDemocraticRevolution@gmail.com **PDRBoston.org**

APPENDIX V: WHY WE CANNOT VOTE THE RICH OUT OF POWER

The Short Answer:

The reason we cannot vote the rich out of power is because a) the billionaires aren't powerful because of winning any election and b) the ruling class (the billionaire class) doesn't hold elections to let people vote it out of power; it holds elections to control people.

The Satirical Answer: See my online, "Do Your Civic Duty and VOTE!"[241]

The Substantive Answer:

Why Does The American Ruling Plutocracy Hold Elections?

Even stodgy academics from Princeton and Northwestern University, who hate to say anything that would make them seem "unobjective," have declared[242] that the data (lots of it, carefully analyzed with sophisticated statistical methods!) show that the United States is an oligarchy, not a representative democracy. Their study concludes:

---

[241] http://newdemocracyworld.org/revolution/vote.html

[242] https://www.cambridge.org/core/journals/perspectives-on-politics/article/testing-theories-of-american-politics-elites-interest-groups-and-average-citizens/62327F513959D0A304D4893B382B992B

"Multivariate analysis indicates that economic elites and organized groups representing business interests have substantial independent impacts on U.S. government policy, while average citizens and mass-based interest groups have little or no independent influence. The results provide substantial support for theories of Economic-Elite Domination and for theories of Biased Pluralism, but not for theories of Majoritarian Electoral Democracy or Majoritarian Pluralism."

"When a majority of citizens disagrees with economic elites and/or with organised interests, they generally lose. Moreover, because of the strong status quo bias built into the US political system, even when fairly large majorities of Americans favour policy change, they generally do not get it."

"Americans do enjoy many features central to democratic governance, such as regular elections, freedom of speech and association and a widespread (if still contested) franchise. But we believe that if policymaking is dominated by powerful business organisations and a small number of affluent Americans, then America's claims to being a democratic society are seriously threatened."

There is enormous evidence[243], besides academic studies, that the United States is ruled by a relatively small set of people with enormous wealth and hence power: an oligarchy or plutocracy or ruling class, if you will.

One of the most powerful Americans was (until his recent death at 101 years of age) David Rockefeller, the patriarch of the Rockefeller family. He controlled a family fortune worth more than one Trillion dollars[244]; his representatives sat (and

---

[243] https://www.pdrboston.org/proof-we-have-a-fake-democracy

[244] http://newdemocracyworld.org/CoR/rock.html

still sit) on the boards of directors of about 108 of the biggest U.S. corporations in all parts of the economy, and he was the president emeritus of the Council on Foreign Relations--the exclusive private "think tank" that determines U.S. foreign policy and whose members implement it as Secretaries of Defense and State, and Directors of the CIA, *etc.*

David Rockefeller was, of course, never elected. In fact, it has been said of him that if he had been made president of the United States it would have been a demotion.

In the United States, money is power; the billionaires have it and ordinary people don't. Billionaires don't become billionaires by winning an election, and so they cannot be un-elected.

How Much Power Does The President Of The United States Really Have?

John F. Kennedy was at first perfectly willing to go along with the agenda of the plutocracy. But after the Cuban Missile Crisis Kennedy feared that the Cold War could result in a thermonuclear war unless it was ended. Kennedy started to end the Cold War--against the will of the plutocracy--with acts such as initiating the Nuclear Test Ban Treaty (to which the plutocracy was totally opposed) and, just before his death, ordering the Pentagon to make plans to withdraw troops from Vietnam (to which the plutocracy was also totally opposed)[245].

Kennedy knew the CIA and its director, Allen Dulles especially, opposed him and so he fired Allen Dulles as Director. But the plutocracy viewed Kennedy as, literally, a traitor to his (upper) class. Because Dulles, and not Kennedy, was acting at the behest of the plutocracy, Dulles, despite being fired as Director of the CIA, continued to direct it from his personal residence and the new official director, John

---

[245] https://www.amazon.com/dp/B005Q07DKY/ref=dp-kindle-redirect?_encoding=UTF8&btkr=1#nav-subnav

McCone, was a mere figurehead. The plutocracy gave Dulles a green light to orchestrate the assassination of Kennedy, which he did[246].

American presidents know where the real power resides in the United States and what will happen to them if they go against it. This is why the promises made during presidential election campaigns have no relation to the policies the elected president actually carries out, as described in great detail for every president from FDR through Obama in my online article, "Voting for President in America: History is Trying to Tell Us Something."[247] Remember when the candidate Obama was for single payer health care and for ending U.S. military attacks on Muslims in foreign lands?

Presidents of the United States have the kind of power that a CEO of a corporation has. CEOs have the power to make important decisions as long as these decisions are for the benefit of the people with the real power--the major owners of the corporation, as expressed by the Board of Directors. Likewise, the President of the United States has the power to make important decisions as long as they benefit the ruling plutocracy, and not otherwise.

The plutocracy does not want a troublemaker in the Oval Office and it will use violence to prevent that from happening. After all, this is a plutocracy that routinely has used the CIA to remove elected heads of state in foreign countries when it felt they threatened its interests. Does it make any sense to believe that this same plutocracy would refrain from violence if it thought its power in the United States, itself, was

---

[246] See https://www.amazon.com/Devils-Chessboard-Dulles-Americas-Government-ebook/dp/B00SFZB93Y/ref=sr_1_1?s=books&ie=UTF8&qid=1455043597&sr=1-1&keywords=devil%27s+chessboard#nav-subnav and http://www.informationclearinghouse.info/article44607.htm and https://www.amazon.com/dp/B005Q07DKY/ref=dp-kindle-redirect?_encoding=UTF8&btkr=1#nav-subnav

[247] http://newdemocracyworld.org/revolution/voting-in-america.html

threatened?

Eisenhower used the CIA to have Patrice Lumumba assassinated[248]. The CIA helped orchestrate the killing of Allende in Chile[249]. The CIA removed Iran's democratically elected[250] liberal prime minister Mossedegh[251]. The CIA removed Guatemala's liberal reformer and democratically elected president, Arbenz[252]. The CIA killed JFK. All of these killings and removals of elected heads of state (and more) were done because the people who control the CIA--the billionaire class--wanted them to be done. Presidents who objected (like JFK) to what the billionaire class wanted got killed as well. Can one seriously believe that a Jill Stein in the Oval Office would fare any better against the CIA than Lumumba and Allende and Mossedegh and Arbenz and JFK? Really?

So, Why Does The Plutocracy Hold Elections?

Elections are an important instrument that the plutocracy uses to control the public. Here are some of the important things that elections do to help the plutocracy remain safely in power:

1. Elections keep people focused on whom to vote for instead of on how to remove the dictatorship of the rich from power in order to have genuine democracy. To the extent that people

---

[248] https://history.state.gov/historicaldocuments/frus1964-68v23/d11

[249] http://www.newstatesman.com/world-affairs/2013/04/why-allende-had-die

[250] The phrase "democratically elected" is a misleading phrase because in virtually all nations the election process is not really democratic in a meaningful sense of the word. Elections in all nations are controlled by an elite ruling class of one sort or another and these rulers do not permit people to elect a government that will truly do what most people want so very much, which is to abolish class inequality. The phrase "democratically elected" is used in this article merely in the sense of having won such an election.

[251] http://nsarchive.gwu.edu/NSAEBB/NSAEBB435/

[252] https://www.academia.edu/3681333/The_CIA_and_Jacobo_Arbenz

are busy engaging one way or another in the electoral process, then to that extent they are busy NOT building an egalitarian revolutionary movement along the lines discussed in Chapter Eighteen. This, not voting, is how it really is possible to remove the plutocracy from power.

2. Elections provide (undeserved) legitimacy to the dictatorship of the rich by making it seem as if it is actually a government freely elected by the people. This undermines the confidence of those who might otherwise work to abolish the dictatorship of the rich, by making them believe they have no right to go against the will of the majority. This is why foreign oppressive and anti-democratic ruling classes also often hold elections, and why Jimmy Carter has gone around the world giving these elections his "Good Housekeeping Seal of Approval[253]."

3. Elections are a good way to implement divide-and-rule. This is what is happened with the Trump versus Clinton campaigns. In truth, Trump and Clinton acted as a divide-and-rule team, as explained in my online article, "The Clinton/Trump Team[254]."

4. Elections are a good way for the plutocracy to ensure that the president will be a person who is capable of getting much of the public to trust him/her enough, at least, to vote for him/her. The long road to the White House--the primary elections to get nominated and then the long general election campaign to get elected--winnows out the inferior (in the sense of being less able to appeal to the public) politicians, so that the elected president will be qualified for the job (which is to get the public to accept, however grudgingly, the policies of the plutocracy.)

5. If the plutocracy did NOT hold elections, it would make it

---

[253] https://www.cartercenter.org/peace/democracy/observed.html

[254] http://newdemocracyworld.org/culture/team.html

crystal clear to everyone that we were living under a dictatorship of the rich and that the only sensible thing to do is to figure out how to make a revolution to remove the plutocracy from power.

But Why Do People Keep Falling For The "Be Sure To Vote" Routine?

Everything said above so far is, to some extent, already known by many people who nonetheless consider "Who to Vote for" the most important decision when it comes to trying to make the world better. Why is this so? One would think that people who know the truth about the United States being, in reality, a dictatorship of the rich, would not take the election game so seriously.

The answer to this riddle is, I believe, the following. Most people, including those who know the truth about power in the United States, believe something that is actually false. They believe that most ordinary Americans oppose removing the rich from power to have real, not fake, democracy with No Rich and No Poor (a.k.a. an egalitarian revolution.)

The truth is exactly the opposite, as one can see from a video[255] of random people-on-the-street interviews in five neighborhoods of Boston. The vast majority of people would LOVE an egalitarian revolution (once they hear what that means.) This is why it really is possible to build an egalitarian revolutionary movement of the majority of Americans that can actually remove the plutocracy from power.

But most Americans think that it is only a tiny, and hence hopelessly weak, minority of Americans who want such an egalitarian revolution. They think this because the mass (and alternative!) media censor all expressions of a desire for an egalitarian revolution (no matter how worded). This censorship makes it seem that hardly anybody else DOES want an

---

[255] https://www.youtube.com/watch?v=95b3SmBYwfU

egalitarian revolution.

Once one accepts the false premise that most Americans are opposed to an egalitarian revolution, it follows perfectly logically that the best one can hope to accomplish is to use the vote to try to win some band aid reforms that will make life better even though these reforms leave the dictatorship of the rich intact and thus keep us on the treadmill of defeat (as discussed in Chapter Fourteen.)

Furthermore, those who accept the false premise (*i.e.,* believe that egalitarian revolution is impossible because hardly anybody wants it to happen) believe, again very logically, that anybody who advocates building an egalitarian revolutionary movement instead of voting is attacking a very possible GOOD in the name of a very impossible PERFECT.

Likewise, because they don't think it is possible to build an egalitarian revolutionary movement, they therefore dismiss as irrelevant the fact that the growth of an egalitarian revolutionary movement is far and away the BEST way to win even short-term reform demands, as discussed in the "Short Term Goal" section of Chapter Sixteen. Nothing makes the rulers more willing to grant our short term demands--for things such as a $15/hr. minimum wage, or better pay and conditions and benefits at work, or affordable health care and college--than a growing egalitarian revolutionary movement that makes them fear there will be a revolution unless they grant such demands.

Yes We CAN Remove The Plutocracy From Power, But Not By Voting

This is what Chapter Eighteen is all about.

APPENDIX VI: NONVIOLENCE OR NON-CRUELTY?

In advocating the goal of removing the rich from power to create an egalitarian society am I advocating violence? This is a question egalitarians are frequently and understandably asked, especially by people who hold to Gandhi's philosophy of nonviolence.

Before proceeding to give an answer to this important question, it is helpful to keep in mind that among those of us who want to remove the rich from power to create an egalitarian society--we're talking about hundreds of millions of Americans and many more world wide--there are disagreements about this question of violence. Therefore we should promote a serious and ongoing discussion among all of us to carefully identify the specific distinct concerns people have and thereby try to resolve our differences on the basis of our shared fundamental values of equality and mutual aid.

In this spirit, I am now going to express my personal views here.

When I think about the question of nonviolence and revolution I think of it by imagining the following scenario, which I think captures the realistic difference between what we would do if we did or did not adopt the philosophy of nonviolence.

Imagine this scenario[256]:

---

[256] This scenario is, of course, just an imaginary scenario. The question of violence by oppressed people against oppressors arises in many other kinds of situations. I wrote about this question of violence in the context of the debate on guns and

There is a very large and popular movement in the U.S. for egalitarian revolution, and the ruling class is about to order the military to violently repress the movement. (Of course I would much prefer that the ruling class give up its power voluntarily without a fight, in which case we could remove the rich from power without any violence at all. We ALL agree on that! But the question is, "What if they decide to use force to remain in power; what do we do THEN?" We can't put all our eggs in the "Let's hope they give up power without a fight" basket, can we?)

For the sake of visualizing this, let's say that, following massive demonstrations across the entire country for egalitarianism and for removing the rich from power there was a huge crowd of demonstrators in front of the White House demanding that the president and his/her staff leave the White House as an indication that the rich were indeed giving up their power.

Now let's say that instead of agreeing to give up their power, the rich instead have ordered the 82nd Airborne Division to protect the White House from the "mob." Furthermore, the rich have ordered the military to violently remove the huge crowd of people (like the cops violently removed the Occupy folks from Dewey Square in Boston and similar places around the country) as a demonstration that the egalitarian revolutionary movement has been decisively repressed and egalitarians should abandon hope that they will ever be able to prevail. In other words, this confrontation between the people and the military is a make-or-break moment for egalitarian revolution, and everybody knows it.

---

gun-control laws in my online article, "Guns and the Working Class" at **http://newdemocracyworld.org/culture/guns2.html** .

Now imagine that the demonstrators are right in front of the soldiers, wondering what will happen next. The demonstrators, of course, hope that the soldiers will refuse orders to attack them. The demonstrators have devoted much effort already to persuade soldiers to join, not attack, the egalitarian revolutionary movement. But the demonstrators know that the soldiers are under strict discipline and would be severely punished--perhaps even executed--if they refused orders and were found guilty of treason. The demonstrators know that even if most soldiers personally support egalitarian revolution, they might still obey orders. Furthermore, the demonstrators know that at least some soldiers as well as some (perhaps many) police (who, unlike soldiers, are trained and conditioned to attack their fellow citizens) would be very willing to attack the revolutionaries when the order is given.

Knowing all of this, and knowing that the order to attack is about to be given to the soldiers, a demonstrator who does not subscribe to the philosophy of nonviolence uses a bullhorn to address the soldiers. She says:

"Refuse orders to attack us. Instead, use your weapons to defend us against those who might violently attack us."

But immediately after this, another demonstrator, who does subscribe to the philosophy of nonviolence, takes the bullhorn and says to the soldiers:

"No, do not defend us with your weapons. We would rather be defeated than to succeed with violence!"

If you were one of these demonstrators, would you be angry or happy on hearing the second, nonviolent, demonstrator's speech?

I would be angry. Here's why. If the soldiers obeyed the nonviolent demonstrator's words, then the likely outcome would be the utter defeat of the egalitarian revolutionary movement. While some--perhaps most--of the soldiers would refuse the orders to attack the demonstrators, the remaining soldiers and probably a good number of police would indeed violently attack the demonstrators and thereby destroy the egalitarian revolutionary movement. Even if there were subsequent egalitarian revolutionary uprisings across the nation, the same scenario would presumably play out: military and police forces (even if only the minority willing to obey orders) would violently repress the egalitarians. After the defeat in front of the White House, soldiers who may previously have been considering disobeying orders would realize now that the revolutionary movement is not going to win and any soldier disobeying orders would be on the losing side and severely punished. Very few soldiers now would disobey orders.

As a result of the defeat of the egalitarian revolutionary movement the rich will remain in power. This means that mass murderers (literally) will remain in power. Countless innocent people will die as a result--people who would have lived had there been a successful egalitarian revolution.

Had the soldiers who supported the demonstrators obeyed the words of the first demonstrator, who did not adhere to the philosophy of nonviolence, then they would have made it clear that they would use their weapons not against the demonstrators but against anyone who attacked them violently--other soldiers or police. This alone would have persuaded any soldier or police officer inclined to attack the demonstrators to think twice about it. Yes, there might have been some violence if any soldiers did attack the demonstrators. The pro-revolutionary soldiers would have used violence to defend the demonstrators against those attacking them violently. So yes, the revolution would have used violence in self-defense, in order to remove from power the mass murderers who control the United States. Countless lives would have been saved!

I hope this scenario helps to clarify what is actually at stake in the question of adhering or not adhering to the philosophy of nonviolence. I believe that Gandhi's philosophy of nonviolence is very wrongheaded, and I spell out my reasons online in "Are You Sure You Hold to the Philosophy of Nonviolence?"[257]

Non-Violence or Non-Cruelty?

I think that for most people who say they believe in nonviolence, their actual concern is non-cruelty. The popularization of nonviolence as a philosophy in the United States rose dramatically only in recent years. Why? I think it is because in recent years we have witnessed violence that is in no way justified as self-defense. I am referring to violence against unarmed non-combatant civilians, violence usually labeled nowadays as terrorism: suicide bombings of people at a bus stop or a restaurant in Israel, the 9/11 attack that killed thousands of civilians, and so forth.

Some people, very wrongly, defend this kind of violence and call it "resistance." **I strongly disagree; I say: 1) Terrorism is not resistance, and resistance is not terrorism. 2) Terrorism is cruelty; it is violence deliberately targeted against noncombatant civilians and it is morally wrong. 3) Violence that is not in self-defense**[258] **is morally wrong**, **and terrorist violence against noncombatant civilians is not in self-defense. 4) Terrorist violence does nothing--absolutely nothing--to weaken the forces of oppression;** in fact it strengthens the oppressors by allowing them to claim they are the ones defending innocent people from harm. (I've been writing on this point for many years; here's one online example from 2006: "Rocket Attacks on Israeli Civilians."[259])

---

[257] http://newdemocracyworld.org/revolution/nonviolence.html

[258] Self-defense in this context means collective self-defense, in other words defending oneself or other people against those *using violence or its credible threat* to force people to submit to unjust oppression or domination.

[259] http://newdemocracyworld.org/old/War/Rocket.htm

The ruling elite has promoted the philosophy of nonviolence (for us, not them!) by making it seem as if violence equals terrorism, so if you're opposed to terrorism you must therefore subscribe to the philosophy of nonviolence. This is an ideological trap in which many people have fallen. Yes, terrorism is violence. But it is NOT violence in self-defense. Terrorism is cruelty. Rejecting terrorism does not necessarily mean rejecting violence in self-defense. It means rejecting cruelty.

There are situations (such as when one's government is controlled by mass murderers) when the actual choice is between violence in self-defense and the perpetuation of extreme cruelty to others.

The philosophy of non-cruelty says that it is morally right to use violence against a person if it is required to prevent that person from violently harming another person. If soldiers in the above scenario used violence (or the threat of it) against other soldiers or police, who were violently attacking demonstrators, in order to protect the demonstrators, then they would be acting in compliance with the philosophy of non-cruelty. The Baha'i faith, for example, opposes violence in revenge for evil, but says (in paragraph 5 of the Baha'l Reference Library's article, "The Justice and Mercy of God"[260]):

> *"The law of the community will punish the aggressor but will not take revenge. This punishment has for its end to warn, to protect and to oppose cruelty and transgression so that other men may not be tyrannical."*

I call upon those egalitarians who presently subscribe to the philosophy of nonviolence to reconsider. Isn't it all cruelty, rather than all violence, that you oppose? Isn't non-cruelty (doing whatever you can to prevent cruelty) a form of mutual aid?

---

[260] http://reference.bahai.org/en/t/ab/SAQ/saq-77.html#pg267

APPENDIX VII: A BORING TECHNICAL DETAIL REGARDING THE SHARING ECONOMY

How, one might ask, would the sharing economy (described in Chapter Four) actually work, from the point of view of a customer walking into a store to obtain an item? How, exactly, would it be determined whether the customer is in a sharing economy with the producer of the item, in which case the product is free for the taking (or rationed equitably by some means democratically determined), or if the producer and the customer are not in the same sharing economy, in which case the customer would be out of luck (although possibly allowed to barter something for the item?

I can imagine it happening this way. People in a sharing economy get an identification card, like a person's driver's license today, with an identification (ID) number. The item in the store (or the service being offered) has attached to it the ID number of a sharing economy that produced the item, or will provide the service, much like a price is attached to these things today.

The customer's ID is inserted into a device (much like the way our credit or debit cards are inserted into a device when we use them to shop today), which is connected to a large database, and the store clerk also scans or types in the ID of the product's sharing economy. The database is searched to see if there is a sharing economy that includes both the customer and the producer of the item, or not. This search returns a simple yes or no answer. If the answer is yes, then the customer can take the product or receive the service for free (or have a chance to obtain it for free if it is so scarce that it is equitably rationed according to need.) If the answer is no, then the customer can only obtain the product or service by offering (to the sharing economy that produced the product or provides the service) something in exchange for it, *i.e.*, by bartering for it.

How feasible is this, technically speaking, in terms of how large a database would be required?

I think it is very feasible, because of the following considerations.

1. Let's assume that there are 30 billion people (much more than the current 7 billion.)

2. Let's define direct and indirect membership in a sharing economy this way: If one is a member of sharing economy A, and A is a member of sharing economy B, and one belongs to B only because of one's membership in A, then one's membership in B is indirect because it is based on one's membership in A. In contrast, one's membership in A is direct if it does not depend upon membership in some other sharing economy. Most people would probably only have direct membership in one sharing economy, although it would be possible for a person to directly belong to more than one sharing economy.

3. Let's assume that everybody is a direct member of ten sharing economies (a wild overestimate in all likelihood.)

4. Let's assume that there are 4 billion sharing economies all together, many of which are smaller ones that are members of larger ones. Here's why this is probably an overestimate. If a sharing economy has, on average, at least ten members (where members may be individual human beings, or smaller sharing economies) then there would be at most four billion

sharing economies (of any size). This is evident if one considers that 30 billion people forming 10-person sharing economies would result in 3 billion (3,000,000,000) sharing economies. If each of these joined nine others like them to make sharing economies each consisting of ten smaller sharing economies, then there would be 300,000,000 of them. And if each of these joined 9 others like them to make larger sharing economies, then there would be 30,000,000 of them. At the next similar step there would be 3,000,000, and then 300,000 and then 30,000 and then 3,000, then 300, then 30 and then 3. Add these all together and one gets 3,333,333,333, which is less than 4 billion sharing economies in total.

How large, then, would the database have to be to have in it all the sharing economies that every individual human being and every individual sharing economy are direct members of? And would this size be large or small compared to datasets that are routinely used today?

First, let's estimate the size of the dataset in terms of "petabytes," which are the units used to measure the size of huge datasets used by Google and such organizations.

Think of the database as having rows and columns. Say there is a row for every human being and also an additional row for every sharing economy (no matter how big or small). There would be 30 billion rows for the human beings and another 4 billion (likely less) rows for the sharing economies, for a total of 34 billion rows.

In each row, there will need to be ten IDs for the ten sharing economies that the person (or sharing economy) represented by that row is a direct member of. This means there would need to be 34 billion times 10 or 340 billion ID numbers in the database (some of which will of course be, say, a zero indicating no sharing economy).

In order for each ID to be distinct, they would require 12 digits. So the total number of digits would be 340 billion times 12, or

4080 billion, or 4.08 trillion digits. Each digit requires one computer "byte" so the database would require 4.08 trillion bytes, or about 4 terabytes. A "petabyte" is a thousand terabytes, so 4 terabytes is 0.004 petabytes.

So, is 0.004 petabytes large or small in the realm of computers today? The answer is, very small. One can see just how small by looking at the number of petabytes various organizations routinely use today.[261] The game World of Warcraft uses 1.3 petabytes. Google, for example, processes 24 (versus our 0.004) petabytes per day--that's six thousand times the size needed to store all the sharing economy data. Facebook has a single "HDFS cluster" with more than 100 petabytes. IBM has a storage array that stores 120 petabytes. The CERN search for the Higgs Boson used 200 petabytes. A supercomputer by Cray, called Blue Waters Supercomputer began being constructed in 2012 and it will have a capacity of 500 petabytes, dwarfing what a global sharing economy computer would ever require 100,000 fold!

A computer with the sharing economy database (which could be located in many computers operated by many different people around the world) could say whether a customer was in the same sharing economy as the producer of a product (or provider of a service) by simply using the database to create a list of all the sharing economies that the customer directly belonged to plus all of the sharing economies those belonged to, *etc.;* then it would likewise create a list of all the sharing economies that the sharing economy of the item belonged to. Then it would see if any sharing economy in the one list was also in the other, and if so the customer and the producer of the item are members of a common sharing economy and the price to the customer is free; otherwise the customer is out of luck.

If there were ever just one huge global sharing economy, a computer would not be necessary at all. People's IDs would

---

[261] https://en.wikipedia.org/wiki/Petabyte

only need to say "member of the sharing economy" or "not member" and the product would need an ID that said if the producer was or wasn't a member, and if and only if both were members the price would be free.

The main point here is that even in the unlikely case that the relationship between sharing economies, in terms of which is a member of which, is very complex, it would still be easy for people to shop much as they do today, using an ID card to enable a store clerk to know whether the product or service was free to them or not. The advantages of being a member of as large a sharing economy as possible would be very evident to all. Those in only very small sharing economies (*i.e.*, not even an indirect member of a large one) or in no sharing economy at all, would have no guarantee they could acquire products and services and their only hope would be if they found a producer of the desired product or provider of the desired service who was willing to barter it for something that unfortunate customer had to offer. Everybody who was willing to contribute reasonably to the economy would have every reason in the world for promoting the trust and solidarity that would enable small sharing economies to merge into larger and larger ones.

APPENDIX VIII: WHO IS IN THE RULING CLASS? WHO RULES AMERICA?

What exactly do I mean by the phrase, "ruling class" (a.k.a. "ruling elite," "corporate elite," "plutocracy" or "upper class")? Who exactly do I mean? Good question.

One quick answer is this: By 'upper class' I mean that top 0.5% to 1% of the population who exercise effective control over the corporations, the banks, the media, the government. I do not mean people who simply have a higher than average income. I mean the people like those amusingly but also seriously described by Kevin Roose, who crashed a Wall Street secret society and wrote about it in *New York Magazine*[262].

Sociology professor G. William Domhoff, who has researched this question for decades, provides a more thorough and scholarly answer and wrote a book titled *Who rules America?* Domhoff describes the ruling class in great detail online[263]. He writes in a Questions and Answers section:

> Q: So, who does rule America?
> A: The owners and managers of large income-producing properties; i.e., corporations, banks, and agri-businesses. But

---

[262] http://nymag.com/daily/intelligencer/2014/02/i-crashed-a-wall-street-secret-society.html

[263] See http://www2.ucsc.edu/whorulesamerica/

they have plenty of help from the managers and experts they hire. You can read the essential details of the argument in this summary[264] *of Who Rules America?, or look for the book itself at Amazon.com.*

The notion--that in so-called democracies like the United States some people act in concert and in secrecy to do things that seriously affect the public's well-being--this notion is dismissed by many people as "conspiracy theory."[265] These

---

[264] http://www2.ucsc.edu/whorulesamerica/power/class_domination.html

[265] Lance deHaven-Smith, in his book, *Conspiracy Theory in America* (https://www.amazon.com/Conspiracy-Theory-America-Discovering/dp/0292743793), points out the following:

1. The Declaration of Independence is a conspiracy theory document. It "connects the dots" (each dot is something King George III did that harmed the colonists) to make the case that King George III was engaged in a secret conspiracy against the colonists.

2. The U.S. Constitution's checks and balances comes from the theory of the Founding Fathers that people in government positions of power will conspire to create tyranny and must somehow be prevented.

3. The young Abraham Lincoln (when he was a legislator) gave a speech in which he "connected the dots" (each dot was an omission or half-truth in President Polk's speech arguing for the need to go to war against Mexico) to make the case that President Polk was conspiring to deceive the public to get it to support a bad war. (Remind you of WMD?)

4. The noted historian, Charles Beard, devoted his scholarship to showing that people in the U.S. government were deceiving the public for selfish and unstated ends, *i.e.*, were engaged in a conspiracy against the public. Beard showed that the U.S. Constitution was designed to serve the private interests of the Founding Fathers, and he showed that FDR, contrary to all of his assertions to the public, secretly used all his power to get the U.S. into WWII, that he conspired with the British to make Japan launch a first strike against the U.S., that he knew in advance that Japan was about to bomb Pearl Harbor and he deliberately kept it a secret from the Pearl Harbor military commanders so he could scape goat their "unpreparedness" and, more importantly, pretend to be shocked at the attack on that "day that shall live in infamy."

5. In the case of the Declaration of Independence and the checks and balances of the Constitution and Abraham Lincoln, nobody considered it wrong in any way to be suspicious of people in government conspiring against We the People; in fact it was considered smart to be thus suspicious.

6. But by the end of World War II, however, Charles Beard was marginalized because of his focus on "inside job" government conspiracy.

7. After WWII, academia switched gears from being suspicious of government conspiracy to dismissing such suspicion as foolish and even dangerous. There are two reasons deHaven-Smith cites for this: Karl Popper and Leo Strauss.

Karl Popper persuaded the academic social scientists that a belief in any <u>particular</u> conspiracy by people in the government was the same as a belief that <u>nothing</u> in history ever has happened except as a result of a secret conspiracy of some individuals to make it happen for some self-interested reason. The absurdity of the latter belief was leveraged (illogically, but effectively nonetheless) to label the former belief absurd. Popper argued that belief in a conspiracy was the secular version of belief in superstition and myths, and that such unscientific beliefs were false and only helped demagogues come to power and replace democracy with totalitarianism. Therefore, Popper argued that such conspiracy theories had to be suppressed.

Leo Strauss, in contrast--but with the same effect as Popper--argued (to his students, which included many of those that became the neocons under G.W. Bush) that many conspiracy theories about government leaders conspiring against democracy were TRUE, and therefore these theories had to be suppressed, because if the people knew these truths they would lose their faith in the leaders and the nation would be weakened. The strength of the nation depends of people believing "noble lies."

So both of these currents in academia contributed to reversing the earlier belief that it was wise to suspect conspiratorial wrongdoing in high places.

people assume that no conspiracies ever happen. But they do. Many are described in "33 Conspiracies That Turned Out To Be True."[266]

An academic study[267] from Princeton and Northwestern University, based on a large amount of data and statistical modeling, concludes we live in a dictatorship of the rich, except it doesn't use that inflammatory phrase; instead its abstract concludes with these words, which mean the same thing:

> *"Multivariate analysis indicates that economic elites and organized groups representing business interests have substantial independent impacts on U.S. government policy, while average citizens and mass-based interest groups have little or no independent influence."*

---

8. Shortly after the Warren Report on the Kennedy assassination came out, the CIA sent a directive (given in full in the book) to all of its officers telling them to counter criticism of that report (in all the mass media they were involved with) by saying how stupid "conspiracy" explanations of the assassination were (many talking points were in the directive, and they were used in the mass media plenty). This drove the nail into the coffin of the "respectable conspiracy theory" and resulted in the situation we have today in which many people can be persuaded to dismiss a theory just by labeling it a conspiracy theory. (This applies to conspiracy theories about American government leaders, not foreign government leaders; it's fine to accuse Vladimir Putin of just about anything!)

---

[266] http://worldtruth.tv/33-conspiracy-theories-that-turned-out-to-be-true-2/

[267] https://www.cambridge.org/core/journals/perspectives-on-politics/article/testing-theories-of-american-politics-elites-interest-groups-and-average-citizens/62327F513959D0A304D4893B382B992B

APPENDIX IX: GLOBAL WEALTH EQUALITY: WHAT WOULD IT MEAN?

How much wealth would people have if all of the wealth in the whole world were shared equally? The total personal (as opposed to government-owned) wealth of the world in the year 2000 was approximately $300 trillion[268].[269] The number of people in the world (including children) in 2000 was approximately 6.3 billion[270]. Do the division and one gets approximately $48,000[271] of wealth per every man, woman

---

[268] http://www.oxfordscholarship.com/view/10.1093/acprof:oso/9780199548880.001.0001/acprof-9780199548880-chapter-19

[269] This number is "Purchasing Power Parity" adjusted, which means it takes into account the fact that some things are cheaper in one country than another. If all personal property in the world were sold and the money then used to buy commodities in the country where that personal property was located, those same commodities would cost $300 trillion if purchased in the United States.

[270] https://en.wikipedia.org/wiki/File:World-Population-1800-2100.svg

[271] This is perhaps too low a figure. Credit-Suisse reports here (for 2012-13), "As already noted, global household wealth equates to USD 51,600 per adult, a new all-time high for average net worth. This average global value masks considerable variation across countries and regions, as is evident in Figure 3." Using this figure of $51,600 instead of $48,000 would mean that perfect global wealth equality would benefit even more Americans than what is asserted based on the lower figure.

and child on the planet, *i.e.,* the global average per capita wealth.

A family of four would thus own a bit more than $190,000 of wealth. The average number of persons per "household" (as opposed to family) is about 2.58[272], so a family this size would have about $124,000 of wealth. To put this in context, in 2002 the median American household net worth was approximately $59,000.[273] This means that half of American households had a net worth that was at least a whopping $65,000 less than what they would have had if global wealth were distributed evenly to every man, woman and child on the planet. Sixty percent of households had a net worth less than $99,999,[274] which means their net worth was at least $24,000 less than if global wealth were evenly distributed.

Furthermore, when I say "at least" such and such an amount less than if global wealth were evenly distributed, this amount is much greater than the figure I cited. Why? Because according to the same source just referenced, 16.9% of households had zero or negative (debts greater than assets) net worth, 9.3% had only between $1 and $4,999 net worth, and 4.8% had only between $5000 and $9,999 net worth. Global equality would mean a <u>huge</u> increase in wealth for these American families. On the high end, of course, some families, like the Waltons who own Wal-Mart, owned billions of dollars' worth of wealth and the Rockefeller family fortune is conservatively estimated to be at least $1 Trillion[275].

---

[272] https://www.census.gov/prod/cen2010/briefs/c2010br-14.pdf

[273] https://www.census.gov/content/dam/Census/library/publications/2008/demo/p70-115.pdf

[274] Table 4 at https://www.census.gov/data/tables/2002/demo/wealth/wealth-asset-ownership.html

[275] http://newdemocracyworld.org/CoR/rock.html

It is well known that the United States is a "rich nation" and most of the world is economically much poorer. It is interesting, therefore, to know that **if all the wealth of the world were somehow magically redistributed among all people on the planet equally, to make the billions of poor people in places like India, Ethiopia, Haiti and Bangladesh equal in wealth to Americans and everybody else, then 55% of American households would be richer, not poorer.** (This underscores how nationality is not a very useful category when thinking about making the world more equal.) Around thirty-five percent of American families would be poorer, among whom are the 8.5% of American families whose net worth exceeded $500,000 in 2002. [same source as above.]

Global Equality Is About Sharing, Not Leveling Down

The goal of global wealth equality is not, however, to redistribute wealth in the simplistic way that the above discussion would imply. The goal is not to "level down" by taking away from any family of four owning more than $190,000. On the contrary, the goal is to "level up" in a manner consistent with preserving a good environment for future generations. The goal is to create an economic and political system in the world in which all people have an equal status economically and politically: egalitarianism as described in Chapter Four.

What About the Well-To-Do?

Here is where the principle of "leveling up" comes in. It's all about how people who value equality and mutual aid decide what a "reasonable" contribution to the sharing economy is. People who live in a region that has a highly developed infrastructure of roads, railways, factories and universities, *etc.,* or in a region with important but scarce natural resources, would probably be expected to contribute more things or provide greater services to a sharing economy than people from poorer regions, at least initially until the poorer regions developed their productive capacities more. In a sharing economy, unlike a capitalist one, everybody benefits when the productive capacity of somebody else improves. It makes it possible for everybody to choose between two pleasant possibilities: everybody works less but still enjoys the same amount of shared economic productivity, or everybody continues to work the same and enjoys greater shared economic productivity. Mutual aid rather than competition is the basis of people's relationships with each other in a sharing economy. People in poorer regions might enjoy less wealth initially than people in richer regions, but over time the result of mutual aid and sharing will lead to greater and greater equality in standard of living across formerly richer and poorer regions.

What does "leveling up" mean for a well-to-do American family with substantially more than $190,000 of personal wealth? Let's say the family owns a $1 million dollar home and owns $5 million worth of stocks. The $5 million in stock represent shares in businesses where people work. In the sharing economy businesses are activities that people do, they are not things that other people own. The $5 million of stock certificates would become just worthless pieces of paper (as would all forms of money itself). The adults in this family would lose their income from these stocks. But if they contributed to the sharing economy in a reasonable (as determined by their local assembly) way then they wouldn't need any "income" because they could take freely what they needed or desired from the stores where products and services were made available (or they could "get in line" so to speak for scarce things equitably rationed in a manner determined by the local assembly, which they could attend as an equal with all others.)

This family would continue to have the most important things that their former income provided: a good place to live and all of the things required for a comfortable and satisfying life, good education, health care, vacations, and security in old age (older retired people, children, disabled people, *etc.* would be members of the sharing economy because their "reasonable" required contribution would be zero.) In many ways this family's lives would be much better than before: the world they lived in would be a friendlier place instead of one in which ruling elites used Orwellian wars of social control to make people fear other nationalities or ethnic groups; they would benefit from the fact that government wealth would be used for things like schools and libraries and hospitals that actually make our lives better instead of things that don't, such as military forces and weapons and "Homeland Security" and prisons; they would share in the far more useful economic productivity of almost four million Americans who presently produce little of real value in our prisons or the military and who would contribute far more if we had a global sharing economy; they would benefit from no longer having to endure mind-numbing and anxiety-producing "ask your doctor about" advertisements and planned obsolescence; those of them who were managers would no longer confront workers in the old labor-management conflict because everybody in the workplace assembly would have an equal say in all decisions and would have equal standards of living; they would no longer have anxiety about where they stood in the hierarchy of wealth and respect from poor to rich; and they would no longer live in a world in which they were resented and disliked by those at the very bottom of an unequal society, or those who were unemployed because the economy, unlike a sharing economy, only employs people if it will make a profit for an employer.

What about the family's $1 million dollar home? They would continue to own that home and live in it. If there were homeless people in the community the local assembly would probably rather house them temporarily in whatever available buildings were suitable and then arrange for the construction of nice homes for them, than resort to having them housed in spare rooms of already occupied large houses. The local assembly might think differently about the multiple mansions that are usually unoccupied and are owned by a family like the Waltons, but this would affect only a very tiny percentage of Americans.

No More Ugly Debates About Who Should Be Paid More than Whom

The global equality as outlined here will mean no more ugly debates about who should be paid more than whom. People won't work for a paycheck; they'll work to be equal members of the sharing economy. Whether they contribute as a teacher or a physician or a janitor, a factory blue-collar or white collar worker, a jet pilot or auto mechanic, an adult student or a person in charge of caring for children, and whether they live in the United States or Bangladesh, if they are in a common sharing economy then they all get "paid" the same: membership in the sharing economy.

APPENDIX X: RACE, CRIME AND EGALITARIANISM

In an egalitarian society with no rich and no poor, will there be vastly less crime (by crime here I mean crimes such as car theft, muggings, home burglaries, murder and rape) than today? The ruling class tries to make us believe that the answer to this question is 'No' because something about black people, not inequality, is what causes criminality. But in truth, the answer is 'Yes," as we discuss here, by carefully examining the reasons why many people (thanks to very sophisticated methods of propaganda the ruling class employs) believe that the cause of crime is black people, not inequality.

Those who say egalitarianism would not substantially reduce crime say the problem is black people--they're just criminal by nature (genetically) or they have a "culture of poverty" that causes them to prefer crime to honest work. They say the solution to crime (to the extent that there even is one) is to give stiff prison sentences to criminals and (to the extent that the problem is cultural rather than genetic) to somehow change the culture of the people prone to criminality while leaving the capitalist nature of society with its enormous economic inequality pretty much the same.

These "stiff-prison-sentences and change-their-culture" people love to cite statistics to make their case, even though (as discussed below) the statistics they cite do not actually make their case at all. They cite the higher rate of murders committed by blacks than by whites, for example. It is apparently true that the murder crime rate is higher among blacks than whites[276] and likewise for other crimes (based on FBI arrest statistics[277]) for which the pattern is that, for most categories of crime, the percent of all arrests in which a black person was arrested is greater than the 12.6% of the population that is black, and the percent of all arrests in which a white person was arrested is less than the 72.4% of the population that is white. Some of this racial imbalance is due to blacks being more likely[278] to be arrested than whites for the same illegal behavior. This is particularly true in the case of narcotic drug arrests (discussed below in the section about the War on Drugs), and also as discussed online.[279] And some of this imbalance is due to outright racial discrimination by police. For example, the *New York Times* in an editorial[280] November 26, 2014 wrote:

> "News accounts have strongly suggested, for example, that the police in St. Louis County's many municipalities systematically target poor and minority citizens for street and traffic stops — partly to generate fines — which has the effect of both bankrupting and criminalizing whole communities. In this context, the police are justifiably seen as an alien, occupying force that is synonymous with state-sponsored abuse."

Still, it seems to be the case that blacks commit crimes disproportionately to their numbers in the population. The question is, what is the cause of this crime? Is it poverty in a

---

[276] http://www.realclearscience.com/journal_club/2013/07/22/youth_homicide_rates_by_race_in_the_us_106602.html

[277] https://ucr.fbi.gov/crime-in-the-u.s/2011/crime-in-the-u.s.-2011/tables/table-43

[278] http://www.huffingtonpost.com/entry/nixon-drug-war-racist_us_56f16a0ae4b03a640a6bbda1

[279] See https://www.aclu.org/files/assets/1114413-mj-report-rfs-rel1.pdf

[280] https://www.nytimes.com/2014/11/26/opinion/the-meaning-of-the-ferguson-riots.html?ref=opinion

society of great economic inequality, or race (*i.e.*, something wrong about black people)? If the cause is poverty, then making society equal (with no rich and no poor) will vastly reduce the problem of crime. On the other hand, if the problem is race then even in an egalitarian society crime will remain a big problem.

Net Worth by Race/Ethnicity - 2002

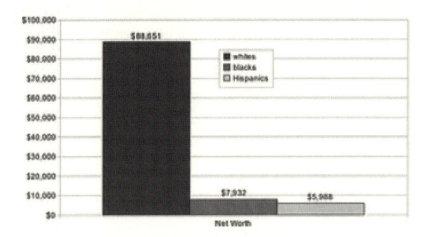

Source: Pew Hispanic Center; The Wealth of Hispanic Households: 1996 to 2002.

Here is some powerful evidence that the cause of crime is poverty, not race. The evidence is reported in an online academic paper[281] titled, "Extremely Disadvantaged Neighborhoods and Urban Crime," by Lauren J. Krivo and Ruth D. Peterson, both of Ohio State University, in the journal, Social Forces, December 1996, 75(2):619-650. The authors analyzed census data for the city of Columbus, Ohio for 1990, specifically data for 177 small regions or "tracts," containing at least 700 persons. Twenty-six tracts were at least 70% black and 122 of them were at least 70% white. A higher *proportion* of the black tracts than the white tracts had extremely high levels of poverty, but the *number* of black and white tracts with extreme rates of poverty were nearly identical.

This study examined the relationship between crime rate and the following factors: poverty, percent of families headed by females, unemployment, employment in professional or managerial occupations, percent of units that are renter occupied, and the percent of the population that is male and in the crime prone ages (15-24). Sophisticated statistical methods were employed, on the basis of which the authors conclude that, "extremely disadvantaged communities have qualitatively higher levels of crime than less disadvantaged areas, and that this pattern holds for both black and white communities." They add, "Overall, average property and violent crime rates are substantially higher in black communities. However, disadvantage has the same patterns of effects on crime in white and black neighborhoods. Hence crime rates for racially distinct areas generally approach one another when structural conditions *[i.e., the factors of poverty, percent of families headed by females, unemployment etc. listed above—J.S.]* are controlled *[i.e., when white and black*

---

[281] http://faculty.washington.edu/matsueda/courses/587/readings/Krivo%20Peterson%201996.pdf

areas are very similar with respect to the structural conditions of poverty etc.—J.S.].

These patterns are particularly striking for violent crime. Gross rates of violence are nearly three times as high in black as in white neighborhoods, but the net race difference *[i.e., when comparing black and white neighborhoods with similar poverty, unemployment etc.—J.S.]* in violent crime is small and nonsignificant for the vast majority of contrasts *[one "contrast" would be comparing black and white neighborhoods that both had low unemployment, whereas another "contrast" would be comparing black and white neighborhoods that both had high unemployment, etc. for the other structural conditions factors—J.S.]* between similarly disadvantaged communities. And even when race differences persist, residents confront much less violence in black neighborhoods with low disadvantage than in either black or white communities with extreme disadvantage. Taken as a whole, these findings clearly substantiate Sampson and Wilson's contention that the sources of crime are invariant across race *[i.e., the same regardless of race—J.S.]* and are rooted largely in the structural differences *[i.e., poverty, unemployment etc.-- JS]* among communities."

The higher rate of crime in black versus white neighborhoods is thus due to the greater poverty and related hardships that blacks experience compared to whites, which is described in great detail online.[282] In an egalitarian society with no rich and no poor, and with no involuntary unemployment, poverty and its associated hardships will be a thing of the past, and "street" crime will be vastly reduced.

Those who try to argue that the cause of crime is a problem about black people, rather than poverty regardless of race, would say something like, "Sure, unemployment and poverty may be associated with a higher rate of criminal behavior no

---

[282] See https://en.wikipedia.org/wiki/Racial_inequality_in_the_United_States and https://www.washingtonpost.com/news/wonk/wp/2015/08/12/black-poverty-differs-from-white-poverty/?utm_term=.29efa634142c

matter what the race, but black fathers far more than white fathers abandon their children, and this in turn causes a culture of poverty mainly among blacks that leads to preferring crime to honest work. How come black fathers do this more than white fathers? It must be something about being black." The famous Moynihan Report of 1965[283] headlined facts such as "Almost One-Fourth of Negro Families are Headed by Females" and "The percent of nonwhite families headed by a female is more than double the percent for whites" and linked this to high rates of youth criminality:

> *"Recent psychological research demonstrates the personality effects of being reared in a disorganized home without a father. One study showed that children from fatherless homes seek immediate gratification of their desires far more than children with fathers present.49 Others revealed that children who hunger for immediate gratification are more prone to delinquency, along with other less social behavior.50 Two psychologists, Pettigrew says, maintain that inability to delay gratification is a critical factor in immature, criminal, and neurotic behavior.51"*

There are two points that these "the problem is blacks" people ignore.

First, while neighborhoods with more female-headed families (both white and black) tended to have higher crime rates, the association between female-headed families and crime is much less than the association between extreme poverty and crime. In the Krivo and Peterson study cited above, the correlation between crime and a high number of female-headed families was only .096 compared to .616 for the correlation with extreme poverty. (Correlation ranges from negative 1 to positive 1; negative values mean when one variable is low the other tends to be high, positive values mean when one is high the other tends to be high also; zero

---

[283] http://www.blackpast.org/primary/moynihan-report-1965

means no association and 1 or negative 1 means the maximum possible association.)

Second, the evidence indicates that it is unemployment (or jobs that pay too little to support a family) that causes men to abandon their families, not the race of the man or anything unique to "black culture." During the Great Depression of the 1930s, the mainly white working class suffered the kind of terrible unemployment that still affects black men today. According[284] to Frederick Lewis Allen's *Since Yesterday: The 1930's in America*[285], a 1940 survey estimated that as many as "1.5 million married women had been abandoned by their husbands."

One account[286] of this period says,

> "By 1933 millions of Americans (we'll never really know how many) were desperate. Out of work and with his family depending on him, the breadwinner, the patriarch, the father/husband bore the brunt of the despair. When he couldn't provide for his family, he felt ashamed and humiliated. Many of these men abandoned their families and became what one has called 'a generation of wanderers,' vagabonds, or hobos. Unable to find work and seeing that each job they applied for had hundreds of seekers, these shabby, disillusioned men wandered

---

[284] https://books.google.com/books?id=ix9zAwAAQBAJ&pg=PA1247&lpg=PA1247&dq=A+1940+survey+revealed+that+1.5+million+married+women+had+been+abandoned+by+their+husbands.&source=bl&ots=wQ5lHnkE2v&sig=fKr0l3sCSt7X13tsx5Y3L4eZiiY&hl=en&sa=X&ei=vX2MU63wK-PNsQStnYD4Aw#v=onepage&q=A%201940%20survey%20revealed%20that%201.5%20million%20married%20women%20had%20been%20abandoned%20by%20their%20husbands.&f=false

[285] https://archive.org/details/sinceyesterdayth001025mbp

[286] The source is "Source 10" in the .doc document that one can download from the link that Google returns for a search for the text fragment (in quotes) "Out of work and with his family depending on him, the breadwinner, the patriarch".

aimlessly without funds, begging, picking over refuse in city dumps, and finally getting up the courage to stand and be seen publicly - in a bread line for free food."

In *Women during the Great Depression*[287] the authors write:

> "In most of the pictures that I took the women look really sad and depress, and they have a reason to be I mean most of them needed too get jobs, plus all of the house work they had that was a lot of work, I think out of all of thing women were the strongest ones, because they had more rolls too play during this times, it was bad, kids and women took this so much worse because, men if they couldn't take this any more, they would just leave and forget about it, but women had to go trough it no matter what they couldn't really run away from life and reality and that's jus the truth."

What happened to predominantly white working class families in the Great Depression demonstrates that high unemployment tends to drive many married men, regardless of their race, to abandon their families because they are ashamed that they cannot fulfill their role as provider. Men in the past left, and in the present leave, their families NOT because of their being in a culture that says they shouldn't provide for their family but, on the contrary, because of being in a culture that says they SHOULD provide for their family and being ashamed at not being **able** to do what they believed they ought to do. When the high unemployment (or lack of jobs that pay a family wage) lasts generation after generation, the negative effects are disastrous.

The greater poverty of blacks compared to whites is largely due to the fact that the enslavement of blacks in earlier generations prevented wealth from being passed down to current generations of blacks, in great contrast to the

---

[287] https://sophiamichellerudy.wordpress.com/

inheritance of such wealth by current white generations. This is spelled out in an academic study[288].

Black-on-Black Crime is Caused by Systemic Racial Discrimination: Here's How it Works:

The people who say, "the problem is blacks" also say that black people far more than white people like to sell drugs instead of doing honest work. What they don't want to admit is that the minimum wage dead-end menial jobs that are the best jobs many black and Hispanic youths can hope to ever get-- jobs that are viewed with great disrespect by all of society including by blacks and Hispanics--are hardly going to seem attractive compared to the allure of dealing drugs, which seems to offer not only much higher pay but also high prestige and a chance to rise up in the "business."

According to the Justice Department[289], "Street gangs, outlaw motorcycle gangs (OMGs), and prison gangs are the primary distributors of illegal drugs on the streets of the United States." And according to a report[290], gang activity accounts for an average of 48% of violent crime in most jurisdictions, and up to 90% in some jurisdictions[291]. This 90% figure refers to what is known as "black on black" crime.

The poorest, predominantly black and Hispanic, people in the United States are told to either accept low paying dead-end jobs that are disrespected by everybody including themselves, or to try to gain wealth and prestige in the illegal gang-controlled drug business which, because it is illegal, can only

---

[288] http://ww1.insightcced.org/uploads/CRWG/Umbrellas-Dont-Make-It-Rain8.pdf

[289] https://www.justice.gov/archive/ndic/pubs11/13157/#relation

[290] https://mic.com/articles/27281/gun-control-debate-gang-violence-accounts-for-half-of-violent-crime-in-america#.Qp12knsUt

[291] https://www.fbi.gov/stats-services/publications/2011-national-gang-threat-assessment

"do business" (compete and enforce contracts) by violent means (as opposed to relying on the legal state apparatus with its official use of violence or its credible threat, as legal businesses do).

The solution to the problem of crime--including "black on black" crime--is an egalitarian society with no rich and no poor, with an economy that is based on everybody being able to work who wants to, and providing everybody who is willing to work everything they need or reasonably desire for free (or equitably rationing scarce things according to need). In an egalitarian society no husband will ever be driven to leave his family for shame at not being able to provide for it. Nobody will feel trapped and forced to choose between abject poverty in a minimum wage dead end job or the lure of escaping poverty by criminal behavior. The crime caused by poverty will vanish and be remembered only as a problem of the past, like legal chattel slavery and explicitly racist Jim Crow laws.

For more hard data and analysis of the crime/race connection see "Incarceration & social inequality" (2010)[292], published by the American Academy of Arts and Sciences, which states:

> *In the last few decades, the institutional contours of American social inequality have been transformed by the rapid growth in the prison and jail population.1 America's prisons and jails have produced a new social group, a group of social outcasts who are joined by the shared experience of incarceration, crime, poverty, racial minority, and low education. As an outcast group, the men and women in our penal institutions have little access to the social mobility available to the mainstream. Social and economic disadvantage, crystallizing in penal confinement, is sustained over the life course and transmitted from one generation to the next. This is a profound institutionalized inequality that has renewed*

---

[292] https://www.amacad.org/content/publications/pubContent.aspx?d=808

race and class disadvantage. Yet the scale and empirical details tell a story that is largely unknown.

Though the rate of incarceration is historically high, perhaps the most important social fact is the inequality in penal confinement. This inequality produces extraordinary rates of incarceration among young African American men with no more than a high school education. For these young men, born since the mid-1970s, serving time in prison has become a normal life event.

The influence of the penal system on social and economic disadvantage can be seen in the economic and family lives of the formerly incarcerated. The social inequality produced by mass incarceration is sizable and enduring for three main reasons: it is invisible, it is cumulative, and it is intergenerational. The inequality is invisible in the sense that institutionalized populations commonly lie outside our official accounts of economic well-being. Prisoners, though drawn from the lowest rungs in society, appear in no measures of poverty or unemployment. As a result, the full extent of the disadvantage of groups with high incarceration rates is underestimated. The inequality is cumulative because the social and economic penalties that flow from incarceration are accrued by those who already have the weakest economic opportunities. Mass incarceration thus deepens disadvantage and forecloses mobility for the most marginal in society. Finally, carceral inequalities are intergenerational, affecting not just those who go to prison and jail but their families and children, too."

For further reading, I recommend a *Guardian* article[293] that puts "black-on-black" crime in perspective, and a

---

[293] https://www.theguardian.com/commentisfree/2016/apr/09/bill-clinton-black-culture-systemic-inequality-problems

siliconafrica.com article[294] about ancient African history that puts any discussion of the African race in more realistic perspective.

How The 18:1 Law Makes The War On Drugs Racist

"Nixon Aide Reportedly Admitted Drug War Was Meant To Target Black People" 'Did we know we were lying about the drugs? Of course we did.'[295]

There is a United States federal law on the books officially named the "Fair Sentencing Act of 2010"[296] that is, in its effect, as viciously racist (deliberately, as will be shown below) as the old and now thoroughly discredited Jim Crow laws that explicitly discriminated against black people. This law, which I call the "18:1" law, is a key part of the legal framework for the War on Drugs; it is one way that the U.S. Government veils its racism so as not to be obvious to the wider general public. Most Americans today wouldn't stand for an explicitly racist Jim Crow-type law. But they tolerate, if they even know about the existence of, the 18:1 law because they don't understand how racist it is. Furthermore, they are influenced by the racist "blacks are innately criminals" stereotype without understanding that if it were not for racist laws (like 18:1, but also others beyond the scope of this book that are the cause of poverty) then there wouldn't be any supposed "real life evidence" (like the disproportionate numbers of black and Hispanics in prison) for that racist stereotype.

One of the main reasons that blacks and Hispanics are disproportionately in America's prisons is because of the 18:1 law. This is how it works, starting with some important, but

---

[294] http://www.siliconafrica.com/terra-nullius/

[295] http://www.huffingtonpost.com/entry/nixon-drug-war-racist_us_56f16a0ae4b03a640a6bbda1

[296] http://www.ussc.gov/research/congressional-reports/2015-report-congress-impact-fair-sentencing-act-2010

little known, background facts, that one can read about in more detail in Carl Hart's book *High Price*[297] (the author is an eminent associate professor of neuroscience at Columbia University).

Fact # 1: There are two types of cocaine: powder, which is snorted (*i.e.,* taken into the nose), and crack, which is smoked. These two types of cocaine are chemically identical except for a tiny difference that makes it possible to burn the latter (and hence smoke it) without destroying the active ingredient, which is the same in both types of cocaine.[298] Snorting or smoking the same amount, by weight, of either type of cocaine has exactly the same pharmacological effect.

Fact # 2: Poor people can buy crack cocaine a lot easier than powder cocaine because unlike powder, the crack is sold in very tiny, and hence cheap and affordable, amounts.

Fact # 3: When a drug is sold in tiny amounts, it means there must be a lot more drug purchase and sale transactions than when the drug is sold in larger amounts.

Fact # 4: When the amounts of drug per transaction are tiny, the people involved tend to be poor, and the location of the transaction tends to be in the street instead of behind fancy closed doors of well-to-do folks.

---

[297] https://www.amazon.com/High-Price-Neuroscientists-Self-Discovery-Challenges/dp/0062015893/ref=sr_1_1?s=books&ie=UTF8&qid=1494456837&sr=1-1&keywords=high+price+carl+hart

[298] "Powder cocaine is chemically known as cocaine hydrochloride. It is a neutral compound (known as a salt) made from the combination of an acid and a base, in this case, cocaine base. This form of cocaine can be eaten, snorted, or dissolved in water and injected. Cocaine hydrochloride cannot be smoked, however, because it decomposes under the heat required to vaporize it. Smoking requires chemically removing the hydrochloride portion, which does not contribute to cocaine's effects anyway. The resulting compound is just the cocaine base (a.k.a. freebase or crack cocaine), which is smokable. The important point here is that powder and crack cocaine are qualitatively the same drug. Figure 1 shows the chemical structures of cocaine hydrochloride and cocaine base (crack). As you can see, the structures are nearly identical." [Carl Hart's High Price, pg. 158-9) (I cannot get the figure from my kindle to this document, but what Hart says is very clearly true.)

Fact # 5: Where there are a lot of illegal transactions on the street, there will be more opportunities for the police to make arrests than where there are fewer transactions behind fancy closed doors.

The result of these facts is that the poorer a cocaine user is, the more likely he or she is to use crack instead of powder and the more likely he or she is to be arrested.

Now it's time to look at:

Fact #6: The amount, by weight, of powder cocaine required to trigger federal criminal penalties is 18 times the amount of crack cocaine required to trigger those penalties (and it used to be 100 times higher).

The result of fact # 6, on top of the previous facts, is that even if the rate of cocaine use by everybody--rich and poor alike--is the same, inevitably the poorest people are not only far more likely to be arrested, they are also far more likely to be convicted of a drug possession crime.

Fact # 7: Blacks and Hispanics are disproportionately poorer than whites[299].

The result of fact # 7, on top of the previous ones, is that even if cocaine use is the same in all racial groups, blacks and Hispanics are far more likely to end up in prison for drug crimes. Dr. Hart reports that, "In Los Angeles--a city of nearly 4 million people--at the peak of the crack epidemic, not a single white person was arrested on federal crack cocaine charges, even though whites in the cities used and sold crack." [pg. 191] "Overwhelmingly, those incarcerated under the federal anticrack laws were black: for example, in 1992, the figure was 91 percent and in 2006 it was 82 percent." [pg.

---

[299]   http://www.pewsocialtrends.org/2011/07/26/wealth-gaps-rise-to-record-highs-between-whites-blacks-hispanics/

192] In fact, an American Journal of Public Health article[300] reports on a study of Chicago youths that found, "compared with African Americans, non-Hispanic Whites had 32.1 times the odds of cocaine-use disorder."

The facts about the disproportionate number of blacks and Hispanics in prison, as well as the injustice of it all and the way it is a "new Jim Crow," are discussed online[301] by Michelle Alexander, the author of *The New Jim Crow: Mass Incarceration in the Age of Colorblindness*.

The 18:1 law, however, is just the tip of the racist iceberg. The supposed purpose of the War on Drugs is to eliminate the use of addictive drugs because, supposedly, the use of such drugs is the cause of terrible social problems. As Dr. Hart demonstrates, however, this theory has no scientific basis in fact. All of the social problems blamed on heroin and cocaine existed prior to their use, and are not caused by their use. Only about 15% of habitual cocaine users are addicted in the sense of the drug preventing them from meeting their job and family responsibilities. Blaming social problems on drugs serves as a way for the ruling class to deflect attention from the real cause--poverty[302] and unemployment that are an

---

[300] http://ajph.aphapublications.org/doi/10.2105/AJPH.2015.303032

[301] http://www.reimaginerpe.org/20years/alexander

[302] In a study [http://www.chop.edu/news/poverty-more-damaging-gestational-drug-exposure] comparing about 112 "crack babies" to about as many non-crack babies, after 23 years of follow up, "The researchers consistently found no significant differences between the cocaine-exposed children and the controls." The organizer of the study concluded: "Poverty is a more powerful influence on the outcome of inner-city children than gestational exposure to cocaine." Medical journal articles on this topic are at https://www.ncbi.nlm.nih.gov/pubmed/21256423 and https://www.ncbi.nlm.nih.gov/pubmed/19686843 and https://www.ncbi.nlm.nih.gov/pubmed/18280843 .

integral part of our capitalist system that is based on, and promotes, extreme economic inequality. It is a way for the ruling class to make people think that blacks and Hispanics are the problem, instead of the plutocracy that rules our nation and keeps it very unequal.

Dr. Hart points to Portugal's way of dealing with drugs as a far more sensible approach (from the point of view, that is, of people who really care about solving social problems rather than from the point of view of a plutocracy that creates these problems as part of its way of controlling us.) In Portugal, users of illegal drugs "stopped by the police and found to have drugs are given the equivalent of a traffic ticket, rather than being arrested and stigmatized with a criminal record. The ticket requires them to appear before a local panel called (in translation) the Commission for Dissuasion of Drug Addiction, typically consisting of a social worker, a medical professional like a psychologist or psychiatrist, and a lawyer. Note that a police officer is not included. The panel is set up to address a potential health problem. The idea is to encourage users to honestly discuss their drug use with people who will serve as health experts and advisers, not adversaries. The person sits at a table with the panel. If he or she is not thought to have a drug problem, nothing further is usually required, other than payment of a fine. Treatment is recommended for those who are found to have drug problems--and referral for appropriate care is made. Still, treatment attendance is not mandatory. Repeat offenders, however--fewer than 10 percent of those seen every year--can receive noncriminal punishments like suspension of their driver's license or being banned from a specific neighborhood known for drug sales."

Dr. Hart reports that in Portugal, "The number of drug-induced deaths has dropped, as have overall rates of drug use, especially among young people (15-24 years old). In general, drug use rates in Portugal are similar, or slightly better, than in other European countries... No, it didn't stop all illegal drug use. That would have been an unrealistic expectation. Portuguese continue to get high, just like their contemporaries and all human societies before them. But they don't seem to have the problem of stigmatizing, marginalizing, and incarcerating substantial proportions of their citizens for minor drug violations."

The American ruling class clearly is not concerned about making things better for ordinary people, and the War on Drugs is not about making things better for ordinary people. It is about fomenting racism as a divide and rule strategy. It is about generating deceitful "evidence" for a racist stereotype in the form of black and Hispanic men thrown in prison and branded criminals for doing what even Barack Obama admitted[303] to once doing--using cocaine.

The War on Drugs increased[304] the prison population from 300,000 to 2 million; it targeted black and Hispanic men because they were black or Hispanic, not because they were using or selling drugs more than whites and not because crime was increasing. This was a bi-partisan racist attack. Bill Clinton's "tough on crime" policies increased the prison population more than any other president. "He and the 'New Democrats' championed legislation banning drug felons from public housing (no matter how minor the offense) and denying them basic public benefits, including food stamps, for life.

President Obama also used his power to increase[305], rather than decrease, the number of black people imprisoned because of the racially biased laws regarding cocaine.

The Civil Rights Movement abolished the racist Jim Crow laws but racist oppression was not abolished; it merely took another form: "From the back of the bus to the front of the prison" or

---

[303] http://abcnews.go.com/Politics/BothSidesAllSides/story?id=2773754&page=1

[304] http://www.reimaginerpe.org/20years/alexander

[305] https://www.blackagendareport.com/content/obama-administration-seeks-keep-tens-thousands-imprisoned-under-unfair-crack-vs-powder-cocai

"The new Jim Crow."[306] As the figure below (giving prison incarceration per 100,000 population, for blacks and whites and the ratio, from a University of Wisconsin proposal to the National Science Foundation[307]) illustrates, Jim Crow was simply replaced with racist prison incarceration, accomplished in large part by the War on Drugs:

In 1975, shortly after Jim Crow became history, the rate of black imprisonment sky rocketed, having been essentially constant for the previous five decades, while the rate of white imprisonment after 1975 rose only very slightly. The oppression of working class blacks after the success of the Civil Rights Movement took a new form, and is arguably worse now than during the years of Jim Crow.

---

[306] https://www.amazon.com/The-New-Crow-Incarceration-Colorblindness/dp/1595586431

[307] http://www.ssc.wisc.edu/~oliver/RACIAL/Reports/nsfAug01narrative.pdf

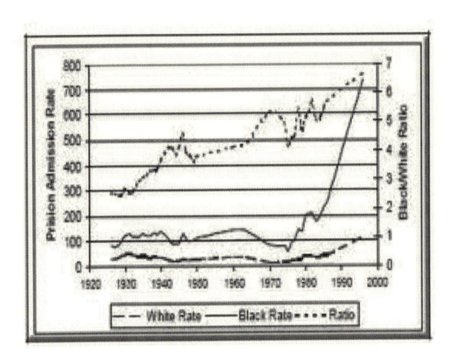

Discrimination in virtually every aspect of political, economic, and social life is now perfectly legal, if you've been labeled a felon." In U.S. federal prisons 41.4%[308] of prisoners are non-white whereas in the U.S. population only 24.9%[309] of the people are non-white. Linking criminality with being black or Hispanic by reminding the public of the disproportionately black and Hispanic character of prisoners (with all sorts of TV shows among other things) fuels racist fears that in turn allow racist policies to continue.

When the ruling class of a nation wrongfully imprisons people to advance a racist strategy of social control, it needs to be removed from power.

---

[308] https://www.bop.gov/about/statistics/statistics_inmate_race.jsp

[309] https://www.infoplease.com/us/race-population/population-united-states-race-and-hispaniclatino-origin-census-2000-and-2010

APPENDIX XI: EGALITARIAN MILITIAS

There have been egalitarian militias in the past, from which we can learn important principles to apply in creating our own egalitarian militias. These principles are:

- The members of the militia are volunteers, not conscripts.
- The members of the militia elect their officers and can recall them if and when they wish.
- The officers are authorized to give appropriate military orders and commands that must be obeyed, but they have no other privileges and wear no special insignia of ranks.
- The entire membership of the militia, as equals, democratically determines fundamental goals.

These principles, in whole or in part, were applied by peasants in the German Peasant War of 1525, by peasants and other working class people in England in their New Model Army in the 1640s, by the American revolutionaries in the Minuteman militia in the 1760s, and by workers and peasants in the anarchist militias of Spain in 1936-9.

APPENDIX XII: TRADE BETWEEN DISTINCT SHARING ECONOMIES

Despite the enormous advantages of being in a very large sharing economy (which may over time persuade everybody on the planet to form one single sharing economy) it may happen that distinct sharing economies form. People in one region may mutually decide to share among themselves but choose not to share freely with people in another region, even though the people in that other region share freely among themselves. There may thus be distinct sharing economies, of varying sizes. What will the economic relation between them be?

Though it is impossible to predict what people will do in the future, it is possible to imagine what are some of the things they might do that are consistent with egalitarian principles in this case.

Certainly the two sharing economies from two different regions could trade with each other. Delegates from each sharing economy could meet to craft proposals for trade that, if agreed to by enough local assemblies in each region to carry out the proposal, would be carried out. For example an agreed amount of lumber would be provided by one region to the other in exchange, say, for an agreed amount of rice or whatever. The sharing economy receiving the lumber would decide democratically what to do with it the same way they decide what to do with any other resource. Ditto for the rice.

Creativity would be called upon, no doubt. What if people in one region wanted to vacation in the other region? Here's how it might happen. The delegates crafting proposals for trade might include a proposal that one region (region A) will provide two-week memberships in their sharing economy to X number of people from the other region (region B) in exchange for something (whatever is agreed upon.) Then region B democratically decides how to select the X people who will get these two-week memberships and they will enjoy a totally free two-week vacation in region A. If the number of people in region B who want to vacation in region A is less than or equal to X, then no rationing is required. Otherwise vacations to region B would be rationed equitably according to need by some reasonable method, as discussed in Chapter Nine.

Additionally, individuals in each sharing economy can trade whatever they have with individuals in the other sharing economy, which is barter. True, barter is problematic, which is why the people in these distinct sharing economies would be better off forming one big sharing economy for all of them. But it's their call.

What could not happen is people using money to buy and sell things with people in another sharing economy. There is no money. The reason there is no money is that egalitarians know what the use of money leads to class inequality and related evils, as discussed in Chapter Six.

APPENDIX XIII: WHY DOES THE ROCKEFELLER FAMILY FUND WANT YOU TO REDUCE YOUR CARBON FOOTPRINT?

This appendix may at first seem out of place in a book about egalitarianism, since it takes a position on a scientific hypothesis about C02 and global warming, a subject on which egalitarian values have no obvious bearing. The laws of nature are the laws of nature, no matter whether one is an egalitarian or a fascist.

The connection between this C02/global warming hypothesis and egalitarianism, however, is this. Many people who want an egalitarian revolution think that it's not the right time to organize an egalitarian revolutionary movement, because there is a more pressing emergency to first deal with: catastrophic global warming caused by human-produced C02 from burning "fossil" fuels. Furthermore, these good people believe that, when it comes to this emergency, the appropriate thing to do is to support whomever advocates reducing our carbon footprint, even if—especially if!—they are rich and powerful people, and regardless of the fact that they are staunch anti-egalitarians.

If I believed that there was persuasive evidence to support the C02/global warming hypothesis that predicts catastrophic global warming unless we dramatically reduce our carbon footprint, then I would direct people's attention to the fact that capitalism is the main obstacle to saving the planet. This is the message of Naomi Klein's book, *This Changes Everything*. But in this case my anti-capitalist message would be challenged pretty effectively by those who could point to the fact that the people leading the charge against using fossil fuels include some of the richest capitalists on the planet, such as the Rockefellers.

What I do believe is that there is not any persuasive evidence to support the C02/global warming hypothesis, and clarity on this fact is important to enable egalitarians to avoid being derailed in their efforts to build an egalitarian revolutionary movement.

FACT #1: THE CLIMATE IS CHANGING (as it always has.)

FACT #2. C02 HAS SOME--BUT NOT NECESSARILY A SUBSTANTIAL OR ALARMING--GLOBAL WARMING EFFECT.

FACT #3: THERE IS NO PERSUASIVE EVIDENCE FOR THE HYPOTHESIS THAT HUMAN-PRODUCED C02 IS CAUSING CATASTROPHIC GLOBAL WARMING (A.K.A. THE "CATASTROPHIC ANTHROPOGENIC GLOBAL WARMING," OR CAGW HYPOTHESIS.)[310]

FACT #4: THE SO-CALLED "97% SCIENTIFIC CONSENSUS" IS MERELY AROUND FACTS #1 AND #2, NOT THE CAGW HYPOTHESIS. THERE IS ONLY

---

[310] Video: "Climate Change: What Do Scientists Say?" by an atmospheric physicist who has published more than 200 scientific papers and taught at MIT for 30 years and is a member of the National Academy of Sciences: https://www.youtube.com/watch?v=Owqly8lkv-c

A 0.3%[311] SCIENTIFIC CONSENSUS AROUND THE CAGW HYPOTHESIS.

FACT #5. THE MEDIA (BOTH MASS AND ALTERNATIVE) CALL PEOPLE WHO AGREE WITH FACTS #1 AND #2 BUT NOT THE CAGW HYPOTHESIS "CLIMATE CHANGE DENIERS."

FACT #6: NO HONEST REPORTER OR NEWS ORGANIZATION WOULD CALL SOMEBODY WHO AGREES WITH FACTS #1 AND #2 BUT NOT THE CAGW HYPOTHESIS A "CLIMATE CHANGE DENIER"; THEY WOULD CALL THEM A DENIER OF THE CAGW HYPOTHESIS.

CONCLUSIONS:

a) THE MASS AND ALTERNATIVE MEDIA ARE ENGAGED IN DELIBERATE DECEPTION ON THE QUESTION OF CLIMATE CHANGE AND C02, DECEPTION DESIGNED TO PERSUADE THE PUBLIC TO ACCEPT THE CAGW HYPOTHESIS BY MAKING IT SEEM THAT THE ONLY ALTERNATIVE IS TO DENY THAT THERE HAS BEEN CLIMATE CHANGE.
b) THE MEDIA ARE OBSCURING THE CRUCIAL DIFFERENCE BETWEEN A) TAKING APPROPRIATE STEPS TO ADAPT TO CLIMATE CHANGE AND REDUCE REAL POLLUTION (C02 IS NOT POLLUTION!), WHICH IS OBVIOUSLY A GOOD IDEA, VERSUS B) ATTEMPTING TO PREVENT CLIMATE CHANGE BY REDUCING OR ENTIRELY ELIMINATING THE USE OF "FOSSIL" FUELS.

READ BELOW TO SEE WHY THE MEDIA ARE DOING THIS.

---

[311] http://www.climaterealists.org.nz/sites/climaterealists.org.nz/files/Legatesetal 13-Aug30-Agnotology%5B1%5D.pdf

The Answer Has A Lot To Do With The Rockefeller Family's Role In American Society

As you can read in detail in this report[312] prepared for Congress in 1974 (when Nelson Rockefeller was nominated by Gerald Ford to be appointed Vice President) the Rockefeller Family fortune at that time was $70 Billion. By 2015 (when I wrote the first draft of this appendix), forty-one years later, it is reasonable to assume that, with compound interest at merely 5% per year, that fortune had grown to at least $517 Billion (and if it merely rose the same as the Dow Jones increased in these last forty-one years it would be $1.33 Trillion[313] and still more than $1 Trillion even if 20% were lost to taxes). This dwarfs the current fortunes of Bill Gates ($76 Billion[314]) or even the entire Walton (owners of Wal-Mart) family ($149 Billion[315]).

Moreover, as the report to Congress shows, the Rockefeller Family fortune is centrally controlled and has been used to give the Rockefeller family corporate control of a very large number of the largest corporations. Here are just some of the many corporations, according to the report, that had multiple interlocks with the Rockefeller Family: General Motors, Exxon, Chrysler, General Electric, Mobil Oil, IBM, U.S. Steel, RCA, Eastman Kodak, Union Carbide, Caterpillar Tractor, Xerox, W.R. Grace, General Foods, Singer, Ralston Purina, Honeywell, Bendix, Colgate-Palmolive, and the list goes on for a total of 108 corporations, including banks, life insurance

---

[312] http://socrates.berkeley.edu/~schwrtz/Rockefeller.html

[313] The Dow Jones Industrial Average rose from 855 in 1974 to 16,253 on September 9, 2015. This is an increase by a factor of 19. Thus if the Rockefeller family's fortune increased in value at merely the same rate as the Dow Jones, it would be worth $1.33 Trillion (with a T) dollars today and more than $1 Trillion if 20% were lost to taxes.

[314] https://www.forbes.com/profile/bill-gates/

[315] https://www.forbes.com/profile/walton-1/

companies, utilities and airlines.

Until his recent death, David Rockefeller was the patriarch of the Rockefeller family. He was the head of a huge private financial empire. He also was directly involved in managing the U.S. government's support for, and protection of, his empire and the social system of capitalism that enables people such as the Rockefellers to enjoy their wealth, power and privilege as a ruling upper class. Thus David Rockefeller had been the chairman[316] of the Council on Foreign Relations (CFR), which is an exclusive "think tank" that essentially determines U.S. foreign policy and provides[317] the key government executives (such as Henry Kissinger and Condoleeza Rice) who have implemented it. Six members of the Rockefeller family are members of the CFR. The domination by CFR members of the top U.S. government posts related to foreign policy is detailed online (up through the Clinton administration[318]) here, and the pattern continues[319].

It is evident why it has been said of David Rockefeller that if he had been made president of the United States it would have been a demotion.

The Rockefeller Family Fund Wants You To Reduce Your Carbon Footprint

The Rockefeller Family Fund (RFF) on its website says[320]:

> "Our program emphasizes public education on the risks

---

[316] https://www.cfr.org/project/david-rockefeller-lecture-series

[317] http://www.cfr.org/about/membership/roster.html?letter=B

[318] http://modernhistoryproject.org/mhp?Article=FinalWarning&C=5.3

[319] http://dissidentvoice.org/2015/04/another-cfr-rhodes-agent-for-secretary-of-defense/

[320] http://www.rffund.org/programs/environment

of global warming and implementation of sound solutions. RFF is interested in the development of initiatives designed to enact aggressive policies at the state and national levels to reduce carbon emissions; ..."

A World Bank website headline[321] reads:

"The Rockefeller Foundation, World Bank Group Innovate to Improve Cities' Access to Funding for Low-Carbon Infrastructure."

The *Guardian* reports[322]:

"Heirs to Rockefeller oil fortune divest from fossil fuels over climate change"

and *RT* reports[323]:

"Rockefeller oil dynasty to 'divest' from fossil fuels," adding that the Rockefeller family announced, "Our immediate focus will be on coal and tar sands, two of the most intensive sources of carbon emissions..." and "In a symbol of the times, America's biggest 'oil family', the Rockefellers, has announced it will get rid of any investments or holdings in fossil fuels from its $860 million charitable fund, and target clean energy instead."

Newsweek headlined[324], "Big Oil Heirs to Say Goodbye to Fossil Fuels" and reported,

---

[321] http://www.worldbank.org/en/news/press-release/2015/02/18/the-rockefeller-foundation-world-bank-group-innovate-to-improve-cities-access-to-funding-for-low-carbon-infrastructure

[322] https://www.theguardian.com/environment/2014/sep/22/rockefeller-heirs-divest-fossil-fuels-climate-change

[323] https://www.rt.com/business/189928-rockefeller-oil-divest-fossil-fuels/

[324] http://www.newsweek.com/big-oil-heirs-say-goodbye-fossil-fuels-272311

> *"The Rockefeller Brothers Fund (RBF), a private charitable foundation with $860[325] million worth of assets as of July 31, 2014, announced Monday that the fund would divest from fossil fuels."*

The New York Times in 2008 reported[326] that the Rockefeller family was using its large holdings in ExxonMobil to pass board of director resolutions aiming to "start moving beyond the oil age" and that, "David Rockefeller, retired chairman of Chase Manhattan Bank and patriarch of the family, issued a statement saying, 'I support my family's efforts to sharpen Exxon Mobil's focus on the environmental crisis facing all of us.'"[327] It also reported, "Kenneth P. Cohen, vice president for public affairs at Exxon, said the shareholders pushing the resolutions were 'starting from a false premise.' He added that the company was already concerned about 'how to provide the world the energy it needs while at the same time reducing fossil fuel use and greenhouse gas emissions.'"

Big Oil Also Wants You To Reduce Your Carbon Footprint

It's not just the Rockefellers who want you to reduce your carbon footprint. It's Big Oil too. There are statements by the major Big Oil corporations on this topic.[328] A typical one is by Chevron:

> *"[W]e recognize and share the concerns of governments and the public about climate change. There is a widespread view that the increase in atmospheric greenhouse gases (GHGs) is a contributor*

---

[325] http://www.rbf.org/about/finance

[326] http://www.nytimes.com/2008/05/27/business/27exxon.html?_r=0

[327] http://www.nytimes.com/2008/05/27/business/27exxon.html

[328] http://citizensclimatelobby.org/wp-content/uploads/2013/07/Oil-Co-Statements.pdf

to climate change, with adverse effects on the environment."

David Rockefeller was a (possibly founding[329]) member[330] of

---

[329] The Club of Rome does not say exactly where it was founded at its initial meeting in Italy in 1968; it's website page about this (no longer a live link, apparently) merely once said:
"A quiet villa and a big bang
In April 1968, a small international group of professionals from the fields of diplomacy, industry, academia and civil society met at a quiet villa in Rome. Invited by Italian industrialist Aurelio Peccei and Scottish scientist Alexander King, they came together to discuss the dilemma of prevailing short-term thinking in international affairs and, in particular, the concerns regarding unlimited resource consumption in an increasingly interdependent world.
There are two theories about at which "quiet villa" the Club of Rome was founded, and they are given, in Italian, at this website [http://www.ticinolive.ch/2012/09/27/il-nemico-comune-dellumanita-e-luomo-labile-presunto-dualismo-del-club-di-roma/], with the following Google translation to English:
There are two theories about the foundation of the Club of Rome:
1. thesis: Aurelio Peccei meets in Rome at the Accademia dei Lincei thirty scholars from around the world to create a sort of think tank free and independent to stimulate debate on the complex dynamics and on the interconnections between the natural systems and the social, technological and economic.
2. thesis: The Club of Rome was created at the Villa Serbelloni in Bellagio, the Rockefeller Foundation. It 'an organization of industrialists, bankers and scientists from 25 countries..."

the Club of Rome, and Al ("An Inconvenient Truth") Gore is a member who chaired[331] its 1997 meeting. The Club of Rome is the premier organization warning about human-produced (anthropogenic) C02 causing catastrophic global warming (a.k.a. "catastrophic anthropogenic global warming," a.k.a. CAGW). Whether a member[332] of the Club of Rome or not, Bill ("the richest man in the world") Gates also warns of the need to entirely eliminate[333] C02 emissions by the end of this century, "get to zero" as he puts it.

Those who think skeptics of the CAGW hypothesis in the scientific community are merely agents of Big Oil, which supposedly denies the CAGW hypothesis, might be surprised to know that the Club of Rome has a very friendly relationship with Saudi Arabia's and Kuwait's rulers--the biggest of the Big Oil personages in the world. The Club of Rome's website[334] reports that its "Hellenic Chapter of the Club of Rome" held a conference titled "A New Development Strategy for Energy and the Economy" January 19, 2011 at the Public Power Corporation Athens Club. In attendance at this meeting were, among others, "Ministers and Counselors from the Embassies of Belgium, the USA, France, Turkey, Croatia, Slovakia, **Saudi Arabia**, Kazakhstan, Korea, and **Kuwait**..." (my emphasis). The Hellenic Chapter of the Club of Rome also held a conference titled, "Economic and Environmental Crises: An Opportunity to Build a Green Society" at the Office of the European Parliament in Greece on April 14, 2009. Attending this meeting was, among others, "Fahad Al-Mansouri, Counsellor from the Royal Embassy of Saudi Arabia."

---

[330] http://www.nndb.com/org/142/000056971/

[331] http://education.jhu.edu/PD/newhorizons/future/articles/rome/

[332] http://www.nndb.com/org/142/000056971/

[333] https://www.gatesnotes.com/Energy/Energy-Innovation

[334] http://www.clubofrome.gr/activities.html

The Club of Rome has another solid supporter: Britain's Prince Charles. The prince solidly backs the Club of Rome's agenda, as is quite evident in a video[335] of Prince Charles addressing the UN's Rio+20 Conference on Sustainable Development in 2012 in Rio de Janeiro, Brazil. Prince Charles tells the conference "its proposition that there has to be proper recognition of the peril we are in is one that I agree with wholeheartedly." He then goes on to say that he even "played host to a preparatory international gathering on board the old royal yacht Britannia in the Amazon delta some fourteen months before ... the first summit twenty years ago." He then lamented "the increasingly dire warnings issued by yourselves and others around the world that we are rapidly breaching one planetary boundary after another have been consistently and alarmingly ignored." This was an unwittingly ironical turn of phrase, given that the British royal family, in the person of Queen Elizabeth, stands solidly with British Petroleum Corporation[336], an oil company that "breached one planetary boundary" in the Gulf of Mexico most undeniably!

A partial list of people who are a member of the Club of Rome or one of its sister organizations (discussed below) includes Al Gore[337], Mikhail Gorbachev[338], Kofi Annan[339], Joseph Stiglitz[340], the Dalai Lama[341], Elie Wiesel[342], Bill

---

[335] https://www.youtube.com/watch?v=8T51m1Sjyzl

[336] http://tampa.legalexaminer.com/toxic-substances/queen-of-england-asks-u-s-supreme-court-to-give-bp-a-pass/

[337] http://www.abc.net.au/news/2007-06-05/club-of-rome-member-warns-against-council/58734

[338] http://www.clubofrome.org/member/mikhail-gorbachev/

[339] http://www.clubmadrid.org/en/miembro/kofi_annan

[340] http://www.clubofrome.net/news/index.html#stiglitz

[341] http://www.clubofbudapest.org/clubofbudapest/index.php/en/

[342] http://www.clubofbudapest.org/clubofbudapest/index.php/en/

Clinton[343] and Jimmy Carter[344]; multi-billionaire David Rockefeller[345] (until he died); and royalty: Juan Carlos I – King of Spain[346], Prince Philippe of Belgium[347], Queen Beatrix of the Netherlands[348], and Dona Sophia – Queen of Spain[349].

The Club of Rome has created sister organizations that work for its aims. One such organization is the Club of Budapest, which describes its connection to the Club of Rome on its website[350] and provides a list of its members[351].

Another organization created by the Club of Rome is the Club of Madrid, which on its website[352] lists the Club of Rome as one of its "Partners." On their website the "World Leadership Alliance Club de Madrid" lists[353] (by my count) 106 members, all of whom are former presidents or prime ministers of a nation, plus others such as Kofi Annan (former Secretary General of the United Nations), Jacques Delors (former

---

[343] http://www.clubmadrid.org/en/miembro/bill_clinton

[344] http://www.abc.net.au/news/2007-06-05/club-of-rome-member-warns-against-council/58734 (Note this also says that Bill Gates is a member of the Club of Rome.)

[345] http://www.nndb.com/people/728/000022662/

[346] http://www.clubofrome.org/members-groups/honorary-members/

[347] http://www.clubofrome.eu/activities/

[348] https://www.clubofrome.org/member/beatrix-wilhelmina-armgard/

[349] http://www.clubofrome.org/members-groups/honorary-members/

[350] http://www.clubmadrid.org/en/our_funding

[351] http://www.clubofbudapest.org/clubofbudapest/index.php/en/about-us/organization

[352] http://www.clubmadrid.org/en/our_funding

[353] http://www.clubmadrid.org/img/estructuras/Brochure_CLUBdeMADRID_2015_WEB.pdf

president of the European Commission) and Javier Solana (former secretary general of NATO).

Billionaire Ted Turner (who personally owns 2.2 million[354] acres in 12 states and Argentina--twice the total acreage of the state of Delaware!) tells Charlie Rose in a video[355] that we have too many people using too much stuff and this is causing global warming that will have us all being cannibals in failed states before long.

Clearly, whether one agrees with or disagrees with the aims of the late David Rockefeller and Big Oil and European royalty and billionaires such as Ted Turner and Bill Gates and the hundreds of former heads of national governments in the Club of Madrid, it is naive to believe that if one protests the failure or reluctance of certain politicians or corporate CEOs to do what these powerful people want them to do as quickly as they want, that one is thereby opposing the wealthiest and most powerful people on the planet. It just ain't so.

WHY Does The Rockefeller Family Fund Want You To Reduce Your Carbon Footprint?

Either the Rockefellers and the host of rich and powerful people in their camp are telling the truth about why they want us to reduce our carbon footprint (*i.e.,* burn less fossil fuel) or they are lying. Let's see how honest these people are, just as one would want to do if serving on a jury trial and a Rockefeller family patriarch were a witness. One way to evaluate a person's honesty on the witness stand is to see if they have or have not lied in the past about other things. So let's take a look at some things that the Rockefellers and "their people" are saying and see if we believe them.

The Club of Rome's Secretary General, Ian Johnson,

---

[354] http://www.businessinsider.com/the-25-biggest-landowners-in-america-2012-10?op=1/#the-irving-family-owns-12-million-acres-21

[355] https://www.youtube.com/watch?v=DSIB1nW4S54

is promoting[356] a book titled, *Enough is Enough*. (The Club of Rome website itself promoted the book when it came out.) The Club of Rome, with this book, is telling the world what its aims are. Here's what that book says:

> *"The 7 billion of us have to do better, and we'd better do better soon. We need to find ways to reverse the climate change we've set in motion and halt the extinction crisis. At the same time we have to eradicate poverty and erase the divide between the haves and the have-nots."* [location 185 (4%) on the kindle version.]

On the Rockefeller Foundation website[357], the president of the foundation, Dr. Judith Rodin along with Jim Yong Kim, the president of the World Bank, say that an aim of the foundation is "Universal Health Care" globally. They lament that:

> *"100 million people fall into poverty each year to pay for health care."*

Rockefeller Foundation president, Dr. Judith Rodin, also expresses a great desire to make sure everybody has a good job. On the Rockefeller Foundation website[358] it asks, "What Exactly Is a Good Job?" There's a photo with a street display of the foundation that says, "GOOD JOBS FOR ALL." We also read:

> *"The Rockefeller Foundation and our partner Purpose[359], found that one in five respondents lack basic benefits like health insurance, dental and*

---

[356] http://www.steadystate.org/discover/enough-is-enough/praise/

[357] https://www.rockefellerfoundation.org/blog/universal-health-coverage-smart/

[358] https://www.rockefellerfoundation.org/blog/what-exactly-is-a-good-job/

[359] https://www.rockefellerfoundation.org/our-work/grants/purpose-global-llc/

vision care, paid vacation, paid sick leave, or paid paternal leave.

"With 83 percent of Americans saying that their employment impacts their overall well-being, we believe that they deserve more than the bare minimum—they deserve the chance to define what a good job means to them."

So now it's time to ask, "Do you believe these people really want what they say they want?" Does the patriarch of a family with a private fortune of at least $517 Billion (and more likely $1 Trillion) truly aim to erase the divide between the haves and the have-nots?

Does Jim Yong Kim, the president of the World Bank that partners with the Rockefeller Brothers Fund and the Rockefeller Foundation, truly lament the fact that *100 million people fall into poverty each year to pay for health care*?

Here's a clue. The World Bank has a notorious history of increasing, not decreasing, misery for the poorest people. Read about it online[360] and watch a video[361] by "economic hit man, John Perkins."

Here's another clue. Before Jim Yong Kim was made the president of the World Bank he was made the director of the Center for Health and Human Rights, at the Harvard School of Public Health where I worked. The Center had for many years sponsored events and published articles about health in Palestine, but had never said that the chief cause of poor health there was Israel's immoral and racist ethnic cleansing of non-Jews (resulting, for example, in women in labor being detained at checkpoints and thus denied access to the nearest

---

[360] http://www.thelancet.com/pdfs/journals/lancet/PIIS0140673605634733.pdf and http://www.thirdworldtraveler.com/IMF_WB/adjust_costs_Dark.html and http://www.globalresearch.ca/what-the-world-bank-actually-does/5396476 .

[361] https://www.youtube.com/watch?v=-osKdUzG_nM

hospital, just because they were not Jewish). I had for years been trying to persuade the previous director of the Center to at least sponsor a symposium where the morality of this ethnic cleansing would be debated in a proper academic manner. I argued that this should be done if for no other reason than the facts that 1) the Harvard School of Public Health had engraved in six languages on the exterior face of its building that "The highest attainable standard of health is one of the fundamental rights of every human being" and 2) the last I heard, Palestinians were human beings. The previous director refused to even sponsor a discussion of the question, privately telling me that the reason was "fear for the reputation of the Center." Fast forward to Jim Yong Kim's appointment as director. One day we were in the elevator together, and I asked him if he would consider doing anything to raise the question of whether Israel's ethnic cleansing was justifiable or not. He said no, he would not. Shortly after his very brief tenure as director of the Center he was appointed president of Dartmouth College, and then shortly after that he was appointed president of the World Bank. He was on the fast track all right, but not a track meant for people who take the side of the have-nots against the haves!

What about the Rockefeller Foundation's goal to ensure that everybody has a good job, as defined by the employee him or herself, with benefits like health insurance, dental and vision care, paid vacation, paid sick leave, or paid paternal leave? To help you decide if he's speaking truthfully about this being his real goal, consider the history of the last several decades in the United States, where David Rockefeller had more power than the president. Economic inequality has skyrocketed. There is huge unemployment and underemployment, college graduates scramble just to get unpaid internships, and hardly anybody has dental and vision care. The "good jobs" have been largely shipped to cheap labor foreign nations and the people who had them are lucky to have a lower paying job with fewer, if any, benefits, instead of no job at all. Unemployment among blacks was around 10% versus the comparable rates for whites, Hispanics and Asians of 4.7 percent, 6.6 percent and 4.0 percent, respectively, according to data released by the U.S. Bureau of Labor Statistics in February 2015)[362], while racist incarceration has climbed to obscene levels and is the "new Jim Crow." Do you really believe that the Rockefeller Foundation means what it says about wanting everybody to have a good job?

If the Rockefeller Foundation can't be believed about wanting to erase the divide between the haves and the have-nots and wanting to prevent people from falling into poverty to pay for their health care and wanting to ensure that everybody has a good job, then why should you believe them when they say that you need to reduce your carbon footprint or else there will be catastrophic global warming?

The Rockefeller Class And The Corruption Of Climate Science

Perhaps you believe the scientific hypothesis that anthropogenic (*i.e.,* human-produced, from C02 resulting from burning fossil fuel) catastrophic global warming is occurring (a.k.a. the Catastrophic Anthropogenic Global Warming, or CAGW hypothesis). If you believe this, it's very likely because you've read that 97% of climate scientists believe it. But it's not true. There's even a peer reviewed journal article that shows it's not true[363]. The *abstract* of this paper reads as follows in its entirety, and my bolding indicates the part most relevant to us:

> **Abstract** *Agnotology is the study of how ignorance arises via circulation of misinformation calculated to mislead. Legates et al. (Sci Educ 22:2007–2017, 2013) had questioned the applicability of agnotology to*

---

[362] http://www.ibtimes.com/black-unemployment-rate-2015-better-economy-african-americans-see-minimal-gains-1837870

[363] See http://www.climaterealists.org.nz/sites/climaterealists.org.nz/files/Legatesetal13-Aug30-Agnotology%5B1%5D.pdf or https://link.springer.com/article/10.1007/s11191-013-9647-9#/page-1

*politically-charged debates. In their reply, Bedford and Cook (Sci Educ 22:2019–2030, 2013), seeking to apply agnotology to climate science, asserted that fossil-fuel interests had promoted doubt about a climate consensus. Their definition of climate 'misinformation' was contingent upon the post-modernist assumptions that scientific truth is discernible by measuring a consensus among experts, and that a near unanimous consensus exists. However, **inspection of a claim by Cook et al. (Environ Res Lett 8:024024, 2013) of 97.1% consensus**, heavily relied upon by Bedford and Cook, **shows just 0.3% endorsement of the standard definition of consensus: that most warming since 1950 is anthropogenic.** Agnotology, then, is a two-edged sword since either side in a debate may claim that general ignorance arises from misinformation allegedly circulated by the other. Significant questions about anthropogenic influences on climate remain. Therefore, Legates et al. appropriately asserted that partisan presentations of controversies stifle debate and have no place in education. [my emphasis]*

Close inspection of the so-called "consensus" for the CAGW hypothesis, in other words, shows the "consensus" to be not 97%, but 0.3%. The illogical and misleading argument for the incorrect 97% figure is explained in great detail in the paper, and it does not take special technical knowledge to follow it. Please read it!

What many climate scientists **do** believe is the following: There was about five times more C02 in the atmosphere during the time of the dinosaurs than today. The earth was as warm or warmer than today about a thousand years ago in what is known as the Medieval Warm Period. That was followed by a cold spell known as the Little Ice Age. Since then the earth has been gradually warming again. C02 may have a very modest warming effect, but historically C02 increases have occurred after, not before, global warming; ocean warming, with a centuries-long time delay, may release C02, making atmospheric C02 more an effect than a cause of global warming. The future is uncertain, but some scientists believe that the current warming hiatus is the beginning of a new cooling period, based on sun activity cycles. And yes, of course we should take steps to adapt to climate change, whatever the climate change may be; but those steps should be based on good science.

You've probably seen, and been frightened by, the infamous "hockey stick" graph that purports to show that global temperature has been low for a thousand years until the second half of the 20th century when it shot up unprecedentedly supposedly because of industrial-produced C02 that started to rise then. Al Gore featured this "hockey stick" graph in his Inconvenient Truth film and it has been widely disseminated to make people believe the CAGW theory. But the basis for the "hockey stick" graph is scientific fraud, as detailed in the book *The Hockey Stick Illusion*[364], by A.W. Montford, which you should also read. The fraud consists of things such as cherry-picking data, *i.e.*, selecting data that gives the pre-determined desired result and rejecting data that fails to do so. The book illustrates how "cherry-picking" has infected paleoclimatology (the study of past climates) by citing a paleoclimatology journal paper[365] in which the author, Jan Esper, shamelessly admits doing it, with these words (about selecting data):

> *"Before venturing into the subject of sample depth and chronology quality, we state from the beginning, 'more is always better'. However, as mentioned earlier on the subject of biological growth populations, this does not mean that one could not improve a chronology [a set of data--JS] by reducing the number of series [subsets of*

---

[364] https://www.amazon.com/Hockey-Stick-Illusion-W-Montford-ebook/dp/B005A54KEM/ref=sr_1_1?s=books&ie=UTF8&qid=1440120454&sr=1-1&keywords=the+hockey+stick+montford

[365] Esper J. *et al*, Tests of the RCS method for preserving low-frequency variability in long tree-ring chronologies. Tree Ring Research. 2003; 59: 81-98 at http://arizona.openrepository.com/arizona/handle/10150/262573 where one can download the pdf file of the actual article

*data--JS] used if **the purpose of removing samples is to enhance a desired signal.** The ability to pick and choose which samples to use is an advantage unique to dendroclimatology [the science of determining past climates from trees (primarily properties of the annual tree rings)--JS]."* [my emphasis]

The author of *The Hockey Stick Illusion*, Montford, after providing this quotation, rightly says, *"...which is a statement to send a shudder down the back of any reputable scientist."* Montford adds, *"Esper argued that he had taken these steps to avoid getting a biased chronology. To some readers, however, they might sound much more like a way of obtaining one. After all, the object of the exercise was to discover what signal was in the tree rings, not to choose a subsection of the rings that gave a 'desired signal.'"*

As Montford describes in detail, the editors of the scientific journal, *Nature*, went out of their way to promote the fraudulent "hockey stick" graph not only by publishing it initially but by severely restricting subsequent criticism of it in their journal and thereby preventing their readers from seeing the full extent of the fraud behind it. Furthermore, despite that journal's policy of requiring authors to make their analysis methods (*i.e.,* computer code in the case of the "hockey stick" graph) available upon request, the editors did not enforce this policy when critics of the "hockey stick" asked for this information.

What Corrupt Science Looks Like

From January 1990 to November 2014, the difference between the mean change in observed global temperature versus the mean change in global temperature predicted by the CAWG hypothesis was dramatic. The predicted increase was 0.69 degrees Centigrade but the observed increase was only 0.34 degrees Centigrade—less than half what was predicted. A graph of these temperatures is included in an article by Christopher Monckton, published January 2015 online,[366] which is the source for the following statements about global temperature up to 2015. The observed temperature change is, as the confidence bounds in the graph indicate, too far below the predicted change to be reasonably attributed to random chance. The CAWG hypothesis has failed the test of science: what it predicted is not what was actually observed.

Another graph (same source) shows no global warming for 18 years 3 months from October 1996 to December 2014; this is known in the scientific literature (which doesn't deny it) as the global warming "hiatus."

Good science works like this. A hypothesis is proposed. To test it, the hypothesis is used to make a prediction about what will be observed. This prediction is stated explicitly and unambiguously before any observation is made. Then the observation is made. If the observation is what the hypothesis predicted, meaning it is closer to what was predicted than could be explained by random chance if the hypothesis were not true (*i.e.,* if the "null hypothesis" were true), then the observation is considered to be statistically significant evidence in support of the hypothesis. Otherwise, it is considered to be NOT statistically significant evidence in support of the hypothesis; the hypothesis fails the test. When a hypothesis fails the test (despite the fact that--as in our case--sufficient data of a sufficient quality was collected so that the hypothesis would be unlikely to have failed the test if it were correct) the scientifically correct thing to do is to try to come up with a better hypothesis. The wrong thing to do is to try to "explain away" the failure of the hypothesis by claiming (*post hoc, i.e.,* after seeing the actual observation) that what the hypothesis REALLY predicted is what was in fact observed. This kind of BAD SCIENCE enables one to defend virtually any hypothesis with clever excuses for its failure to predict what was actually observed. For example:

---

[366] https://wattsupwiththat.com/2015/01/03/the-great-pause-lengthens-again/

Bad Scientist: "The earth is not spherical, it is flat."

Good Scientist: "Let's put your hypothesis to the test."

Bad Scientist: "Good idea. My flat-earth hypothesis predicts that if we go to the beach and look at the horizon when a Tall Ship first becomes visible, we'll see the top and bottom of the ship at the same time, not the top first as would be predicted by the spherical earth hypothesis."

[After they return from the beach]

Good Scientist: "Looks like your flat earth hypothesis failed the test; we both clearly saw the top of the ship before the bottom."

Bad Scientist: "That's only because--who knew?--the bottom (hull) of the ship was painted blue and it was harder to see against the blue water than it was to see the white sail against the blue sky. My flat earth hypothesis was actually confirmed."

Good Scientist: "Really? But when the ship got close to us we could plainly see that the hull was painted red."

Bad Scientist: "True, and that means we have made an important discovery! Marine paint that looks blue from a distance looks red up close. I'm going to publish this fact in the Journal of Paintology."

Climate scientists who defend the CAGW hypothesis have resorted to BAD SCIENCE. They are publishing articles in prestigious journals such as Nature that attempt to "explain away" the global warming hiatus in order to maintain credibility for the CAGW hypothesis despite that fact that it has failed its test.

Thus *Nature* published an article[367], titled "Recent global

---

[367] http://www.nature.com/nature/journal/v501/n7467/abs/nature12534.html

warming hiatus tied to equatorial Pacific surface cooling," which "explains away" the CAGW's failure by saying, "Here we show that accounting for recent cooling in the eastern equatorial Pacific reconciles climate simulations [*i.e.,* the predictions of the CAGW hypothesis by computer programs incorporating that hypothesis—J.S.] and observations."

Nature also published an article[368], titled "Recent intensification of wind-driven circulation in the Pacific and the ongoing warming hiatus," which "explains away" the CAGW's failure by saying,

> *"Here we show that a pronounced strengthening in Pacific trade winds over the past two decades— unprecedented in observations/reanalysis data and not captured by climate models—is sufficient to account for the cooling of the tropical Pacific and a substantial slowdown in surface warming through increased subsurface ocean heat uptake...This hiatus could persist for much of the present decade if the trade wind trends continue, however rapid warming is expected to resume once the anomalous wind trends abate."*

So, according to these bad scientists, the CAGW hypothesis is still true, despite failing its test, because of *"recent cooling in the eastern equatorial Pacific."* No, it's because of a *"pronounced strengthening in Pacific trade winds."* But wait! There's more. There are 52 different ways[369] the failure of the CAGW hypothesis has been "explained away" by bad science. Perhaps the leading way the failure of the CAGW hypothesis is explained away is the theory that the heat from global warming doesn't affect thermometers in the air because it's all going into the ocean by melting the polar ice instead. But this

---

[368] http://www.nature.com/nclimate/journal/v4/n3/abs/nclimate2106.html

[369] https://wattsupwiththat.com/climate-fail-files/list-of-excuses-for-the-pause-in-global-warming/

argument is numerically flat out false[370].

Note, by the way, that whatever the climate does in the future, get warmer or not, the CAGW theory about how C02 affects global temperature is not the theory that will explain it; this theory has already been shown not to make correct predictions and even if, like the broken clock that is right twice a day but clearly not giving the correct time otherwise, its predictions are sometimes true, that does not constitute evidence for the theory. (The same author, Christopher Monckton, who published the article in 2015 cited above, published an updated article[371] in January 2017. The same very large difference between what the CAGW hypothesis predicts and what has been actually observed remains the case.)

The question is, how come bad science has taken over in climatology? Scientists and science journal editors come from a long tradition of being very determined to understand the sources of bias, especially unintentional bias, and very careful to use methods designed to prevent bias. The whole purpose of the hypothesis testing procedure described above is to prevent bias in conclusions. In areas of science where Big Money does not have an agenda that it wants science to back up, scientists perform good science and journals weed out bad science. So why has bad science taken over climatology? Why do the most prestigious journals, such as Nature, publish bad science and severely restrict criticism of it in the journal?

The answer to the above questions that is most likely the true one is this. Billionaires such as the Rockefellers and Ted Turner and Bill Gates and royalty, for whatever reason, want people to believe that if they don't dramatically reduce their carbon footprint by reducing the burning of fossil fuels, then

---

[370] https://wattsupwiththat.com/2016/05/18/ingenious-or-misleading-rational-for-the-pause/

[371] https://wattsupwiththat.com/2017/01/07/when-will-the-pause-in-global-temperature-return/

there will be catastrophic global warming and the end of human civilization. And these billionaires and royalty have enormous power in society, the kind of power that controls the mass media, the kind of power that makes or breaks an individual's career (the author of the "hockey stick" paper, Michael Mann, was only a recent Ph.D. when he published his "hockey stick" paper, but then he was catapulted to being the preeminent scientist in paleoclimatology), and the kind of power that can bend scientific journal editors in the direction of bad science to support the CAGW hypothesis.

Why, Really, Is The Rockefeller Foundation Telling Us To Reduce Our Carbon Footprint?

Just because David Rockefeller told us (in a video[372] of his speech, for example) that he was trying to save the world from *"the spectre of an alarming and possibly catastrophic disaster to the biosphere we live in,"* that doesn't mean that was his real aim, any more than the Rockefeller Foundation's claim of wanting to ensure that everybody has a good job means that is its real aim, or that the Club of Rome's claim that it wants to erase the divide between the haves and the have-nots means that that is its real aim.

Nor is it likely that billionaires and royalty, with access to the same information that yours truly has, are unaware that the claims for the CAWG hypothesis are unfounded.

So what, then, is the real reason why David Rockefeller told us that the *"spectre of an alarming and possibly catastrophic disaster to the biosphere we live in"* haunts us and the only way to make it go away is to stop producing so much C02 from burning fossil fuels?

The obvious answer is that David Rockefeller (when he was alive) and the other billionaires and royalty in his camp want people to believe that it is vital, for the sake of saving human

---

[372] https://www.youtube.com/watch?v=OrSq3jbl1NQ

civilization, to drastically reduce fossil-fuel-based industrial production. Whatever their **real** reason is for wanting to reduce this type of industrial production, they apparently don't think it is a sufficiently convincing or appealing reason to get the world's population to accept, never mind embrace, such a goal. Catastrophic global warming, on the other hand, will, they feel, "scare be bejesus" out of people and make them passionately support lowering material productivity however much may be necessary to avoid using fossil fuel. Promises to provide a good job for all and to *"erase the divide between the haves and the have-nots,"* they hope, will help even more to persuade people to follow the leadership of Rockefellers and other upper class climate fear mongers.

Before considering why the Rockefellers *et al* want to abandon the use of fossil fuels, let's note another reason why they like making people fear anthropogenic catastrophic global warming. This reason can be gleaned from the writings of intellectuals whom David Rockefeller relied upon to think for him and act in his interests.

In 1991 the Club of Rome published a report, titled *The First Global Revolution*, authored by Alexander King and Bertrand Schneider. The authors write:

> *"There appears to be a general loss of the values which previously ensured the coherence of society and the conformity of its individuals. In some places this has been the result of a loss of faith in religion and the ethical values it promulgates. In other cases it stems from a loss of confidence in the political system and those who operate it."* [pg. 41]

> *"In searching for a new enemy to unite us, we came up with the idea that pollution, the threat of global warming, water shortages, famine and the like would fit the bill. In their totality and in their interactions these phenomena do constitute a common threat which demands the solidarity of all peoples. But in designating them as the enemy, we fall into the trap about which we*

have already warned, namely mistaking symptoms for causes. All these dangers are caused by human intervention and it is only through changed attitudes and behaviour that they can be overcome. The real enemy, then, is humanity itself." [*pg. 115:* This is the entire text of a sub-section titled "The Common Enemy of Humanity is Man" and it concludes the chapter it is in, titled "The Vacuum"]

In 1997 David Rockefeller's protégé, Zbigniew Brzezinski, published *The Grand Chessboard*. Brzezinski, with David Rockefeller, founded[373] (and Brzezinski, appointed by Rockefeller to be the Executive Director, ran) the Trilateral Commission[374], an organization[375] of the corporate and government elites in Europe, the United States and Japan; and Brzezinski was President Jimmy Carter's National Security Advisor from 1977-81. (Just to remind us of what that means, recall that Carter increased military aid to Indonesia's President Suharto who used it to occupy East Timor and to kill 200,000 East Timorese. Carter also backed Ferdinand Marcos of the Philippines and the Shah of Iran, both notoriously anti-democratic and brutal rulers. Carter similarly backed the murderous Somoza regime in Nicaragua and had the U.S. Army School of the Americas train 250 Salvadoran officers and non-coms for El Salvador's brutal and violently repressive military that blew up every union meeting place and opposition newspaper as it killed opposition leaders.) In his book, Brzezinski writes:

"More generally, cultural change in America may also be uncongenial to the sustained exercise abroad of

---

[373] https://www.thomhartmann.com/forum/2015/05/zbigniew-brzezinski-admits-he-founded-trilateral-commission-david-rockefeller

[374] http://www.4rie.com/rie%205.html

[375] http://www.thirdworldtraveler.com/Engdahl_F_William/Rockefeller_Plan_SOD.html

genuinely imperial power. That exercise requires a high degree of doctrinal motivation, intellectual commitment, and patriotic gratification. Yet the dominant culture of the country has become increasingly fixated on mass entertainment that has been heavily dominated by personally hedonistic and socially escapist themes. The cumulative effect has made it increasingly difficult to mobilize the needed political consensus on behalf of sustained, and also occasionally costly, American leadership abroad...In addition, both America and Western Europe have been finding it difficult to cope with the cultural consequences of social hedonism and the dramatic decline in the centrality of religious-based values in society. [location 3225 in the kindle version]

"Unfortunately, to date, efforts to spell out a new central and worldwide objective for the United States, in the wake of the Cold War, have been one-dimensional. They have failed to link the need to improve the human condition with the imperative of preserving the centrality of American power in world affairs. Several such recent attempts can be identified." [location 3267 in the kindle version] [Brzezinski then cites the failure of the following: "the advocacy of 'assertive multilateralism' in the Clinton administration, the "notion that America should focus on global 'democratic enlargement'", the "elimination of the prevailing injustice in the global distribution of income," the "shaping a special 'mature strategic partnership' with Russia," "containing weapons proliferation," "safeguarding the environment," and "combating local wars."]

The theme here is clear: some new Big Idea (a veritable new religion) must be found with which to get the masses to follow the leadership of the upper class; it needs to restore *"the coherence of society and the conformity of its individuals."*

The elite have been grappling with the problem of finding such a Big Idea. After 2001 it seems the elite decided to go with "The War on Terror" but apparently David Rockefeller and company thought and think something better is also required. (Brzezinski, for example, says in an online article[376], that the War on Terror is in many ways harmful and far too unsophisticated ideologically to be the basis of American power in the world for the long term, and (in another online article[377]) how he identifies the threat of Global Warming as the real threat.)

In the period of feudalism, the Big Idea that enabled the upper class to control the masses was the idea that if one did not obey the Church (and its anointed royalty and aristocracy) one would suffer hellfire and brimstone for an eternity. This was a powerful idea indeed! Even people (such as Pascal famously[378]), who were very skeptical of the "eternity in hell" threat, reasoned that if there were even the slightest chance that it were true then it's safer to assume it is true and obey the rulers than to disobey them and risk finding out the hard way that eternal hell is the consequence.

Today the upper class climate fear mongers argue that we must put aside fighting for economic equality and against environmental pollution caused by profit-driven capitalists (such as BP and its destruction of much life in the Gulf of Mexico just to make a buck) because the "real enemy" is human-caused catastrophic global warming that can only be defeated if we all unite behind people like the Rockefellers and Al Gore and Bill Gates and Prince Charles to reduce our CO2 "footprint"; furthermore, if we don't do what these people say we must do, then the consequence will be even WORSE than an eternity of personal suffering in hell--it will be the end of the human race entirely because of climate catastrophe. How convenient is the anthropogenic catastrophic global warming

---

[376] http://www.washingtonpost.com/wp-dyn/content/article/2007/03/23/AR2007032301613.html

[377] http://www.nytimes.com/2012/04/08/books/review/zbigniew-brzezinski-and-robert-kagan-on-the-state-of-america.html?_r=0

[378] https://en.wikipedia.org/wiki/Pascal%27s_Wager

thesis! How much safer is the world for the likes of Rockefellers and royalty when the masses are persuaded that the enemy is not a small but extremely privileged upper class but rather that *"The real enemy, then, is humanity itself."*

Why Does The Rockefeller Foundation Want To Stop Using Fossil Fuels?

Independently of the question of global warming, the Club of Rome has been saying since its founding publication in 1972, *The Limits to Growth: A Report for the Club of Rome's Project on the Predicament of Mankind,*[379] that world population and material production--regardless of whether the energy is from fossil fuel, nuclear or solar--need to be limited because the world is finite. *The Limits to Growth* book does not single out fossil fuels from other things such as minerals (aluminum, chromium, *etc.*), the finite supply of which also constitutes a limit to material growth. Everything is finite, so why does the Rockefeller Foundation focus on fossil fuel?

Very likely, here's why. The Rockefellers, along with others in the billionaire and royalty upper class, are thinking ahead. They have apparently concluded that material growth on this planet cannot go on forever. But this creates a big problem for the upper class. Why? The ideological basis for the legitimacy of the capitalist upper class has, since the time of the Industrial Revolution, been based on its claim that its economic system--unlike the old feudal system it overthrew--increases economic production and will keep increasing it more and more and more forever. The Rockefeller Foundation sees that, "Houston, we have a problem!" What to do?

The solution that the Rockefeller Foundation is laying the groundwork for is this. Change the basis of legitimacy for the upper class enjoying its immense wealth, power and privilege. Change it from the claim that it will increase economic production forever to the claim that it will RESTRICT economic

---

[379] https://en.wikipedia.org/wiki/The_Limits_to_Growth

production and consumption in order to save the planet and human civilization. The Rockefeller Foundation apparently believes that it will be much harder to persuade the masses to live with less economic production and consumption if the argument is "Use less non-renewable resources so people have some in the future" than if the argument is "Save the planet and human civilization from imminent destruction!"

By focusing on fossil fuel, rather than non-renewable resources in general, The Rockefeller Foundation kills two birds with one stone: it can use the "Save the planet from climate catastrophe!" argument to justify ending the use of CO_2-producing fossil fuel, and by ending the use of fossil fuel it thereby dramatically reduces ALL economic production.

The future that the Rockefeller Foundation is preparing us to accept is one in which the upper class will be like the old feudal upper class. It will be the owning (not productive) class; it will be the class that owns the wealth of the planet, keeps the lion's share for itself, and doles out the rest to the masses in quantities small enough--as the masses will be told *ad nauseam*--to avoid *"the spectre of an alarming and possibly catastrophic disaster to the biosphere we live in."*

What Should We Do?

As long as society continues to be ruled by a privileged, wealthy, powerful, anti-democratic upper class, science will be subservient to that upper class. Ordinary people know this, and will therefore have every reason in the world to distrust scientists no matter whether the things scientists say are true or not. (This is why more and more people are starting to disbelieve what scientists tell them today, about things such as the benefits of pharmaceutical drugs versus alternative therapy, the safety of vaccinations, and even whether CO_2 is causing catastrophic global warming.)

In order for people to have confidence in scientists who study things such as climate and the limits to growth due to finite resources, we need to abolish the class inequality that prevents people from trusting such scientists. Until people trust scientists, and until--therefore--people have abolished class inequality to have genuine democracy and equality (*i.e.,* egalitarianism), they will not be able to democratically make important social decisions based on trusted scientific knowledge, and they will not willingly make sacrifices (such as producing and consuming less) that **may**--or may not[380]--indeed be called for. This is why, no matter what the truth is about climate and limits to growth, we need to make an egalitarian revolution.

---

[380] Or may not! An article [https://phe.rockefeller.edu/docs/Nature_Rebounds.pdf], authored by (interestingly) the Director of the Program for the Human Environment at The Rockefeller University (Jesse Huntley Ausubel), cites tons of data that indicate that Americans' use of non-renewable resources (land and minerals, etc.) leveled off and even in some important cases declined starting around 1970, contrary to all the dire predictions (based on the current trends) at that time. And a video [https://www.youtube.com/watch?v=eA5BM7CE5-8] presents data indicating that the population of the world is also leveling off, contrary to alarmist reports that it continues to be increasing exponentially.

APPENDIX XIV: HOW THE AUTHOR LEARNED WHAT CAUSES A POLITICAL SEA CHANGE

I learned what causes a sea change in people's political behavior at Dartmouth College, in 1969, a year after I graduated. Here's the story.

As a student at Dartmouth from 1964 until my graduation in 1968 I was very opposed to the War in Vietnam. With less than a dozen other like-minded students and a couple of anti-war faculty members, we tried to persuade other students to oppose the war too. But it was initially tough going. We distributed leaflets and engaged in informal dorm discussions and so forth, but saw little evidence that it was accomplishing much. We also stood in a "peace vigil" with a large sign that said simply "PEACE." We did this every Wednesday at noon on the grassy "Common" in the center of the campus, for years.

During my last year before graduating we organized a "teach-in" against the war. We invited as speakers not only nationally known opponents of the war, like the editor of *Ramparts* magazine, but also one of the government's chief defenders of the war, the Assistant Secretary of State for Southeast Asian Affairs, whose last name, if I recall correctly, was Dean.

The teach-in was one of the first such teach-ins in the nation. Hundreds of Dartmouth students came to it to hear the pro-war government representative confront the anti-war speakers. Many hoped to see the government demolish the anti-war side. What they saw, however, was very different. Faculty members who were experts on Southeast Asia exposed lie after lie uttered by the Assistant Secretary of State, to his face, and students in the audience saw that the man could not defend his lies credibly. It was a memorable experience for me. I saw conservative fraternity types who came to cheer the Assistant Secretary of State look in disbelief as it became clear the war was based on nothing but lies. I saw in the expressions on their faces that they were abandoning their support of the war. And each of them saw the same thing in the faces of the others.

The teach-in had two "roving microphones" so that people in the audience could participate with not only questions but also comments of their own. The pro-war side was fully represented, and failed—in the sight of all—to stand up to scrutiny.

That was 1968.

The following year I stayed around as an SDS [Students for a Democratic Society—the big anti-war organization at the time, of which we anti-war students at Dartmouth had constituted ourselves a chapter] regional traveler (my first job after graduating.) We continued to hold our little "peace vigils" with eight or ten people every Wednesday at noon, not knowing what else we could do.

Then one day the Dartmouth Conservative Society put out an edition of their newspaper with a headline calling for "Splatter Warfare" in Vietnam. They advocated dropping nuclear bombs on North Vietnam. As bad as that was, they did something else that frightened us even more, because we knew it was really going to happen. They called for a pro-war demonstration in one month, on a Wednesday, at noon, on the "Common" exactly where they knew we would be.

We felt nothing but dread as the terrible day approached, knowing that in order to save face we had no choice but to continue our peace vigil no matter what. I remember wishing that somehow I could snip the space-time continuum to jump over the dreaded day without having to actually experience it.

When the awful day did nonetheless arrive, I approached the Common from a distance and what I first saw there was fifty students holding pro-war signs. I said to myself, "Oh shit!" But then I saw something else. It was something I'd never seen before or expected to see. It was a long "snake" of people that winded all over the entire grassy Common. It consisted of 1500 people. And they were holding anti-war signs! This on a campus at which the entire student body consisted of only 3,000 students.

This Was The Day Everything Changed.

The previous day we viewed ourselves as a tiny minority among a majority that disagreed with us. On this day we learned that we were the majority.

We held an SDS meeting to discuss what to do. We decided to do something that, previously, we would never have even dreamed of doing in a million years—forcibly occupy the administration building and demand the abolition of the military reserve officer training program on campus, ROTC, that produced 2nd lieutenants for the war.

I distinctly remember something that happened at the next SDS meeting, just before we occupied the administration building. One student at the meeting, who had never shown any initiative or much enthusiasm for anything before, was holding in his hands an electric drill and some lock hasp hardware. I asked him, "What's that all about?" He replied, "Well, if we're going to take over the building, we should remove their locks and install our own." This was when I realized there had been a sea change. People were actually doing things—concrete acts of resistance and rebellion—that a couple of weeks ago nobody in their right mind would have even considered. A few days later hundreds of students took over the administration building. They ordered the deans to leave. When one dean refused to leave, they grabbed the chair he was sitting in and carried it, with the dean, down three flights of stairs and deposited him outside on the grass. And yes, we replaced the old locks with our own.

The College called the police and forcibly removed students from the building after a couple of days, arresting forty and placing them in jails scattered all over New Hampshire in order to make it hard to mount a protest because supporting friends and relatives would be dispersed to distant jail locations. The College even, at first, refused to provide the jailed students materials to study for final exams, knowing that failing grades would mean they'd lose their student deferment and be drafted into the military.

In response to the College's crackdown, many more hundreds of students protested, and a student strike developed. The faculty passed a resolution calling for ROTC to be abolished. The Trustees of the College held an emergency meeting and concluded that the College could not resume normal operations with ROTC on campus. They abolished ROTC. And it stayed abolished for ten years.

The Most Important Lesson Of My Life

I learned the most important lesson of my life at Dartmouth—a year after graduating. The lesson is this. It takes two things to cause the kind of political sea change that led students at Dartmouth to take the collective, militant action that, alone, could have abolished ROTC—action that, before the sea change, would have been considered out of the question. The two things are these: 1) People must know that their anti-establishment beliefs and aims are morally right. 2) People must know that in having their anti-establishment beliefs and aims they are not only morally right, but also a majority.

To make a revolution, people must 1) know they are morally right in wanting one, and they must also 2) know that, in wanting a revolution, they are in the majority.

The strategy for building a revolutionary movement is to use tactics designed to ensure that people know both of these things. Either one, by itself, is not enough. Both, in combination, however, cause a political sea change. When this happens, people on their own initiative will do amazing things, like the fellow who showed up with the drill and hasp.

When the sea change occurs, there will be a need for organization just as the building takeover at Dartmouth required organization. But before the sea change has occurred, the goal of our organizations is to do what it takes to create the sea change, which is not the same thing as carrying out the kinds of collective actions that can actually make a revolution.

As more and more Americans are realizing that we have only a fake democracy controlled by the rich, the first requirement for revolution—that people know it is morally right to want one—is getting easier and easier to meet. It is the second requirement—people knowing that, in wanting a revolution, they are the majority—that is our great challenge to meet. The ruling class's mass media are not persuasive when they try to argue that the rule of the rich is morally right, but they have been quite successful in persuading the public that, contrary to the truth, only a fringe minority wants revolution. We need to figure out ways of letting people learn that it's a majority, not a minority, that knows we have a fake democracy and wants a real one with no rich and no poor, and knows it will take revolution to get it. When we do this, the sea change will change the world. Nothing will be the same.

APPENDIX XV: WHY SOLDIERS WILL JOIN US

To remove the rich from power in the United States we need to persuade a critical mass of members of the American military forces to refuse to obey orders to attack the egalitarian revolutionary movement and instead use their weapons to help defend this movement from those who would attack it. A big reason for believing this is possible is that in 1975 the American ruling class was forced to withdraw from Vietnam in ignominious defeat because American GIs refused[381] orders to fight the Vietnamese peasants in the National Liberation Front.

If American GIs refused to attack Vietnamese peasants--foreigners about whom they had no prior knowledge and about whom they had been drilled with racist "kill the gooks" propaganda in their boot camp training--think how much more likely it is that GIs in the future will refuse to attack fellow Americans calling for an egalitarian society that the GIs themselves want too. Yes, people in the military now are volunteers in contrast to draftees in the Vietnam war days, but a) it's really a "poverty draft" today and b) whatever reason a person enlisted, keeping the rich in power was not one of them.

The story of the GIs' refusal to fight in Vietnam is told in the book, *Soldiers in Revolt: GI Resistance During the Vietnam War*, by David Cortwright, first published in 1975 and re-published in 2005.

---

[381] https://en.wikipedia.org/wiki/USS_Kitty_Hawk_riot

The following are excerpts from this book. Col. Robert D. Heinl, Jr., however, presents the same story, in his online article in the Armed Forces Journal, 7 June 1971, titled "The Collapse of the Armed Forces."[382]

[start of excerpts]

[Pg. 269-70] [A] survey found that during the height of the GI movement in 1970-71, one out of every four enlisted persons participated in dissident activities, with an equal percentage engaging in acts of disobedience. The combined results showed a startling 47 percent of low-ranking soldiers engaging in some form of dissent or disobedience, with 32 percent involved in such acts more than once. If frequent drug use is added as another form of resistance, the combined percentage of soldiers involved in disobedience, dissidence, or drug use came to an incredible 55 percent. The Army's own investigation thus showed that half of all soldiers were involved in some form of resistance activity--a truly remarkable and unprecedented level of disaffection. ...

The Army's study...confirmed what GI activists themselves understood. Contrary to popular impression, soldier opposition was far more concentrated among volunteers than among draftees.

[pg 261-2] A decade after the publication of *Soldiers in Revolt*, its central thesis was confirmed by former Army Captain Shelby Stanton in his book *The Rise and Fall of an American Army*...Stanton was a wounded combat veteran who offered a startling picture of the crisis that gripped the U.S. military in Vietnam...He also provides important data on the extent of combat refusals.

[pg. 267-9] Within Vietnam itself, the disintegration of morale and discipline sapped the very heart of military capability.

---

[382] https://msuweb.montclair.edu/~furrg/Vietnam/heinl.html A Counterpunch article also has material from this book at http://www.counterpunch.org/2014/10/10/g-i-resistance-to-the-vietnam-war/

Here is how Stanton describes it:

Serious disciplinary problems resulted in disintegrating unit cohesion and operational slippages. In the field, friendly fire accidents became more prevalent as more short rounds and misplaced fire were caused by carelessness. There was an excessive number of "accidental" shootings and promiscuous throwing of grenades, some of which were deliberate fraggings aimed at unpopular officers, sergeants, and fellow enlisted men.

"Fragging," of course, was a new word, coined from the lexicon of GI despair and resistance, meaning an attack with a fragmentation grenade...Gung-ho officers, eager to push their men into battle, often became the victims of assault by their own men. Stanton reveals that after the bloody ten-day battle of Hamburger Hill in May 1969, embittered troops placed a notice in their underground newspaper offering a reward of $10,000 for fragging the officers in charge. ...

In the elite 1st Cavalry Division alone, supposedly one of the Army's premier units, there were thirty-five instances of refusal to fight during 1970. Some of these incidents involved entire units... All of this suggests that when commanders sent forces into battle, they had to worry not only about what the other side would do, but what their own troops would not do. In the face of such pervasive non-cooperation, combat effectiveness crumbled.

In Vietnam, an American army that was supported by the most lavish firepower in military history, that never lost a battle, nonetheless lost the war. Vietnam confirmed that military and technological power alone can never assure victory if the cause is unjust and lacks popular support.... Combat refusals, unauthorized absences, fraggings, widespread indiscipline, racial rebellion, antiwar organizing, underground newspapers-- all combined to undermine military effectiveness and purpose. The Army had to withdraw from Vietnam to save itself. This was a key factor in the U.S. defeat. The resistance and dissent of ordinary GIs made the Vietnam War unwinnable and changed the course of history.

[end of excerpts]

U.S. Soldiers Refuse Nixon's Order To Scab On U.S. Postal Workers Strike

In 1970 U.S. postal workers waged a **nationwide** strike. It was a "wildcat" strike, meaning that the official postal worker union opposed it and tried to stop it. President Nixon called in military troops to sort the mail. But, "stories commonly told of troops unable to master mail-sorting in a few days but also sympathetic to strikers—some of whom had been called up as reservists and were working next to them."[383] No doubt much of the inability "to master mail-sorting" was due to sympathy for the strikers and unwillingness to scab on their strike. This illustrates that it is one thing for the rulers to give orders to soldiers, but it is something altogether different for the orders to be obeyed.

---

[383] http://savethepostoffice.com/who-remembers-nationwide-postal-wildcat-strike-1970-and-why-does-matter/

APPENDIX XVI: AN EGALITARIAN FOREIGN POLICY

An egalitarian foreign policy would be the policy mutually agreed upon by sovereign local assemblies of egalitarians. It is likely that very large regions—the size of nations or continents even—would in this manner have a single foreign policy. In my opinion such a foreign policy should include:

#1. Having a very strong self-defense force at home against any potential invasion by enemy military forces or missiles, *etc*. What this would require is open to discussion, but whatever it requires we should make sure to have it.

#2. Giving as much support (ideological and material) as possible to the pro-egalitarian forces in nations ruled by anti-egalitarian regimes, so that egalitarian revolution spreads.

#3. Never deliberately directing, or threatening to direct, violence against non-combatants. This means destroying nuclear[384] bombs unilaterally. It also means never invading other nations to direct violence against non-combatants as the U.S. did in Vietnam and Iraq.

#4. Promoting economic self-sufficiency as much possible, and trading (bartering) with non-egalitarian societies on the basis of mutual agreement as long as this does not contradict #2 above.

---

[384] http://original.antiwar.com/lawrence-wittner/2016/09/12/isnt-time-ban-bomb/

BIBLIOGRAPHY

Murray Bookchin, *To Remember Spain: The Anarchist and Syndicalist Revolution of 1936**

Agustin Guillamon, *The Friends of the Durruti Group: 1937-1939**

Peter Kropotkin, *The Conquest of Bread**

George Orwell, *Homage to Catalonia**

Sam Dolgoff, ed., *The Anarchist Collectives**

Gaston Leval, *Collectives in the Spanish Revolution**

David G. Stratman, We CAN Change the World: The Real Meaning of Everyday Life (Online at http://www.newdemocracyworld.org/old/Revolution/We%20Can%20Change%20the%20World%20book.pdf .)

* You can find this online by searching for the author and title.

ABOUT THE AUTHOR

John Spritzler is the author of *The People As Enemy: The Leaders' Hidden Agenda in World War II.* He may be contacted by email at spritzler@comcast.net.

Spritzler is the editor of the websites: NewDemocracyWorld.org and PDRBoston.org .

Spritzler is a retired Senior Research Scientist (biostatistician) at the Harvard T.H. Chan School of Public Health, and presently lives in Boston, MA, USA

Made in the USA
Columbia, SC
24 October 2018